David,

With since[re]
[appre]ciation for shar[ing]
your editorial gifts
with me —
wishing you God's best
in all you do —
would welcome
your feedback ... if you
have time —

With appreciation,

Tom Sine

NEWCHANGEMAKERS.COM
TWSINE@GMAIL.COM

"Tom Sine has been engaged in the struggle for social justice for many years. In *Live Like You Give a Damn!* he lifts up the new generation of activists and social entrepreneurs who are taking the baton from his generation and doing wonderful, necessary, and world-changing work all over the globe. The justice challenges of our time demand an unprecedented response from Christians and all those of faith and conscience, and the witness of millennial activists in response to this challenge fills me with the same hope for a better future that Tom articulates so well in this book."

—JIM WALLIS, *New York Times* bestselling author of *America's Original Sin: Racism, White Privilege, and the Bridge to a New America*; President of Sojourners, and editor-in-chief of *Sojourners* magazine.

"Tom Sine's incisive curiosity about how the greater good can be realized in our time is contagious. This book, his most hopeful and personal, is a real gift to the church and emerging generations. For the sake of the poor, the planet, and the future of our neighborhoods and cities, let's join Tom and live like we give a damn."

—MARK SCANDRETTE, Founder of Reimagine, Author of *FREE: Spending Your Time and Money on What Matters Most*

"Above all this is a book about hope and imagination. Tom weaves together ideas, dreams and stories of people and communities who are changing the world one community at a time. And it's infectious. You find yourself wanting to meet with friends over a meal and start sparking ideas talking about what you can do together in your own locale to make a better world. It's refreshing that Tom resists collapsing life solely into a church sphere and focuses rather on change in the world through social enterprise and community endeavors. It's then that church begins to make sense reimagined as a community in mission participating with God and the community around towards its healing. And of course, given Tom's previous love of Jesus' parable, it's still one mustard seed at a time!"

—JONNY BAKER, Church Mission Society Director of Mission Education, Anglican Church UK

"At a time when the church is falling short in bringing Good News to those who need it most, Sine observes that there is a blossoming movement among millennial entrepreneurs to facilitate social change and community renewal. I encourage church leaders of all stripes to read the stories of changemakers in Sine's book and ask themselves how they can foster this kind of energy and social transformation in their own congregations and communities."

—SARAH WITHROW KING, Deputy Director, Evangelicals for Social Action at the Sider Center of Eastern University

"In his new book, *Live Like You Give a Damn! Join the Changemaking Celebration*, Tom Sine has written a compelling book filled with stories and portraits of hope at a time filled with cynicism, hatred, and negativity. Instead of focusing on the evil in the world, he introduces us to people and places where love, justice, and an audacity to try what others are afraid to imagine become the catalyst for changemaking for the benefit of others. Inspiring and challenging!"

—NOEL CASTELLANOS, CEO and President, CCDA

"*Live Like You Give a Damn!* is one of the best snapshots of millennials in action today. It captures the optimism and determination of the young men and women actively working to change the world. His enthusiasm and hopefulness for what God is doing through the next generation is contagious and inspiring. *Live Like You Give a Damn!* is a much-needed addition to the ongoing conversation of community renewal and social innovation."

—AMANDA ALLEN, PhD student in Intercultural Studies with a concentration in Development, Asbury Theological Seminary

"With every fiber of his body, Tom Sine is compelled to look up and out towards the new horizon and report to us what he has seen. *Live Like You Give a Damn!* rouses us to join the movement of a generation of global social entrepreneurs who are changing the world with creative solutions to complex problems. At the heart of this book you can hear his desire that we see what he has seen, a social and cultural revolution arising from the fragmentation of our times, propelled by human creativity and energized by the compassionate love of Jesus. This is a book for our times and a guiding light to our future."

—J. DEREK McNEIL, Academic Dean, Seattle School of Theology and Psychology

"Futurist Tom Sine gives us a whirlwind tour of changemakers (including many Gen Y & Z's) who are creatively engaging in the opportunities and challenges we face in our collective economic, political, social, and environmental lives. This book will animate your *imagination* and help you *innovatively* live into God's future. Read it with your team, reflect together, and find your life by living it for the sake of others!"

—JR WOODWARD, National Director, V3 Church Planting Movement; Co-author, *The Church as Movement*

"Tom Sine takes us on a journey that moves at dizzying speed through time and many places. In doing so he brings to the surface some of the amazing changemaking that is flowing from the creativity and energy of millennials, and the new possibilities opening up through rapid technological change. He highlights the power of social enterprise as an arena for the playing out of God's plan for a just and renewed world. This is an exciting and energizing ride that I am sure will help many people in realizing their own potential in a world of disruption and dazzling change."

—TIM COSTELLO, Chief Executive, World Vision Australia

"From Cambodia to Nigeria, Australia to Canada, Portland to New York, young adults are founding businesses and organizations that blur easy but false distinctions between work and charity, profit and empowerment. These young social entrepreneurs are not waiting for the church to wrap up theological and doctrinal battles; they are waiting for the church to join them and *do something*. While the Pew Research reports that millennials make up an increasing portion of religious 'nones,' Sine illustrates through countless stories that they are far from 'dones' when it come to Jesus-like engagement and Kingdom-oriented visions of society. Sine provides crucial guideposts for the journey of changemaking that he has learned from these young leaders: ignite imagination, anticipate opportunities, choose with purpose, and empower others. *Live Like You Give a Damn!* is indispensable reading for anyone weary or leery of capitulating to the bankrupt narratives of blame, greed, and excess. Highly readable, inspiring, and motivating, this book is ideal for individuals, small groups, Sunday School classes, and college and seminary students."

—ANDY BRUBACHER KAETHLER, Assistant Professor of Christian Formation and Culture; Director, Center for Faith Formation and Culture, Anabaptist Mennonite Biblical Seminary

"For too long, Christians have used our faith as a ticket into heaven, and ignored the world around us. We've promised people life after death, while many folks are asking if there's life before death. At times we've been so heavenly-minded that we haven't been much help here on earth. Tom Sine's new book invites you to see another version of Christianity, and it is all about bringing heaven to earth. Let this book inspire you to do something with your life that leaves off the fragrance of Jesus and moves the world closer to God's dream for it."

—SHANE CLAIBORNE, Author of *Irresistible Revolution* and *Executing Grace*; Member of the Simple Way

"I first encountered Tom Sine more than thirty years ago in Toronto. He won't remember the lively conversation I had with him after he'd talked about *The Mustard Seed Conspiracy*, but I knew I'd met a man filled with a passion for the way of Jesus and eager to invite others onto that journey. Over all these years Tom has been imagining and re-imagining all that is involved in following a radical Jesus in the midst of massively transformative, confusing times. *Live Like You Give a Damn!* continues that journey. It is a passionate invitation to awaken, not just to the crises of our time or the anemic life of cultural Protestantism, but to see what the Spirit is gestating and dare to join the Jesus movement today."

—ALAN ROXBURGH, Missional Network

"Tom Sine's new book is a great introduction to his life-long message of making change and seizing opportunities. It's as fresh and inspiring in 2016 as *The Mustard Seed Conspiracy* was in 1981."

—BRIAN MCLAREN, Author; Speaker; Activist

"*Live Like You Give a Damn!* is Tom Sine at his best . . . and it's a must-read. With the wisdom and clarity of a hopeful prophet Tom insightfully reads the signs of our times—some of which should sound alarms in us—yet all the while points to the new wine of the Spirit. This book is an invitation of God through real stories of fresh expressions borne of radical disciples of Jesus. This book is a study resource for colleges, seminaries, and congregations to enable us all to more fully put God's compassionate purposes first in our lives, communities, and congregations."

—DWIGHT J. FRIESEN, Associate Professor of Practical Theology, The Seattle School of Theology & Psychology; Co-Author, *The New Parish*, *Routes and Radishes*; Author, *Thy Kingdom Connected*

"This imaginative and prophetic invitation to envision a church that exists for the sake of others is an urgent call for pastors, students, and practitioners who are tired of status quo Christianity. Sine captures the creative and entrepreneurial spirit of millennials and everyday people who are committed to a mustard-seed kingdom and an experience of 'the good life' that is not captive to comfort, self-interest, and fear. For many years, I've appreciated Sine's passion for social change and his deep conviction that the future has a church. May we listen intently—even amidst disorientation—as we long for that future together."

—DAVID LEONG, PhD, Associate Professor of Missiology, Seattle Pacific University and Seminary

"Hopeful, timely, practical, and sincere are a few words to describe *Live Like You Give a Damn!* Sine invites the reader to explore the world-changing practices that will create our better future. The reader can journey alongside him as he urges us to join the changemaking celebration. It is an enlightened look at how millennials are shaping the future for the better, and an invitation to join with him in joining them. A true opportunity to expand our vision of the future's church!"

—ROMANITA HAIRSTON, Vice President, US Programs, Transformational Engagement, World Vision

"Tom Sine makes my head whirl. Just when I think I could maybe settle down a bit, he comes along and turns me upside down—in a thoroughly good way! Tom combines research, personal experience, a wise head, and a passionate heart to call us to be innovators and entrepreneurs and so to change the way things are, both within and without the Church."

—RUTH VALERIO, Churches and Theology Director, A Rocha UK; Author of *L is for Lifestyle: Christian Living that Doesn't Cost the Earth*, and *Just Living: Faith and Community in an Age of Consumerism*

"Everyone should read this book. Young changemakers looking to remember that we are not alone in this work. Those who are wondering what the future might possibly hold for church and for those following the Jesus way. Older generations who are struggling to understand new generations and new movements both in and outside of the church. *Live Like You Give a Damn!* is Tom's ongoing work to empower Generations Y and Z. Read this book. Be inspired. Join the movement. Live like you give a damn."

—REBECCA SUMNER, Lead Pastor, Our Common Table, Everett, WA

"Tom Sine has crafted a hopeful and powerful tour of what God is doing through people who are breaking new ground and taking big risks. What Tom does so well is uncover and shine a blazing light on the innovative ways people are engaging their local places. It's filled with spicy descriptions and prescriptions of changemaking. You will be passionately stirred to dream big dreams and live like you give a damn!"

—DAN WHITE JR., Co-founder of the Praxis Gathering; Author of *Subterranean: Why the Future of the Church is Rootedness*

"Warning: don't read this book unless you're ready to hear not only the call to change the world, but also real ways to do it. Tom Sine looks at today's innovators among the under-35s, who lead the way in social entrepreneurship and community empowerment—the two streams of God's new changemaking revolution. The call here is to join young social innovators, many of whom are beyond the church, to take a real, practical, and exciting part in God's transforming mission."

—AL TIZON, Executive Minister of Serve Globally, Evangelical Covenant Church

"So many of us know that the church is in desperate need of change. We need to regain our imaginations and bring dreams into reality. We need brave changemakers who are willing not only to shake the status quo, but also to be part of cultivating a better reflection of the Kingdom of God, here and now. I am thrilled to have material to pass on to other dreamers, collaborators, changemakers, and bridge-builders that will inspire, challenge, and encourage. We need this kind of hope."

—KATHY ESCOBAR, MA, Co-Pastor of The Refuge; Author, *Faith Shift: Finding Your Way Forward When Everything You Believe is Coming Apart*

"*Live Like You Give a Damn!* tantalizes the imagination and ushers people into a world of possibility. Tom turns our attentions to millennials and social changemaking. This book is eminently readable, overflowing with practical examples of change that cut across the broad spectrum of Christianity, and positioned to draw the reader into a world of hope: fed by Scriptures and lived by the church. A must-read!"

—GREGG A. OKESSON, PhD, Dean, E. Stanley Jones School of World Mission and Evangelism, Associate Professor of Leadership and Development, Asbury Theological Seminary

"One of my beloved colleagues recently made this statement, 'Our church is set up to make a point but not a difference.' Such a truth has not resonated with me so deeply in a long time. Tom Sine has, in this book, begun building the bridge between making the point and making the difference. I am grateful for it and after reading it I want to say, 'Let's be church like we give a damn!'"

—GREG RICKEL, Bishop, Diocese of Olympia

"'The alarm is going off—all over the planet,' Tom Sine announces. We no longer have the luxury of living our lives, raising our young, operating our businesses, and leading our churches as though the context in which we live is stable and predictable. It's not. If you're put off by the title, then maybe you need his message most. He's intent, not on condemning the church, but awakening it to the call to the creative changemaking celebration as we live our lives for what matters most, by giving Christ a chance to express his hope through us."

—RICHARD DAHLSTROM, Author, *Colors of Hope*; Pastor, Bethany Community Church, Seattle

"Tom Sine has lifted the fog and given us a glimpse of the future awaiting us. It invites imagination. His message is directed especially, but not exclusively, to a younger generation of social entrepreneurs who are creating new ways to make a difference. They have the compassion and creativity to bring about the needed changes in our communities. The good news is that we can join them if we are ready to put God's changemaking purposes more fully at the center of our own lives and churches. Sine's message is grounded in an insightful reading of scripture and is richly illustrated with examples of changed lives and communities."

—Edgar Stoesz, Author, *Doing Good Better*; Former Director of Overseas Outreach for the Mennonite Central Committee; Former Chairman of the Board, Habitat for Humanity

"Tom Sine's incisive analysis has long helped us understand the challenges to be faced in the future by both the church and the wider community. In this book, he takes us one step further, reminding us to recognize the seeds of hope—practical responses which enable us to recognize new possibilities by joining young change-makers so we too can become more a part of God's solution. Tom invites us all to imagine and create innovative ways to engage that change in ways that reflects God's loving purposes for a people and a world."

—Gary Heard, Minister, The Eighth Day Baptist Community; Dean, Whitley College Theological School, The University of Divinity, Australia

"Social innovators and other changemakers are bringing the future to us in remarkable, powerful ways. Tom Sine serves here as a wonderful, insightful tour guide into this new world. He wants Christians to become part of the changemaking celebration. An inspiring book. I hope it reaches a wide audience!"

—L. Gregory Jones, Williams Professor of Theology and Ministry, Duke Divinity School

"Tom Sine's latest book is an invitation to learn from a life-long, incredibly curious, insightful, and hopeful student of the possible. Tom draws on a range of influencers— from middle school-aged youth to East African food entrepreneurs, to diverse theologians to internet activists, in laying out his case that in the midst of political sideshows and soaring costs of living, there are signs of hope that should inspire us all to get up, get dirty, and live like we give a damn."

—Brian Howe, Founder and Member of the Board of IMPACT Hub Seattle

"*Live Like You Give a Damn!,* is unlike any other Christian reading I have picked up and it is the perfect time for you to read it. In this book, Tom addresses the issues within the church today and gives tangible ways to solve them. He examines the why's and how's and he challenges all of us to be changemakers for a better tomorrow. As a millennial, I am already finding ways to carry out the lessons I learned in planning to create social enterprises and my current efforts through H.O.P.E to empower those at the margins."

—Jensen Roll, Age 22, Founder, H.O.P.E. – Helping Other People Eat; Degree in Social Entrepreneurship, Elon University, 2016

"Tom's book motivates me to encourage upcoming generations as they lead us into creating a better world. He's spread a savory feast of stories about social enterprise and innovation for us to sample, effectively making the case that God is using the dreams and visions of 'Generation Next' to stir the church to action. He has given us a great gift in his decision to follow and support young people, and in this compelling invitation to join him."

—SUNDEE T. FRAZIER, Coretta Scott King New Talent Award-winning author for children, including Cleo Edison Oliver books (about a 10-year-old entrepreneur)

"Tom Sine's new book sparks the imagination and gives us all permission to move beyond the pew and the comfy chair into positive action for God's Kingdom. Rather than feeling behind or left out of this fast-paced crazy world, Tom helps us see how we can learn from, and partner with, millennials to help others and our world. It's time for us to dream big and get out there again, loving and practically serving our neighbors and the world."

—LILLY LEWIN, Author, *Sacred Space*; Worship Curator; Founder, ThinplaceNashville and @freerangeworship.com

"Tom has consistently spoken to the heart of the narrative issues of our time. Our fundamental values and life decisions have been narrowed by the dreams of our culture. Frequently we run out of steam to live the life of kingdom purposes of God that we long for. Too often we have separated our spiritual selves from our work and the public good. This book renews focus and ignites thinking, dreaming, and longing for what could be. If, like me, you are wanting to not waste the precious years you have, this is the book to read and discuss in your church."

—MATT ARONEY, Assistant Minister, Newtown Erskineville Anglican Church, Australia

Live Like You Give a Damn!

Live Like You Give a Damn!

Join the Changemaking Celebration

Tom Sine

Foreword by Walter Brueggemann

CASCADE *Books* · Eugene, Oregon

LIVE LIKE YOU GIVE A DAMN!
Join the Changemaking Celebration

Cascade Books
An Imprint of Wipf and Stock Publishers
199 W. 8th Ave., Suite 3
Eugene, OR 97401

www.wipfandstock.com

ISBN 13: 978-1-4982-0625-9

Cataloging-in-Publication data:

Sine, Tom.

Live like you give a damn! : join the changemaking celebration / Tom Sine ; foreword by Walter Brueggemann.

xxii + 206 p. ; 23 cm. —Includes bibliographical references.

ISBN 13: 978-1-4982-0625-9

HB ISBN 13: 978-1-4982-0627-3

1. Christianity—Forecasting. 2. Church and the world. 3. Entrepreneurship—Moral and ethical aspects. 4. Creative ability in business—Moral and ethical aspects. 5. Social entrepreneurship. I. Brueggemann, Walter. II. Title.

BR121.2 .S5548 2016

Manufactured in the U.S.A.

To all those in Gen Next who are leading
this Changemaking Celebration;

to a new crop of parents committed to growing
compassionate, creative, and changemaking kids;

and to educators and youth workers committed to growing
compassionate, creative, and changemaking young adults as well.

Contents

Foreword

TOM SINE IS FILLED with energy. He writes with energy. He transmits energy to his readers. The reason for his energy is that he has seen a lively linkage between the deep *promises* of the gospel and the concrete *practices* of people who move out toward new futures with imagination, energy, and stamina. The connection of *promise and practice*, in Sine's horizon, effectively bypasses the current paralysis of the church, which is too much trapped in fearful despair and preoccupation with survival. His book is a practice-grounded summons to do otherwise.

Sine has a gift for new suggestive phrasing that helps us see afresh. Try these:

Changemaking celebration.

The gift of disorientation.

Dreaming and scheming.

The future you want to inhabit.

The mustard seed empire of Jesus.

The age of imagination.

These phrases (and many more like them) are filled with quite concrete exposition, characterized by new energy and new possibility that are being performed in many places. Sine's geography is expansive and ecumenical as he cites many specific embodiments of the work of imagination: Goshen, Bellingham, Alberta, Melbourne, and Pleasant Valley in Haiti. In all of these places Sine identifies folks who are engaged (I would say) in gospel obedience, but who do so without too much focus on the gospel and with no worry about obedience. Rather, they are caught up in the wonder of experiment, empowerment, and entrepreneurial investment out of which astonishing local things happen.

The bet that Sine makes is that the future is enacted by the emerging cadre of millennials who are not locked into or held back by or committed to old formulations, old institutional structures, or old treasured procedures. These are folks who will try anything, some of which may work in powerful ways to bring about healthy change, to create new neighborhoods and new healing transformations. They are alert to political reality and to the economic crunches produced by current economic arrangements; they know it can be otherwise.

This quite remarkable book in fact refuses our recurring questions about the future of the church. Sine does not make much of it, but I judge that his work is grounded in a theology of the Holy Spirit (to be sure, the Spirit of Christ!), the Spirit as wind, energy, force that will not linger over old patterns and boundaries. The book is a witness to Spirit-given energy and guidance, as the Spirit keeps the church young. In sum, his numerous case studies remind me of the narrative of the young church in the book of Acts in which the church is on the move in ways that transform and that cannot be stopped even by the frightened, bewildered imperial authorities. It is also an invitation to the not-young to join in such risky conduct, a joining that we variously find difficult and want to resist. The provocative title of the book suggests that in reality we have given too much of a damn for old structures and procedures. When we relinquish, new energy and imagination and courage are given for alternatives. I am glad to commend this exposition that exhibits quite concretely ways to revision, reimagine, and reperform the gospel. More than that, it invites us out of the narrative of old ways, out of our comfort zones, to new modes of life that may seem at first to be inconvenient in the extreme but that very soon may turn out to be joyous fulfillment in coming down where we ought to be. Such fresh, imaginative engagement will surely yield a "well done" from the Lord of the church who makes all things new.

Walter Brueggemann
Columbia Theological Seminary
January 25, 2016

Acknowledgments

So many friends and associates journeyed alongside me in the completion of this book. I am particularly grateful for Christine's support and our good collaborators at Mustard Seed Associates. These include: Forrest Inslee, Katie Metzger, Stefan Schmidt and Andy Wade. I am very appreciative for Lisa San Martin's keen editorial assistance.

A team of readers were of great value in helping me to clarifying what I was attempting to communicate as well as identifying my slip ups—including Tom Balke, Heidi Unruh, Chris Smith, John Pattison, Josh Packard, David Bronkema, Andy Brubacher Kaethler, J. D. Walt, Gary Heard, Trevor Thomas, Rosa Lee Hardin, Kevin Jones, John Talbot, Brian Howe, Jon Plummer, Liz Colver, Gregg Okesson. Larry Lake, who taught creative non-fiction writing at Messiah College, was a Godsend. He guided me as I struggled to incorporate some creative non-fiction in my narrative.

Sincere thanks to the team at Cascade Books. It feels like I am working with a very large and engaging family, including Charlie Collier, my editor, who was very clear and helpful in his guidance. Jacob Martin's assistance was invaluable in polishing the manuscript for publication. Suzy Logan helped me, under James Stock's careful guidance, to get our marketing platform carefully constructed.

I am particularly appreciative for Keith Anderson, President, and Derek McNeil, Academic Dean, at the Seattle School of Theology and Psychology for making it possible to launch this book at the Inhabit Conference in 2016. I am grateful to all those who not only read this book but also sent us their stories of ways God is using their mustard seeds in innovative ways to be a difference and make a difference in these turbulent times.

I dedicate this work to three groups of people. First, the book is dedicated to the growing number of those in Gens Y and Z who are investing their lives in making a real difference in the lives of their neighbors near and far—as well as those who want to join them. I not only dedicate this book to them, I want to do everything I can to help these young change-makers launch and challenge others to join them.

Second, this book is also dedicated to parents committed to raising compassionate kids in this age of entitlement. For example, a friend of mine has just ordered a copy of Jan Johnson's classic book *Growing Compassionate Kids* because he wants his daughter to learn to focus more on the needs of others. I met a family who takes their two young teens to Thailand every summer to teach teens English as a second language. Of course in the process they not only get to know other teens and another culture, their parents report they are being changed as well as learning how to collaborate with others to bring change. Still other parents are committed to seeing their kids grow not only into caring for others but also into caring for those in their own families. So they assign everyone in the family a list of chores and make sure everyone follows through. They report that they are seeing their offspring becoming more fulfilled by learning to both care for those in their own family and neighborhood and launch their own lives in ways that they can become more involved in changemaking celebration in their communities.

Third, this book is dedicated to educators and youth workers committed to growing compassionate, creative, and changemaking young adults. The Mennonite Colleges in Canada and the U.S. were among the first Christian colleges in North America to require students to have a cross-cultural experience as a requirement for graduation. For example, Canadian Mennonite University in Manitoba sponsors an unusual program for their students called Outtatown Discipleship School. Essentially, this is an experiential program where groups of students go to Guatemala, Burkina Faso, and an urban community in Winnipeg to better get to know God, themselves, and the beauty, pain, and diversity of God's world.

Nathan, one of the instructors, encourages students to use "this is an opportunity to see the world differently . . . to see it through the eyes of Jesus." Bethany, who was a part of a student group that went to Guatemala, discovered that "God's love is not passive or timid . . . it is a powerful active force!" Not surprisingly, many of these grads go on to join this "powerful active force" through their careers in urban empowerment, environmental stewardship, or working with at-risk high-school students in their discretionary time. This book is dedicated to all those in Gen Next and all those who are seeking to join this changemaking celebration. It is also dedicated to all those parents, youth workers, and educators that are seeking to empower them to create their best communities, their best world, and in the process their best lives in these troubled times.

Introduction:
"The Clock Is Ticking!"

Join the Changemaking Celebration

"THE CLOCK IS TICKING for this tomato," stated Nnaemeka Ikegwuonu, a social entrepreneur from Nigeria, holding up a single red tomato. This was the opening line to a very imaginative social enterprise proposal called ColdHubs[1] that he presented during the Fledge Session at Impact Hub Seattle on July 6, 2015. He described an inventive new refrigerated food storage unit—essentially, a shipping container with solar-powered refrigeration—for produce in communities where no electricity is available. Then Nnaemeka demonstrated how these refrigerated storage units could be located in public markets throughout Nigeria, dramatically expanding the life of that tomato from two days to twenty-one days for a modest storage fee. This would mean a dramatic increase in the fresh food supply for consumers, greater income for farmers and vendors, and an enormous reduction in agricultural waste.

Nnaemeka Ikegwuonu plans to scale ColdHubs up to serve public markets all over Nigeria and then expand this social enterprise to other countries in Africa. His simple, scalable invention illustrates the power of social enterprise to impact millions of people.

The clock is ticking, and not only for produce but also for people and the planet. The clock is ticking for sixty million refugees from the Middle East who are seeking a safe haven for their families. The clock is ticking for tens of millions of young people who can't find work, not only in the Middle East and Africa but also in Europe and in all corners of the globe. The clock is ticking for the earth, as we seem unable to stop dumping our garbage in the ocean and the atmosphere. As we race into the

---

1. See www.coldhubs.com.

2020s, the clock is ticking for all of us because the rate of change seems to be accelerating and we could all face daunting new challenges.

Announcing Some Very Good News

I have some very good news—and some really bad news. The good news first. God seems to be at work not only through people of faith but also through people of compassion who are bringing welcome change to our world in what some are calling an "innovation revolution." In the last ten years there has been a veritable explosion of new forms of social innovations, like the Cold Hub, all over the planet.

The good news just gets better. Much of this new changemaking is being led by young innovators from Gen Y (those born between 1981 and 1997) and Gen Z (those born between 1998 and 2014). Since Gen Y and Gen Z are the first digital generations, they seem to be more aware of the daunting social, economic, and environmental challenges facing our world. Most importantly, a surprising number of them are determined to do something about it. Even though research also shows that some in Gen Y and Gen Z do feel more entitled, I want to join, support, and learn from those who want to use their lives to have an impact on the lives of others.

I think what we are witnessing, however, is a changemaking celebration more than an "innovation revolution." I suspect you will also celebrate the sense of satisfaction and significance changemakers often seem to experience as they create and discover in ways that make a real difference in the lives of others. I believe the Spirit of God may well be using the lives of these young social innovators, who are largely outside the church, to entice and challenge those of us in the churches to become much more a part of this remarkable new movement that is making such a difference in the lives of our most vulnerable neighbors. Why would any follower of the servant Jesus want to settle for less and miss the best—discovering how God can more fully use our lives to make a little difference in our troubled world?

On our global tour we will visit an array of often younger social innovators who through groups like the Transitions Town network in Britain, Australia, and the US, are fashioning more sustainable, resilient, and flourishing local communities—and are having the time of their lives doing it. You will also meet this new generation of social entrepreneurs from all over the planet who are creating a range of new businesses with social and environmental missions that are making a difference in the lives of millions of our neighbors.

These generations also seem to resonate strongly with Pope Francis's challenge to care much more for both the vulnerable and the environment. On February 15, 2015, Pope Francis very directly challenged leaders in the church to follow Jesus by embracing a gospel of "compassion and action." He declared, "The gospel of the marginalized is where our credibility is found and revealed."[2] This message urgently needs to be heard not only by leaders within the Catholic Church but also by the entire Western church as we race into the 2020s. As I share some daunting bad news, I think you will see why Pope Francis's challenge to all of us in the church to become "people of compassion and action" couldn't be more timely.

And Now for the Bad News: Does the Future Have a Church?

The clock is also ticking for the church in the West! While the church is enjoying rapid growth in China, a number of African nations, and other countries, this regrettably is not true for many churches in the United States, Canada, Australia, Britain, and other Western nations.

I have had the opportunity, over more than three decades, to be a consultant in futures research and innovative planning, working with and learning from leaders in mainline denominations like the Presbyterian Church (USA), the Evangelical Lutheran Church in America, the Mennonite Church, the United Methodist Church, and the American Baptist Church. I remember, in the early 1980s, showing leaders of a number of mainline denominations that not only were their denominations beginning to gray but their attendance was beginning to decline significantly as well. Now, however, leaders of mainline denomination are not only much more aware of often sharp decline lines but are scrambling to find ways to reverse the decline. Alan Roxburgh, in a thoughtful analysis of the efforts of denominational leaders to deal with the hemorrhaging they are facing, calls this "the great unraveling" of the "Eurotribal denominations."[3]

2. O'Connell, "Pope Francis: 'The Gospel of the Marginalized Is Where Our Credibility Is Found and Revealed.'"

3. Roxburgh, *Structured for Mission*, 11–35.

These days I find it is often the leaders of evangelical denominations who are struggling with denial about the potential long-term impact of declining attendance and aging populations in many of their congregations as well. Diana Butler Bass observes in *Christianity After Religion*, "Churches in the Southern Baptist Convention, the Missouri Synod Lutheran Church and the conservative Presbyterian Church in America are reporting losses that resemble declines their mainline counterparts suffered in the 1970s . . . Indeed, the first decade of the twenty-first century could rightly be called the Great Religious Recession."[4]

While some ethnic and immigrant churches in the West are experiencing more growth than most white churches, the ticking of the clock seems to be accelerating in mainline denominations in the West. In North America they are declining at a rate of 1 to 4 percent a year. Leaders in these denominations increasingly express concern about how declining numbers are also causing serious reductions in resources they are able to invest in local and global mission. In fact, I hear growing numbers of leaders in these organizations ask the urgently important question, "Does the future have a church?"

Lovett Weems, a leader in the United Methodist Church, offers us an arresting answer. In an article in Faith and Leadership, he uses the provocative phrase "death tsunami" to describe his view of the future of many mainline churches, including his own. Essentially, he argues that the current rate of decline is not constant. Since many of our mainline congregations are comprised of members of the Silent generation (those born between 1925 and 1945) and Boomer generation (those born between 1946 and 1964), the rate of decline will accelerate. Weems urges us to wake up to this huge tsunami wave that is headed our way while we still have time to act. He predicts that this trend is likely to accelerate most rapidly after 2020.[5]

To compound this growing crisis, we are losing the under forty at a rate we have never seen before. I am sure that many readers are aware of the Pew Research Report titled "Millennials Increasingly Are Driving the Growth of the 'Nones.'" The "nones" are those who identify as being not affiliated with any religious group. Whereas only 11 percent of the Silent Generation describe themselves as unaffiliated, for the millennials

---

4. Bass, *Christianity After Religion*, 19–20.
5. Weems, "It Is Not Enough to Be Right."

the figure is more than three times as high, at 35 percent.[6] Some of the major concerns expressed by millennials who have left our churches include a lack of authenticity, a lack of involvement in working for social and environmental change, and the preoccupation with institutional maintenance.

A second group of people increasingly leaving our churches are the "Dones." According to Josh Packard and Ashleigh Hope, authors of *Church Refugees*, these Christians, who are multigenerational, are leaving churches in the US because, like many millennials, they are looking for ways to invest in working for change in the lives of their neighbors.[7] In the concluding chapter, I address these concerns more directly, exploring ways to draw upon both the compassion and creativity of Gen Next to innovate not only new forms of changemaking but also new forms of faithful communities for times like these.

To make matters even worse, levels of participation in both mainline and evangelical churches in the West have also been declining for well over a decade. As we race into the 2020s, I predict we are likely to see not only an accelerating decline in numbers but also a dramatic decline in the investment of time and money in projects to empower our most vulnerable neighbors.

A number of mainline churches still sponsor seminars on social justice and environmental stewardship. Many evangelical congregations continue to sponsor an annual missions conference that reflects their global concerns. However, in working with a spectrum of mainline and evangelical churches in North America I have found that although many congregations contribute to the local food bank or rescue mission, they rarely sponsor a single ministry in their own communities that would enable their neighbors or communities to become more self-reliant.

The problem with food banks is that while they do help people meet their immediate food needs, they do little to enable them to move beyond a lifestyle of dependency. When aging churches close down, support for the food banks also disappears. Of course, as I will show you in subsequent chapters, there are congregations involved in a range of alternatives to the charity model of care. For example, Bridge of Hope[8] enables local congregation all over the US to develop a team of eight to twelve people

---

6. Lipka, "Millennials Increasingly Are Driving the Growth of the 'Nones,'" par. 4.

7. Packard and Hope, *Church Refugees*.

8. See www.bridgeofhopeinc.org.

who receive training in how to mentor a single parent and her children to empower them to become more self-sufficient. Janice and her son, Tony, met with their support team at their Chicago church every month for a year to share a meal and a conversation. The team enabled Janice to find a good job and a safe place near the church to live. I urge all of our churches to become involved in this kind of serious empowerment.

Don't we all need to wake up to the stunning new reality that "business as usual" will no longer serve? Is it possible that large numbers of churches have settled for simply being chaplains to the dominant culture? Is it possible that they have settled for simply helping nurture us in a fairly private faith while enabling us to limp through our week? Is it possible that we could be missing out on God's best—discovering how God could use our mustard seeds to join those who are creating their best neighborhoods, their best world, and, in the process, their best lives?

Walter Brueggemann, in his recent book *Sabbath as Resistance*, offers readers a clear alternative to the dominant "culture of now." He argues that the dominant "culture of now" is preoccupied with a driven acquisitiveness, consumerism, and self-involved lifestyles. He reminds us that Jesus calls us away from mammon, "the culture of now," to a new Sabbath way of being by redefining what is important, what is of value, so that we have time for both devotion to God and care for our neighbors. Brueggemann states, "Sabbath is an arena in which we learn to recognize that we live by gift and not by possession . . ."[9]

What Is God Stirring Up?

"The dance on the Berlin Wall is the Dance of God. The songs sung in the streets of Soweto at the release of Nelson Mandela are the songs of God. And the prayers for the peace of Jerusalem are the prayers of God."[10] This summary of promise I called people to in my book, *Wild Hope*, expresses the kind of hope God was stirring up in the early 1990s. Now, as we race into the second decade of the twenty-first century, the good news is that the Creator God is still at work stirring up new possibilities. I believe one of the ways God is at work today is in stirring up people, largely outside the church, to challenge all of us to invest our lives and resources more

9. Brueggemann, *Sabbath as Resistance*, 85.
10. Sine, *Wild Hope*.

fully in joining those who are working for change in the lives of our most vulnerable neighbors.

Remember that in Matthew 25 Jesus admonishes us that as we care for the urgent physical needs of our neighbors we are expressing our love for Christ. Of course, the ministry of the church also includes calling people to become followers of the radical way of Jesus and planting communities of faith. However, I will argue that to be authentic followers of Jesus we need to start by embracing a more authentic whole-life faith, which entails investing more of our time in being more present to both God and to neighbors—if we want those outside the church to take us seriously. However, we also need to plant new churches that are much more invested in compassionate changemaking, instead of focusing so much of our resources on the needs of those of us under the tent.

Walter Brueggemann observes that the great crisis in our world today "is a crisis of the common good." He reminds us that concern for the common good "reaches beyond private interest," which has become the driving force of the global economy. He also reminds us that concern for the common good is both the vocation of the children of Israel and those of us who follow Jesus.[11] Isn't the call to work for the well-being of both humankind and God's good creation central to what it means to be a follower of Jesus?

As we focus on our calling to work for the common good, I have been particularly challenged by the ways God seems to be stirring up the empathy, compassion, and imagination of people largely outside the tent to remind us that our neighbors and neighborhoods matter and real change is possible. As the authors of *The New Parish* put it, "God is up to something in neighborhoods, on the ground, in real places. The church in all its diversity, needs to figure out how to join in."[12]

Why Am I Inviting You to Join This Changemaking Movement?

After I take you on a very quick tour of this changemaking celebration, I think you too will see some of the remarkable potential of these new forms of social innovation to make a lasting difference in the lives of our neighbors as we work with others for the common good. I will show

11. Brueggemann, *Journey to the Common Good*, 1, 2.
12. Sparks et al., *New Parish*, 77.

you that the clock is also ticking for our current forms of funding social change, as we describe the likely cutback in social spending by Western countries as well as a likely cutback in missions funding by churches in the West. It will become clearer why these new forms of changemaking are so essential to our common future.

The purpose of our journey together is not simply to learn more about this changemaking celebration; I want to encourage you to join it. Consider this an invitation to discover how God might use your mustard seed to make a difference in ways you might find surprising and welcome. Remember, "Jesus let us in on an astonishing secret: God has chosen to change the world through the lowly, the unassuming, and the imperceptible. 'Jesus said, "With what can we compare the kingdom of God, or what parable shall we use for it? It is like a grain of mustard seed, which when sown upon the ground, is the smallest of all seeds on earth; yet when it is sown it grows and becomes the greatest of all shrubs, and puts forth branches, so the birds of the air can make nests in its shade"' (Mark 4:30–32)."[13]

For whatever reason, God has chosen to use the insignificant and ordinary to change the world, which should give us all a little hope! I want to invite you to ask the Creator God to ignite your imagination to join others in creating our best communities, our best world, and in the process our best lives—in ways that both advance something of God's purposes and respond to some of tomorrow's urgent opportunities and challenges.

Why I Am Inviting You to Journey with Me

First, I want you to sample some of the savory new forms of changemaking and see the real difference they make in the lives of our neighbors. But this book, unlike the others I have written, is also a personal challenge to myself to learn to live more consistently. God is prodding me to get out of the bleachers and onto the field of play again—to join those making a difference in my own community. I have always been a slow learner, and I am so grateful for God's mercy and grace, over many years, as I seek to follow in the way of Jesus.

Therefore, for the first time, I will share a bit of my own story and my struggles as I try to learn to become a more faithful disciple of Jesus.

13. Sine, *Mustard Seed Conspiracy*, 11.

This will include revealing some of my own blind spots and learning moments. This kind of writing is called "creative non-fiction." I hope this will make the narrative a little more interesting as we travel together.

Throughout this book, I am attempting to persuade those over 35 to solicit the ideas and initiatives of the under 35. As a result, at times it may seem I am only addressing older readers. However, I am also seeking to write directly to those in generations Y and Z, for whom I have much regard. I also need to confess that I have never been so aware of being a privileged, aging white American male than as I was writing this book. I am increasingly aware of how this limits my cultural perspective.

Now I want to introduce our little community. Christine and I live in an intergenerational community, called the Mustard Seed House, here in Seattle. We and our fellow community members live on three floors in an old 1910 house. Forrest Inslee, who is a professor of community development, and his thirteen-year-old daughter, Kayra, live on the top floor. We usually have students living in the basement apartment. Christine and I live on the middle floor with our Golden Retriever, Bonnie.

We share a meal together every week where we also talk about what God is stirring up in our lives and pray for one another and our community. We garden together at least once a month since we are attempting to raise 30 percent of our produce on an urban lot. Christine is also busy offering seminars on gardening and spirituality and hosting a very active blog site called Godspace.[14]

My favorite thing to do in our community is to cook food from all over the world for friends from all over the world. (Most have survived.) For example, at our first barbecue of the summer on July 5th, we enjoyed hosting twenty-two friends who grew up in Argentina, Kazakhstan, Egypt, Australia, and Mexico. At this post-Fourth of July event, we celebrated God's work for the common good in all nations. We prepared a meal of grilled zucchini from our garden and red peppers, grilled free-range chicken, a spicy Sine family barbecue sauce, a Tex-Mex black bean salsa salad, corn on the cob, a Hawaiian fruit plate and other munchies, plus a selection of brews and beverages. Christine led us in a liturgy of God's loving work in all nations. This book is really an invitation to discover a more festive way of life.

14. See www.godspace-msa.org.

Is This Book for You?

If you're not content to simply make a living, keeping your nose above water, and you feel that endlessly pursuing more will never be enough, this book is for you. If you're a person of faith who's no longer satisfied with a status-quo Christianity that has little impact on the lives of those outside the tent, this book is for you. If you're looking for a faith that calls you beyond yourself, this book is for you. If you're a young person who has left the church or is looking for a reason to stay, this book is for you. If you're searching for a more authentic whole-life faith and creative ways God can use your mustard seeds, in concert with others, to be a difference and to make a difference, this book is also for you.

This book is also for anyone looking for a resource that will introduce them to a broader range of new possibilities in terms of how to follow Jesus in difficult times. It is designed to be a study book and a user's manual for reimagining how to create lives and communities of faith with a difference—for campus ministries, colleges, and seminaries, as well as church study groups. There is an online study guide and a forum for those who want to share what God is stirring up in their lives, neighborhoods, and local churches (www.newchangemakers.com).

One heads-up as we begin journeying together. I have "the gift of disorientation." Over the years I have found myself traveling to places where I never planned to go. A good example: I once visited the Taizé Community in France for an overnight stay. The next morning I got up extra early. I gave myself forty minutes for my ten-minute walk to the bus stop, because I wanted to have a buffer in case my "gift" kicked in. Two hours later I found myself wandering through the cow pastures of southern France. I finally retraced my steps back to Taizé, discovering I had turned right when I should have turned left. Eventually, I caught the bus and later a train and made it to my next stop, Madrid. Of course, if I had been traveling with Christine we would have arrived in Madrid on time. But then I never would have made the acquaintance of those lovely cows I met along the way. As you and I travel together, I will attempt to stay on course. I invite you to discover what God is stirring up today and learn how you can be more a part of it in all our tomorrows.

1

Touring, Sampling, and Savoring
the Changemaking Celebration

First Stop: San Francisco

OUR PLANE TOUCHED DOWN at San Francisco International Airport on a stunningly beautiful blue-sky September morning in 2013. I was there to attend the SOCAP[1] Conference because I wanted to learn about new forms of social innovation that are reportedly making a lasting difference in people's lives all over the planet. However, I got much more than I bargained for. I invite you to join me as we not only get a little taste of SOCAP but as we savor tasty examples of the global changemaking celebration.

My first taste of this celebration came as I ate an early morning breakfast of granola and yogurt with my friends at the Sojourner Community[2] in the Mission District. My attention was caught by a rich array of murals in this predominantly Latino neighborhood as I was headed to catch my bus. Suddenly, I was confronted by an arresting portrait of Archbishop Óscar Romero. He seemed to be looking directly at me. This imposing mural is painted on one wall of St. Peter's Catholic Church. It captured for me a sense Archbishop Romero's hope for a future that transcends our present world of violence and injustice. This turned out to be a great image to start what would turn out to be a day of remarkable discovery.

1. See www.socialcapitalmarkets.net.
2. See churchofthesojourners.wordpress.com.

11

I boarded a bus crowded with students, which headed down Van Ness Boulevard and past Redding Elementary School, where I attended my first four years of school. I got off the bus at the end of Van Ness, at the edge of the San Francisco Bay, and walked past the Muni Pier, where I fished on a number of Saturdays as a kid. Then I hiked up over the hill. As I reached the crest I could see the iconic Golden Gate Bridge against the brilliant blue sky.

Directly below me, I spotted Fort Warden, an old military base left over from World War II that has been repurposed as a conference site. I headed down the hill and toward the loud music blaring from a huge inflated tent where SOCAP 13 was beginning. I found myself with nearly two thousand mainly younger social innovators as well as a host of investors and representatives from foundations like the Rockefeller and Bill Gates foundations. I sat in the front row so I could see both the stage and most of the audience. My friend Brian Howe, who heads up Impact Hub Seattle,[3] came in and sat beside me, and I greeted him as the moderator, Rosa Lee Harden, stood to welcome us.

Suddenly a blast of wind off the bay hit the inflated tent and violently shook it for several minutes. Some people edged toward the exits and others of us simply grabbed our chairs. However, what happened over the next three days arrested my attention much more than that blustery beginning. SOCAP, which stands for social capital investment, was started ten years ago by Rosa Lee Harden and her husband, Kevin Jones. Rosa Lee Harden is an Episcopal priest with a background in business. Kevin Jones is a serial business entrepreneur who is running an important venture called Good Capital. Its mission is "to accelerate the flow of capital to enterprises that create innovative market-based solutions to inequality, poverty and other social problems and in doing so amplify their total impact."

There are at least a dozen events like SOCAP all over the planet, including the Skoll World Forum on Social Entrepreneurship, which meets in Oxford, the Clinton Global Initiative, the Feast, and Ted Talks that are held at several locations in the US and around the world. There is also a global network of Impact Hubs[4] from Sao Paulo, Johannesburg, Zurich, and London to Sydney, Toronto, New York, and Seattle. These are essentially incubators where those who want to develop new social in-

---

3. See www.impacthubseattle.com.

4. See www.impacthub.net.

novations gather to help one another create and launch these novel ways to have an impact.

The Changemaking Celebration: Two Streams

Essentially, I am breaking this changemaking celebration into two distinct streams.

The Social Entrepreneurship Stream

Social entrepreneurship creates enterprises that do good by doing well. A growing number of social entrepreneurs are creating innovative new businesses whose primary mission is to have a social and environmental impact. The authors of *The Solution Revolution* explain what makes social entrepreneurship possible: "Converging factors have made this kind of social innovation more attainable. Technology and greater access to venture capital and other funding enable organizations with innovative business models to scale rapidly. Powerful collaboration tools enable citizens to work directly with peers to solve problems."[5]

The Community Empowerment Stream

This entails creating new ways to enable our neighborhoods to increase their capacity for mutual care, sustainability, resilience, and celebration for both the good times and the tough times. Social innovators in this stream often join others in their communities to draw from their shared dreams, imaginations, and local resources to create new forms of community empowerment. The community empowerment stream of changemaking has been around for a while but new expressions are being created every day. "There is a growing movement of people with a different vision for their local communities. . . . In many nations, local people have come together to pursue a common calling," affirm John McKnight and Peter Block in their book *The Abundant Community*.[6]

As you will see, numbers of these social innovators in both streams are imagining, creating, and launching a remarkable range of new forms of social innovation. Those who succeed often have a surprising level of

5. Eggers and Macmillan, *Solution Revolution*, 6.
6. McKnight and Block, *Abundant Community*, 1.

impact. J. Gregory Dees, in the *Stanford Social Innovation Review*, explains why he feels that recently there has been a significant increase in social innovation: "We are moving toward a more open-solution society, one in which people of all walks of life are encouraged to apply their creativity and talents to crafting innovative solutions to social problems and increasing their impact."[7] In other words, we are witnessing the rapid spread of connectivity and democratization of the Web, which is helping accelerate this rise in the rate of social innovation and social discourse in working for the common good.

Join Me for a Global Tour of This Changemaking Celebration

Sampling the Social Entrepreneurship Stream

I want to give you a quick taste of the kinds of social innovation that ignited my imagination at SOCAP 13. Savor every sample and keep your iPad or a notebook handy so that you can write down any creative new possibilities God stirs up for you. Let's fly to Heathrow International Airport outside of London to meet a recent university grad named Aaron Jones. Then we will board a flight with Aaron bound for Cambodia.

Transforming Concrete Bags into Good News

Aaron Jones completed his degree in international enterprise and business development at the University of Essex in the UK. Like many other millennials he is very concerned about the twin issues of social justice and environmental stewardship. So he knew he would never be satisfied with simply finding a comfortable job in business and finance in London.

Aaron made a decision toward the end of his schooling to take a gap year in Southeast Asia to learn more about the realities of people's lives in that region and about possible ways to have a small impact. He found what he was looking for in a Cambodian market—used concrete bags. He was intrigued by the designs of tigers, elephants, eagles, and cobras on these bags. They sparked his imagination.

After doing vigorous research, Aaron took the plunge. He located some startup funding and launched Fikay Eco Fashion.[8] This small social

---

7. Dees, "Toward an Open-Solution Society," par. 1.

8. See www.fikay.co.uk.

enterprise transforms the concrete bags with their emblematic animal designs into new designer products. These include purses, iPhone cases, wallets, and shopping bags. These products are a real hit among the eco-conscious in Europe.

Fikay employs women in Cambodia and pays them twice the minimum wage. Aaron explains that this new business not only provides workers a better income but also teaches them valuable skills that enable them to "have a sustainable, effective way out of poverty."[9] For every product sold, money is given to build schools and provide educational resources in the regions in which the bags are produced. Also, instead of flying the bags from Cambodia to Britain, Aaron has created a slower delivery route by sea that reduces the carbon footprint for the transportation of these products.

Aaron recently invited his friends and patrons to join him at the Clock Tower in London for a four-course meal called Cambodian Fusion to celebrate a very good year for Fikay and those who benefit from this social innovation. I can smell the Cambodian green curry . . . how about you?

Weaving Natural Thai Fabrics into Economic Empowerment for Women

Katie Metzger, a member of our team at Mustard Seed Associates,[10] completed a master's degree at Northwest University in international community development. She took a course in social entrepreneurship with Forrest Inslee. She and one of her classmates, Danielle Neufeld, have launched a new venture called Same Thread. They have developed a new line of women's fashion, using Thai fabrics and natural dyes, for the American market. Same Thread hires women in northern Thailand and pays them a living wage to give them a real alternative to working in the sex trade to support themselves and their family.[11] Katie and Danielle recently celebrated a very successful beginning, raising $12,000 through a Kickstarter campaign to get their social enterprise launched. I wish you could have been with us for their celebration at Chef Cafe, an Ethiopian restaurant here in Seattle. We celebrated with a huge array of Ethiopian

9. Mead, "Fikay Eco Fashion," par. 5.

10. See www.msaimagine.org.

11. See www.facebook.com/samethread.

dishes, including two of my favorites: gomen, a spicy collard dish, and a festive vegetarian platter.

Aaron, Kathy, and Danielle are all members of the millennial generation or Gen Y. As mentioned earlier, this generation seems to be more motivated than previous generations to create businesses that are designed to have a social or environmental impact. The millennial generation is beginning to change not only the profile of work but their view of charity as well. "The traditional model of doing social and charitable good when you have reached a certain level of economic wealth, namely later in life, is no longer viable," states Claritta Peters, a student involved in the social enterprise movement in the UK. This generation wants their entire lives to make a difference, not just to contribute a share of their discretionary resources as they prosper.[12]

Watch out for Gen Z! They are the first social media generation, and a surprising number of them seem to be hardwired to be changemakers too. The BBC has suggested a couple of names for this age cohort. The one I like best is "Rainbow Generation," since this will be the most racially diverse generation in most of our Western countries.[13] Charlotte Seager, writing in the Business Insider, asserts that Gen Z will be even more committed to changing the world than Gen Y and will likely be more entrepreneurial,[14] which bodes well for the continued growth of this promising changemaking celebration—and that's very good news for our common future!

Joining the Social Entrepreneurship Stream

Redeemer Presbyterian Church in New York was one of the first to start new entrepreneurial ventures, and a few other churches are considering this form of changemaking. Most schools of business in Christian colleges now offer courses in social entrepreneurship. Seattle Pacific University has launched a new program in Social Entrepreneurship Education, for church leaders to enable them and their congregations to become more effective change agents in their own communities.[15] Spencer Burke is collaborating with the Disciples of Christ to offer a master's

12. Seager, "Generation Y," par. 12.

13. Alsop, "Why Bosses Won't 'Like' Generation Z," par. 6.

14. Peterson, "Millennials Are Old News," par. 7.

15. See www.spu.edu/cse.

of divinity degree at Hatchery L.A., in what he calls "a Silicon Valley of church innovation."[16] Burke coordinates this educational venture that is already working with their grads to create "common cause communities in the way of Jesus" and to develop innovative approaches to making a difference in the lives of their neighbors in Los Angeles.

Can you see the potential impact of scaling up these kinds of social enterprises to improve the lives of tens of millions of people? Now I want to invite you to join me as we fly to Portland, Oregon, to visit the first of several examples within the community empowerment stream.

Sampling the Community Empowerment Stream

Transforming Paint and Brushes into Good News

You don't need to be a business entrepreneur like Aaron or Katie to be involved in creating new ways to make our world a better place. You simply have to find others in your own community who want to make a little difference and make a beginning.

I want you to meet Brandon Rhodes and some of his friends in the Lents neighborhood of Southeast Portland. As we arrive on a warm Saturday morning in June, we see Brandon and about eighteen others of different ages and cultural backgrounds gathering with paintbrushes plus loads of enthusiasm.

Weeks earlier these neighbors had used their imagination to come up with ideas to help people in their low-income neighborhood become better connected. It began when fifty neighbors came together and did some brainstorming. They started quite simply by asking for everyone's ideas of what they might do to create a little more pride in their neighborhood. Someone mentioned that one of the major things that distinguished this small community is the beautiful array of trees.

The four most prominent trees were the maples, firs, pines, and oaks. Ideas started popping. This led to them to paint a mural of trees right on the pavement in that intersection. This band of "artists" brought paint and brushes and got to work. First they painted the outline of the four trees pointing out in all four directions. In the center of the intersection the

---

16. See www.hatcheryla.com.

roots of the four trees formed an elegant Celtic knot. They even posted a video on YouTube documenting and sharing their project.[17]

As they were putting the finishing touches on this very beautiful piece of public art, people came from everywhere in the Lents neighborhood to view their work and to celebrate. As they circled the stunning, freshly painted picture in the intersection, the participants reported that the project not only connected them but also pulled them together right into the Celtic knot.

And the attraction grew. So many neighbors came to see the artwork that they began to run out of food. One good neighbor ran a couple blocks to Amigos del Sol and returned with some two hundred taquitos filled with meat and cheese that kept the party going. Can you smell the taquitos? Are you beginning to savor this colorful community innovation? Stay with me as we fly from Portland to a very different community in Detroit.

Transforming Vacant Buildings into Good News

Neighborhoods and communities around the world are determined to take much greater responsibility for their common life, including the natural order that sustains them. For that reason, many communities begin as Wendell Berry advocates: by seeking to increase their own local food self-sufficiency. That includes protecting what Berry calls "the natural foundations of the human economy": soil, water, and air.[18]

For example, in the Brightmoor neighborhood of Detroit, residents of all ages farm back yards, front yards, and vacant lots to increase local food self-sufficiency. Some of the young people are selling their produce at local farmers' markets. According to Detroit city councilman James Tate, people in Brightmoor are experiencing "a sense of accomplishment in a community that has seen so much disinvestment."[19]

Jeff Adams, who lives in the neighborhood, had been looking for an entrepreneurial opportunity to provide jobs for his unemployed neighbors. Jeff's background is in marketing automotive products. An opportunity came, and a vertical gardening business called Artesian Farms was

17. "Community Roots" Intersection Repair: www.youtube.com/watch?v=spyhz2 jjUBI.

18. Berry, "Thoughts in the Presence of Fear," XXV.

19. Satyanarayana, "Urban Farming Invigorates Detroit Neighborhood."

born in an empty manufacturing building. He found investors and started putting neighbors to work.[20] Jeff has just harvested some fresh carrots for us to sample—my first taste of produce from vertical gardening.

As you consider joining this important new celebration it is important to remember that changemaking is not easy. Any readers who have sought to create new forms of community empowerment more than likely have discovered that these ventures don't always succeed. However, I will share some of the best resources I have found that may make it easier for you to join those who are discovering they can make a real impact.

This Is Your Invitation to Join the Dreamers and Schemers!

Join me as we return to the SOCAP Conference for the final plenary address. As I sat back down in the same seat in the tent for the final plenary at SOCAP 13, I found myself reeling from the dozens of examples of social innovation I had sampled over the past three days as you might be from the innovations you just sampled as we traveled together. I had no idea how to respond to this remarkable feast of new ways to do real changemaking.

Van Jones, the progressive voice on CNN's Crossfire, was our final plenary speaker. "You guys are here to invent the future!" he shouted. He reminded us of Dr. Martin Luther King's compelling dream for a future of reconciliation and justice for all people. Then he added, "You need to create new dreams and schemes . . . I want to support the future you want to invent!" Not surprisingly, the nearly two thousand social entrepreneurs gave Van Jones a rousing ovation as the conference concluded.

On my flight back to Seattle I read over my pages of notes and reflected on the fact that I couldn't remember ever being in a space with so many people who wanted to invest their lives in making a difference. I was impressed by the sense of empathy and compassion that seemed to motivate many of them. God got my attention by showing me how many of them were already "dreaming and scheming" to make a positive impact in the lives of others.

As I flew home, God deeply convicted me through the commitment and risk-taking of these social innovators. I suddenly realized that even though I had written books about reaching out to neighbors, it had been years since I had been down on the field of play. As the plane landed in

20. Gallagher, "Vertical Farming Sprouts in Detroit's Brightmoor District."

Seattle I realized that I needed to change. I wrote in my journal that I would try to find some way to actually get back in the game.

I could hardly wait to talk with Christine. Part of the rhythm of our lives together is going out to breakfast on Sunday morning and journaling before we go to church. On this particular morning we happened to go to the Portage Bay Cafe, which prides itself on serving only local, sustainable food. We hadn't eaten there for about three years. As I looked up from the menu I noticed that all the wait staff were wearing black Portage Bay Cafe T-shirts that read, "Eat like you give a damn!"

"That's it! I need to join these social innovators and start living like I give a damn," I blurted out, which startled our waiter. Since that personal wake-up call I have found three new ways to begin living like I give a damn:

1. After much searching for an opportunity, I have volunteered with my friends at Seattle Mennonite Church and Lake City Future First. For the first time in years, I am getting out of the bleachers and back on the field of play. I have joined our neighbors in north Seattle in their efforts to create a more resilient and flourishing local community, particularly for the most vulnerable. I encourage readers to discover those in your own communities who enjoy making a little difference.

2. I have also decided to join those who are committed to empowering a new generation of changemakers who want to use their lives to make an impact. I started by challenging the huge gathering of friends that just helped me celebrate my eightieth birthday. Rental prices for students here in Seattle are extremely high. So I invited my friends to ask people in their churches to consider joining Christine and me in providing rental space in their homes, at below market value, for students from the Seattle School of Theology and Psychology. Many of these students want to invest their lives in fashioning new expressions of the changemaking celebration, but the costs of getting started are making it extremely difficult.

3. I also realize, as an older white, privileged male that there is still much in my life I need to change to become a more authentic follower of the radical way of Jesus. First, I simply need to develop the discipline to listen more carefully to God and those around me, including taking more time for biblical reflection. I also need to become more disciplined in stewarding my time and learn to stay on

top of my email and blog posting. Thankfully, I have found a new spiritual director at Saint Joseph's Catholic Church who is willing to help me up my game a bit.

I am deeply grateful for God's mercy and grace in my life every waking moment. However, I am no longer content with a status-quo way of life. I am joining those who want to change and grow and live like they give a damn—for life in these challenging times!

I do realize that the title of this book may be off-putting to some of my Christian friends. However, I am using this phrase because I believe we have a very small window of time in which to take our personal faith much more seriously, reinvent our churches, and join forces with the many people who are already seeking to create their best communities and their best world—and in the process their best lives.

I also realize some of my readers are already highly involved in making a difference in their workplaces and in their neighborhoods. However, I hope this book motivates all of us to do two things: to invite God to ignite our imaginations, and to join those who are creating new ways both to be a difference and to make a difference, so that we can all more fully participate in this new changemaking celebration.

Dreaming, Scheming, and Launching at SOCAP 14

Return with me now to San Francisco on another mostly blue-sky day one year later for SOCAP 14. This time Van Jones offers the lead-off address. He reports, with evident enthusiasm, that he followed his own advice from SOCAP 13. After that conference he got busy doing his own "dreaming and scheming." He acted on the deep concern he had voiced the year before about the huge number of young people in schools in poorer communities from both Gens Y and Z who have little chance of achieving a decent way of life. With the help of some influential friends, Jones created a remarkable new opportunity for their future.

Van Jones shouted at us, "Yes we code!" He explained that this program was part of the answer to the question of how to address the urgent educational needs of young people in underfinanced schools. #YesWe-Code[21] is designed, with the support of leaders from Silicon Valley, Main Street, and Wall Street, to educate one hundred thousand students in poor schools in how to become high-level computer programmers. The

21. See www.yeswecode.org.

impact on the lives of bright and creative young people will be enormous. Today when these students graduate, not only do they have very limited job opportunities, but many of the jobs they qualify for don't pay a living wage. They tend to have a much higher rate of unemployment and underemployment than older adults.

This program will empower young people who, when they learn to code, could have starting salaries that range from $60,000 to $70,000 a year. These young people will also likely create a range of innovative new apps and products using their own imaginations. This, of course, will also be a boost to our entire national economy and make many of our communities much stronger as well.

Where Does This Celebration of Changemaking Begin?

Many of the changemakers I am introducing you to are not people of faith, but often they are people of compassion. Shouldn't we become people of "compassion and action" too? Shouldn't we who are followers of Jesus express our love for both God and neighbor in more concrete ways? Lets start where many of the changemakers start—by imagining new ways we can join in making a real impact in the lives of our neighbors, as you will do in our next chapter on creativity. This is an invitation to discover how God can enable us to unleash the potential of our imagination, to create new ways to be a difference and make a difference. Peggy Taylor and Charlie Murphy, writing in *YES! Magazine*, state, "Creative expression opens the door to the inner world of our imaginations: it is here that we make meaning of our lives; it is here that motivation takes root. The more creative we are, the more capacity we have to imagine what's possible and make those visions real."[22] *YES! Magazine* is one of the best resources I have found to keep you abreast of what is being stirred up on the innovative edge.

Dreaming and Scheming

This is your invitation to "imagine what is possible and make those visions real." Find a friend or two or a small group in your church. Get out your iPad or a notebook and begin by responding to some questions:

22. Taylor and Murphy, "10 Things Creative People Know," par. 5.

1. What are some changemaking ventures that are already having an impact in lives of neighbors in your community or somewhere else in the world that you might join?

2. What are some new dreams for changemaking that God is stirring up in your imagination that could make a real difference in the lives of your neighbors locally or globally?

3. Where can you find a small group where you can work with others to begin reordering your life so that you can free up more time to be present to both God and neighbor?

4. How do you plan to celebrate every step forward as you seek to become more a part of the changemaking celebration?

Are you beginning to see the potential of this new changemaking celebration? Why don't you join others in the kitchen shaking and baking, dreaming and scheming? Let me give you a little overview of the rest of our journey together so you are ready to travel.

GPS for Our Tour of the Changemaking Celebration

Here is the itinerary for our journey together that starts in the kitchen of creativity.

Introduction: "The Clock Is Ticking!": Join the Changemaking Celebration

Chapter 1: Touring, Sampling, and Savoring the Changemaking Celebration

Chapter 2: Igniting Our Imaginations Today to Create Our Best Tomorrows

At the very center of this changemaking celebration is remarkable creativity. I will invite you to discover how God can ignite our imaginations to create both innovative forms of changemaking and new ways of living as we join others in creating our best tomorrows. In chapters 2 though

8, I will break each chapter into two distinct conversations to give you more time to reflect and engage all the opportunities in this changemaking celebration.

Chapter 3: Anticipating New Opportunities to Create Our Best Tomorrows Today

We are racing into a future of accelerating change and surprising new opportunities. I will invite you to join those who are identifying new opportunities and then create innovative ways to engage these new opportunities—making a difference in both the lives of our neighbors and our own lives as well.

Chapter 4: Choosing Changemaking Purposes Today for All Our Tomorrows

We also live in a world filled with many competing narratives, aspirations, and dreams for all our tomorrows. Therefore, it is essential that we define a clear sense of purpose for our social innovations and our own lives and communities that more directly connect to a more compelling sense of something of God's loving purposes for people and the planet.

Chapter 5: Imagine New Community Empowerment Today to Create Our Best Neighborhoods Tomorrow

We will explore a range of innovative approaches to community empowerment that include sustainable local business and environmental networks, innovative forms of mutual care and economic cooperatives, local investing, and new community celebrations. Then I will outline the steps to create a new form of community empowerment.

Chapter 6: Imagine New Social Enterprise Today to Create Our Best World Tomorrow

I will give readers a fuller sampling of this stream to illustrate the potential of social entrepreneurship and innovation to promote the common good locally and globally. Then I will present steps and resources that entrepreneurs and their collaborators use to create new social enterprises.

Chapter 7: Imagine Living on Purpose Today to Create Our Best Lives Tomorrow

One of the things that impresses me most about this changemaking revolution is the numbers of innovators who are not only creating purpose-focused innovations but also often creating more purpose-focused, disciplined lives through life coaching. I will show followers of Jesus how we can create our best lives not only by living with a clearer sense of purpose but also by developing more innovative ways to more fully live into those purposes.

Chapter 8: Imagine Gen Next Joining Us to Create Our Best Churches for Tomorrow

I will encourage readers to invite the voices of Gen Next to discover what their creative ideas are for not only changemaking but also to help us reimagine and reinvent both our churches and our own lives. We will offer practical ways to 1) create churches for others, joining those who are creating innovative ways to make a lasting impact in the lives of our neighbors; and 2) become people for others by joining those who are reordering their personal lives to put first things first and to discover the good life of God . . . creating better parties.

What are God's dreams, not only for our lives but also for our neighbors and our world? Pope Francis has an answer to this question, an answer that stems from his frequent contacts with the marginalized and forgotten. He reminds us of the clear focus of God's dreaming: "I prefer a church which is bruised, hurting and dirty because it has been out in the streets, rather than a church which is unhealthy from being confined and *clinging* to its own security."[23] Doesn't dreaming and scheming, for followers of Jesus, always begin by trying to glimpse something of God's dream for a people and a world, and then joining it?

---

23. Francis, *Evangelii Gaudium*, 49.

2

Igniting Our Imaginations Today
to Create Our Best Tomorrows

"Dreaming and Scheming" on the Innovation Express!

"Last call for the Innovation Express!" The conductor's voice echoed through the station on a sunny San Francisco morning in 2013, and twenty-five millennials began boarding a vintage 1950s train complete with a domed observation car, an elegant dining car, and sleeping cars.

The Millennial Trains Project, a nonprofit organization supported through crowdfunding and other contributions, is one of the most imaginative expressions of the new changemaking celebration. What I found most fascinating about this trip—the first in a series of transcontinental train trips with the same function—was its design as an innovation incubator on wheels. The twenty-five millennial passengers were selected on the basis of their current and potential work as social innovators. Each Millennial Train stops in seven key cities to visit new expressions of social innovation in the United States.

The train also serves to create a space for learning and invention, as key entrepreneurs and innovation leaders are invited to mentor their younger counterparts in their new ventures, some of whom were already at work creating new innovations, while the rest brought creative possibilities to work on during their trip.

Remember that the millennials—those born between 1981 and 1997—are the first generation of "digital natives." As we have seen, they tend to be more globally aware. They care about the well-being of the workers who make their clothes. They also they care about issues of racial justice, social justice, and environmental stewardship. Not surprisingly, the passengers on this Millennial Train trip were eager to learn about innovative ways to use their lives to work for change.

The train stopped in strategic cities that are experiencing a resurgence of entrepreneurship and innovation. For example, in Omaha, the innovation has primarily been driven by creative leaders who have purchased rundown warehouses and converted them into workable, livable spaces. In Denver, the Downtown Denver Partnership is creating hubs for startups with the intention of making the city the number one destination for young entrepreneurs in America.

Listen to the insights of a sampling of the millennials who were a part of this first transcontinental venture: "We created a community that valued creativity, curiosity, collaboration, and introspection and we pushed each other to push our ideas further," Travis Korte reported. Web Barr expressed surprise: "What I thought would be a cool trip across the U.S. by train was so much more. It was an incredible way to learn about the intersection of innovation, community space, entrepreneurship and philanthropy." And Autumn Carter added, "I felt like a part of a community and network that believe in the vision of this generation."[1]

Several of these young innovators actually gave birth to new forms of changemaking during their cross-country journey: "Daniella Uslan . . . met with local food purveyors to understand how they recycle their food waste and subsequently launched a social enterprise to repackage and sell salvageable food waste. Jenny Gottstein used a fictional zombie apocalypse as a framework for disaster preparedness training."[2]

CONVERSATION 1—DISCOVERING YOUR CREATIVITY

Followers of Jesus: Unleash Your Imagination!

While most of us will not have the opportunity to board one of the Millennial Trains, we can all find ways to join these young innovators by learning how to unleash our imaginations. We too can create imaginative

---

1. The Millennial Train Project: www.millennialtrain.co/impact.
2. Slade, "Crowdsourced Incubator on Track," par. 6.

new ways to be a difference and make a difference in our communities and in our own lives and families as well.

We can join those on the innovative edge in our communities and churches who are creating their best communities, their best world, and in the process their best lives. We can join those who are unleashing the potential of their mustard seeds to create and launch new possibilities that both engage some of tomorrow's challenges and advance something of God's loving purposes for a people and a world.

I want to suggest a radical proposal for followers of Jesus—that *all of life* is a "design opportunity"! I am not only inviting you to create new forms of changemaking; I am also urging you to consider creating new ways of being. I am asking you to consider the possibility that following Jesus is much more than a spiritual add-on to your "real life." I believe it is a call to a more radical whole-life faith, a wonderful opportunity to reimagine and reinvent our entire lives so that we more authentically reflect something of the aspirations and values of Jesus and that first community. We are called to live into values that are often in direct conflict with the aspirations and values of the dominant global culture.

I am a huge fan of Walter Brueggemann and his important writings. *The Prophetic Imagination*, published in 1978, was the first of his books that arrested my attention. There he wrote, "The contemporary American church is so largely enculturated to the American ethos of consumerism that it has little power to believe or to act. This enculturation is in some way true across the spectrum of church life, both liberal and conservative . . . This enculturation is true not only of the institutional church but also of us as persons."[3] I suspect this is significantly more true today than when the book was published—true not only in our churches, but even more so in our lives and families.

Walter Brueggemann's remedy is to encourage us to develop a "prophetic imagination," to create ways of living as well as new ways of acting that are clearly at counterpoint to the establishment imagination. Brueggemann proposes, toward the end of his book, that our decision to follow Jesus is a decision not only to embrace a different view of reality but also to join those creating new forms of countercultural community.[4]

Doesn't embracing this view of discipleship open the door to viewing all of life as a new design opportunity? Doesn't it open the possibility

3. Brueggemann, *Prophetic Imagination*, 11.
4. Ibid., 96.

to creating new forms of housing that emphasize the values of community and hospitality over the values of autonomy and acquisition? Doesn't it also open the door to creating new ways to celebrate around themes of homecoming, reconciliation, and Jubilee? Wouldn't it also open the door to beginning to alter our timestyles so that we have more time to be present to both God and neighbor?

The Coming of an Age of Imagination

What has made it possible for so many people in our communities and in some of our congregations, in the last ten years, to "dream and scheme" and create innovative new forms of changemaking? I credit it, in part, to the coming of a new Age of Imagination.

The Information Age we entered in the early years of this new millennium has implications for how we access and utilize information as a society, and expands the opportunities for creative participation for all of us. Dr. John Vanston of Technology Futures, Inc., elaborates: "The almost unlimited amount of information being produced, together with increasingly effective techniques for increasing and processing this information, means that, in the future, success will not depend upon the amount of information one can gather, but rather on how imaginatively individuals and organizations can employ this information. Thus I am convinced that we have entered a new age—the Age of Imagination."[5]

In other words, one of the gifts of the Information Age is the democratization of access to this swelling universe of information. As a consequence the world of imagination, innovation, and creativity is no longer the exclusive domain of a small elite, of technologists, business entrepreneurs, or artists. We are all welcome to try our hand at preparing festive new possibilities that have never been seen before. The good news is that we can all become dreamers and schemers, shakers and makers.

In an important article in *Forbes*, Rita King urges us to view this new age of information as a new Age of Imagination: "We can collectively imagine and create the future we want to inhabit before we lose that chance."[6]

---

5. Vanston, "In the Age of Imagination," par. 4.

6. King, interview with Drew Hansen, "Imagination," par. 9.

Waking Up to the Risk of Missing the Age of Imagination

Is it possible that many of us who are followers of Jesus could miss the opportunity to create "the future we want to inhabit" because we fail to take our God-given imagination seriously? Let me be clear: I am not suggesting for a moment that there is no innovation in the church. In fact, for more than thirty years I have enjoyed reporting on the innovative edge in both society and the church.

Until recently, however, innovation has come almost exclusively from the leaders of our churches and Christian organizations. A friend of mine who belongs to a megachurch related that his pastor often states that his congregation "lives in terror of his returning from a conference or having read another book because he will have yet more innovative ideas for them to implement."

Over the past twenty years, Christine and I have offered futures/creativity workshops for congregations called *Imagine That!* We invite participants in a Saturday workshop to choose a small creativity group, each with a different topic, to create new possible ways to make a difference in their neighborhoods, their congregations, and their own lives. Invariably, participants tell us that this workshop was the first time they had ever been asked for their ideas at church.

I suspect that we could all learn from firms like Apple and Google the importance of inviting creative input from everyone in the organization. We could also learn from firms like these how to more thoroughly research best practices in terms of Christian innovation in other churches and Christian organizations—that could stimulate our creativity.

In *The New Conspirators: Creating the Future One Mustard Seed at a Time*,[7] I was delighted to report that a number of younger Christian leaders in Britain, Australia, Canada, and the United States stopped waiting for leaders to invite their ideas. In the early 1990s they started taking the initiative in creating new expressions of the church as well as new ways to make a difference in the lives of others. For example, when Alan Hirsch was a lad he started an innovative missional church-birthing program in Melbourne, Australia, called The Forge. I was impressed by the innovative process The Forge used not only to invite students' ideas for new missional churches but also to help these young innovators launch their new models.

7. Sine, *New Conspirators*.

In other words, it is essential that our congregations and Christian organizations not only invite creative input from everyone but also enable them to develop and launch their most viable new ideas. Remember, as we discussed in the last chapter, if the future is going to have a church, then we need to invite and take seriously the creative ideas of Gen Y and Gen Z in particular. If we enable the young in our neighborhoods or churches to launch their most viable ideas for changemaking or reinventing our churches, then they would have a sense of ownership—which, I suspect, is the key for their leading the church into the 2020s.

Discovering That We Are All Creators!

As children of the Creator God, we are all creative. Like the students on the train, we can all learn new ways to unleash the potential of our imaginations. Creativity is not the exclusive province of people like Mark Zuckerberg, Sergey Brin, or Kurt Cobain. Of course, some of us may not have used our imaginations much recently. However, I assure you God can ignite all of our imaginations and enable us to dream, scheme, and give birth not only to new possibilities for our own lives and families but also to new ways to make a difference in the lives of others as well. We can all become much more a part of this new Age of Imagination.

Discovering How We Can Create "the Future We Want to Inhabit"!

This changemaking celebration is at its core a celebration of imagination. People all over the planet are waking up to the opportunity to imagine and create new possibilities for their neighborhoods, the larger world, and their own lives. I am finding more and more people who, like the millennials on the train, are intrigued by the remarkable potential of unleashing our imaginations to create "the future we want to inhabit." Many of us don't want to miss out on being a part of this Age of Imagination. Yet in many cases, we don't know where to begin.

Wouldn't you like to discover how God might ignite your imagination to create innovative new ways to *be* a difference and *make* a difference—to engage new opportunities in ways that advance God's loving purposes for a people and a world?

I suspect the easiest way for most of us to begin reconnecting to our imaginations is to travel back to childhood. Think of your own childhood: what are some of your most compelling memories of experiences or times when something stirred your imagination? Was it in an experience in your grandparents' home, perhaps, or while on a vacation with your family, or creating a clubhouse with your friends?

One of my own earliest memories of having my creativity stirred is of a time way back in the 1940s, when I was six years old and living with my parents in San Francisco.

Creativity in the Kitchen

As the trolley car clanged its way up the steep Powell Street hill from Fisherman's Wharf to Nob Hill, I was standing on the trolley's running board and used my left arm to hang on for dear life. My right arm was wrapped around a huge shopping bag full of live, squirming crabs. My dad, Tom senior, was hanging on to the post next to me and toting an even larger bag of prawns, fish, clams, and loaves of sourdough French bread.

This was the first time I had experienced this unusual shopping experience with my dad, but it wouldn't be the last. My dad worked hard all week helping construct ships in Alameda to transport troops during World War II. At the time, meat was rationed, but seafood was abundant and inexpensive. My dad became motivated to see what he could cook up in our small kitchen.

My mom, Katherine, and I were both surprised and delighted that my dad, with the help of a couple of seafood cookbooks, began to create a host of new tasty seafood dishes. My favorite was his version of Crab Rangoon using fresh crab, shrimp, cream cheese, spinach, leeks, and artichoke hearts. Soon our small apartment on the second floor was open for seafood sampling many Saturday afternoons. We became very popular with our neighbors on all three floors.

I was so impressed with my dad's creative achievements that I started learning to cook and create in our kitchen as well. One of my early specialties was pancakes. One Sunday morning I fried three absolutely perfect pancakes for my breakfast. I slathered them with butter. Then I reached up on the top shelf for the brown bottle. I poured its contents all over my three lovely pancakes, took a bite, and almost perished.

Somehow I had grabbed the vinegar instead of the syrup. There was no more batter, and no way back.

That was one my earliest discoveries—even our best creative ideas can lead to failure. For those who are active in changemaking, however, those failures provide important lessons. Very often, ventures launched with these lessons in mind are more successful, since they are informed by what we have learned from our setbacks.

Creativity in the Classroom

My six-year-old creativity was ignited by more than my dad's seafood feasts. It was also ignited by Miss Laverne in my first-grade class at Redding Elementary School in San Francisco.

Miss Laverne was a very quiet and retiring teacher. I never would have guessed that she had a wonderfully wicked imagination. Halfway through the school year, Miss Laverne made a very unusual request. She asked eleven of my twenty-two classmates to bring wooden orange crates to class. She asked the rest of us to bring in some scrap pieces of wood and any cardboard we could find in our neighborhood. Miss Laverne brought an assortment of saws and hammers that were designed for smaller hands, and she put us to work in small groups. I can remember how awestruck we kids were several weeks later when we beheld what we had fashioned.

There stretching across the back of our large classroom was a train complete with an engine. The engine was simply a large oil drum connected to a box, with large wheels we had fabricated out of old cardboard. She showed us how to make wooden wheels for each of the eleven orange crates. We also put two wooden seats in each orange crate, so we had enough space to seat all twenty-two students. Then we painted it, and we were ready to roll.

Back in the 1940s, field trips were virtually unheard of because school budgets were tight. So we created our own field trips. Twice a week for the rest of the year Miss Laverne would have us all board our train. Students took turns studying and preparing to be tour guides to different locations. When we "arrived" at our destinations, we would clamber off our train and visit different sites, from the canneries of Monterey to the gold fields near Sacramento.

You can imagine how these excursions ignited our imaginations as well as enriched our learning. The two experiences described here—learning how to cook and becoming a train tour guide at the age of six—have had a lasting impact on my imagination.

Creativity in Global Competition for Kids

Kayra Inslee was seven years old when Christine and I first met her and her dad, Forrest Inslee. Forrest is a gifted professor who teaches courses on both community development and social entrepreneurship in the Seattle area. Forrest and Kayra have really become family and now live in community with Christine and me.

We particularly enjoy watching Kayra grow up. Until recently, her life seemed to be focused on interests common to kids her age: soccer, sleepovers with friends, and a growing appreciation of art. Though already a creative kid at heart, Kayra's imagination was ignited by a particular discovery she and her friends made after her ninth birthday: an organization called Destination Imagination.[8]

Destination Imagination is a global organization whose stated purpose is to "teach the creative process from imagination to innovation . . . to help student teams learn to be creative in every aspect of their lives." Kayra and a small group of her friends have become keen participants since that discovery.

Kayra, now thirteen, and her friends, who are members of Gen Z, have taken part in innovation competitions with teams of students from all over the world. These teams are inspired to combine art, science, math, and engineering methods in new ways to meet challenges that are posed to them. Victory goes to the most innovative, thought-provoking, and effective solutions.

This year Kayra and her team won the regional and state competitions for their age group, then moved on to the Global Finals—touted as "the world's largest celebration of creativity"—in Knoxville, Tennessee.

Imagine the scene: a stadium full of nearly eight thousand students. The energy is palpable as more than fourteen hundred teams from all over the world compete and, more importantly, befriend each other—teams not only from North America but also from Asia, Africa, the Middle East, and Latin America.

8. See www.destinationimagination.org.

The teams work throughout the year, prior to Globals, to research and develop a specific academic category. Kayra's team recently faced a challenge in the science category: how to survive in extreme environments.

The team proposed a whimsical scenario through which to explore the challenge: survival inside the human stomach! They spent months researching everything from corrosion-resistant materials for survival suits to social strategies for staying alive. They then created a performance, complete with props and functional devices, to demonstrate their scientifically grounded, innovative solutions through humor, art, and design.

While the competitive dynamic of Destination Imagination adds an element of fun, Kayra explained that it's not really the point: "We get to learn so many things, like a really fun way of doing school. For the challenges, we sometimes have to figure out how to design and build something in a short time, with just the materials they give us. Or sometimes they give us a problem through a story, and we have to think in new ways about a solution that maybe no one has thought of before—and then we might have to perform the solution!"

Forrest also reported from his perspective as both a father and an educator: "Students invariably do better in school; more importantly, they become better creative thinkers and problem-solvers, and learn to work together as teams."

According to one study carried out by the University of Virginia's Curry School of Education, "Students who participated in the activities and tournaments provided by Destination Imagination outperformed comparable students who had not participated in Destination Imagination on assessments measuring creative thinking, critical thinking and collaborative problem-solving."[9]

Preparing a New Generation of Changemakers

One of the groups that is doing the best job equipping Generation Next to become an active part of the creative edge of this changemaking celebration is Ashoka. Bill Drayton founded Ashoka in 1980. Ashoka is heavily invested in enabling people all over the planet to ignite their creativity so they can learn to become changemakers. They have almost three thousand Ashoka Fellows in seventy countries. One of the programs that I find

9. See the Destination Imagination website, under the heading "Proven Results": www.idodi.org/get-involved/administrators.

most intriguing is Ashoka's Youth Venture. They are enabling more than five thousand youth in a number of different countries to develop their creative problem-solving skills in small groups. Unlike Kayra's Destination Imagination team, who were focusing on a hypothetical problem, students in Youth Venture learn to come up with creative ways to solve real problems right in their own communities.

For example, Jessie Mehrhoff, also a thirteen-year-old Gen Z-er in Wilmington, Connecticut, started a creative action group called Green Teens at her high school. Green Teens convinced the school to install a new composting system in the cafeteria to transform waste into compost. Green Teens has also become effective as green ambassadors in their community, influencing neighbors to create more sustainable lifestyles by using reusable shopping bags and replacing their old light bulbs with compact fluorescent bulbs. What might happen in your home, church, or community if you invited the young to discover the satisfaction of creating and launching new ways to make a real difference where they live?

Dreaming, Scheming, and Creating

Now it is your turn. Get out your iPad or notebook.

- Think about your own story as you grew up: What are some experiences that ignited your creativity? Write those areas down to share with family or friends.

- Start taking regular creativity "recesses" and set aside time and places to unleash your imagination. Then identify one of your areas of creative interest today, such as creating a new app, a new form of an electronic game, writing song lyrics, or creating a wild new recipe. Write down your innovative new ideas and share them with a friend.

- Now I invite you to follow in Kayra's footsteps and find a couple of friends to walk the streets of your community and spot some challenges your neighbors are facing. Then begin dreaming and scheming of new ways you might enable yourself and those in your community to solve those problems or perhaps create a festive neighborhood party.

Now I am going to offer a quick introduction to the origins of this innovation revolution. Then I will introduce some new ways that you can join others in discovering how God can ignite your imagination to create innovative new possibilities for both your own life and the lives of your neighbors.

CONVERSATION II—JOINING THE INNOVATION REVOLUTION

Dropping into Innovation Central

In *The Innovators*, by Walter Isaacson, we are offered a sweeping history of the "Digital Revolution": "The digital vision looked into the future and saw unimagined possibilities of representing, recombining and communicating information—and doing so fast, robustly, cheaply and globally."[10] No one had previously expected such a remarkable explosion of creativity and innovation, which gave birth not only to the Digital Revolution and the Imagination Age but also to the new social innovation movement as well.

Notably, Isaacson suggests that this remarkable explosion of innovation that has placed Silicon Valley at the center of the innovation universe doesn't simply originate from the imaginations of talented engineers and business entrepreneurs. He suggests that it is also a product of a range of cultural movements that have played a major role in shaping the culture of the Bay Area over the last forty years. These movements include the Whole Earth movement, organic farming communes, the "Homebrew hackers," free speech activists, social justice advocates, and all kinds of hobbyists and "makers."[11]

Tim Brown, the head of IDEO, also seems to believe that some of these broader impulses are essential to the emergence of the field of social innovation. He observes, "A purely technocratic view of innovation is less sustainable now than ever." What we need are innovative new products and new forms of social innovation "that balance the needs of individuals and society as a whole; that tackle the global challenges of health, poverty,

---

10. Shapin, Review of *The Innovators*, par. 2.

11. Ibid., par. 8.

and education; new strategies that result in differences that matter and a sense of purpose that engages everyone affected by them."[12]

Discovering a World Swept Up in the Age of Innovation

Not surprisingly, in this Age of Innovation we are seeing a rapid increase in all kinds of centers of innovation all over the planet—from Europe, Britain, and Australia to an innovation boom in China and early start-ups in Africa. Some of the more established North American centers for innovation include the MIT Media Lab, the Center for Imagineering at Disney, and Lincoln Center Education, which sponsors Imagination Conversations for professionals across the US.

In the past decade, we have also witnessed a remarkable multiplication of Impact Hubs and similar organizations all over the world. These Impact Hubs are really birthing centers for primarily younger innovators who want a supportive community in which to imagine, create, and launch new forms of social innovations that could have a significant social and environmental impact.

Hackathons are one of the most recent forms of innovative problem-solving, and they are sweeping the planet like a firestorm. Not only tech firms but also businesses of all sizes, nonprofits, and new social enterprises are utilizing them. Hackathons are competitions that employees join outside of their regular work lives and that involve working in small groups to create inventive ways to solve difficult problems.

For example, Harry's, a New York–based firm that sells shaving gear, annually donates 1 percent of its sales and time to nonprofits, in cooperation with an AmeriCorps program called City Year. The mission of City Year is to persuade young people to volunteer a year of their lives to work in urban impact programs. They sponsor an annual hackathon and have fun doing good. Laura Zax, director of social innovation at Harry's, reported that she has "never seen her peers more motivated than during a hackathon. It is the natural friendly competition of a hackathon and the ticking clock that keeps people on their toes."

For this event, four members of City Year picked the winners whose presentations came out of their group brainstorming. Believe it or not, one firm gave the first-place winner a cow, the second-place winner a goat, and the third-place winner a pig.

12. Brown, *Change by Design*, 3.

In keeping with its social mission, Harry's simply rewarded their winners with the fact that they helped a charitable organization recruit more young men and women to volunteer a year of their lives to make a difference in the lives of vulnerable people in the city.[13]

Back in Silicon Valley, a number of high-tech firms, including Apple and Google, have their own centers for imagination and innovation, affectionately called "skunk works." Undoubtedly the most notorious is Google's secret lab, called Google X.

According to Chris Urmson, who heads Google's autonomous (driverless) cars project, "Co-founders Page and Sergey Brin 'have this idea that incremental improvements are not good enough. The standard for success is whether we can get these into the world and do audacious things.'"[14] Google X doesn't limit itself to creating driverless cars and Google Glasses. It is also constantly shopping around for other entrepreneurs whose work is on the edge furthest out.

One of the most audacious innovations that Google has invested in recently is being developed by an "augmented reality" startup called Magic Leap. They are in the early stages of creating a new visual experience that, frankly, I have a hard time visualizing. Apparently, Google believes it has promise—it has become a major investor.

"If Google has its way," asserts Rony Abovitz, the founder of Magic Leap, "hammerhead sharks will swim through your office, elephants will fit in the palm of your hand and dragons will fly among the birds." According to Abovitz, "Magic Leap is going beyond the current perception of mobile computing, augmented reality, and virtual reality . . . We are transcending all three, and revolutionizing the way people communicate, purchase, learn, share and play."[15]

While we are likely to continue to see remarkable forms of innovative new technology created, I am most interested in what is called "human-centered design." The innovation firm that seems to have the most experience in "human-centered design" is IDEO, which began in Silicon Valley in 1991.

13. Pullen, "Problem Solved," 58–60.
14. Stone, "Inside Google's Secret Lab," par. 9.
15. Gelles and de la Merced, "Google Invests Heavily," B7.

Welcome to Innovation as "Human-Centered Design"

IDEO has made its name by enabling a range of corporations to create innovative new products and services. For example, they were instrumental in helping Apple create its first mouse and 3Com the Palm V handheld organizer. By using "human-centered design," they enabled a host of other corporations, such as Procter & Gamble, to create innovative new products addressing consumers' needs that the firms had never considered.

IDEO is the standard-bearer of a broader revolution. In 2006, Stanford University started the D-School, which helps businesses improve innovation and reduce complexity. And in Britain, the Design Council and the Royal Society of the Arts are also strong advocates of design thinking.[16]

"A growing proportion of IDEO's work in re-engineering services is for NGOs and governments. Oxfam employed the firm to redesign its core product, gift giving. Singapore asked it to revamp its systems for handling applications for work permits."[17]

Essentially, "human-centered design" is a unique approach to innovation that focuses first on the people to be served—whether by a corporation, a humanitarian organization, or a social enterprise. In other words, there is a strong emphasis on human participation.

Relying on consumer research is not nearly as useful for the creation of innovative new solutions as spending time with the actual consumers. According to Tim Brown, "A better starting point is to go out in the world and observe the actual experiences of commuters, skate boarders and registered nurses as they improvise their ways through their daily lives . . . Their actual behaviors . . . can provide us with invaluable clues about their range of unmet needs."[18]

Graduate students, for example, have used design thinking to attempt to create an innovative way to enable more premature infants to survive in poor countries. Initially, they focused on creating a new product for hospitals in India. But after they actually traveled to India and met families that were struggling to help their preemies survive, they changed their focus.

16. Brown, *Change by Design*, 224.
17. *The Economist*, "Back to the Drawing-Board."
18. Brown, *Change by Design*, 40–41.

They realized they needed to create an innovative resource for parents, rather than hospitals. Through a creative collaboration with engineers, they designed what looks like a small sleeping bag with a heating element to increase the likelihood of premature infants surviving.

When the students field-tested their model with parents, they discovered they had to make another modification. The original model had a small heating gauge that parents could adjust for different settings. The students learned that the people they were working with had a strong belief that "Western medicine was too hot" and they were turning the heat settings to levels that put the infants at risk.

Their solution was quite simple. They removed the gauge with multiple settings and simply replaced it with an "on" switch. How can people of faith incorporate the insights of human-centered design in joining those creating new forms of changemaking?

Innové: Inviting Millennials to Design New Forms of Changemaking

Pastor Daniel Harrell was surprised when he learned that his congregation, Colonial Church in Edina, Minnesota, had received two million dollars from a recent land sale. He said the church was committed to investing at least 20 percent of those funds "outside the walls."[19] They started by creating a new organization called Innové, which has dedicated itself to "growing new ideas to serve the world." This is the first church I have found that holds a contest as a means of inviting millennials to create and launch new forms of social innovation that make a difference in the lives of their neighbors in their larger community.

In 2013, Brian Jones, the minister of mission who coodinates Innové, announced their first contest. They invited those under the age of thirty-five in their community, regardless of whether they were church affiliated or not, to submit proposals for new forms of social entrepreneurship that could make a difference in the lives of their neighbors in the Twin Cities area.

One hundred thirty-nine young applicants submitted their ideas. Innové picked six winners, to whom they offered startup funding. The winner's circle included everything from an alternative loan association to serve low-income workers who were becoming dependent on predatory

19. Sunde, "When a Church Matches Missions with Entrepreneurship," par. 1.

payday loan groups to the Twin Cities Mobile Market, designed to serve those in "food deserts" who don't have access to fresh produce and reasonably priced food. One of the surprising aspects of this story, aside from the generosity of the church, is the generosity shown by numbers of businesspeople and other leaders in the congregation, who volunteered as coaches and mentors to get these important ventures launched.[20]

Join me as we visit the Twin Cities Mobile Market and Leah Driscoll, who not only came up with this creative social innovation but has been very busy since the contest launching this innovative venture. I encourage you to Google Twin Cities Mobile Market. On Facebook you can see a picture of the first city bus covered with pictures of fresh fruit and vegetables. This first bus has been transformed into a grocery store on wheels and is busy serving some of the underserved communities in the Twin Cities. Leah is now raising money for a second bus.

What is remarkable to me is that Leah followed the essential steps outlined in human-centered design process.

- *Empathy*: Human-centered design emphasizes how essential it is to get to know the beneficiaries as the first step. Leah Driscoll had done extensive research and gotten to know the underserved in the Twin Cities before a contest was ever imagined. Her empathy motivated her to make it the major focus of a master's degree in nonprofit management at Hamline University.

- *Opportunity*: Human-centered design emphasizes the importance of paying greater attention to the changing social and economic contexts in every community in order to identify new opportunities. In her research Leah discovered a need that presented a huge opportunity in the Twin Cities. She learned from her research that more than 176,000 people in Minneapolis and 98,000 in St. Paul who are low-income live in a "food desert."

- *Purpose*: Tim Brown suggests that "an overarching purpose" is essential to creating an innovative way to address the opportunity.[21] Leah's purpose couldn't be clearer: to insure that "healthy affordable food should be accessible to everyone. It shouldn't be a luxury."[22]

---

20. French, "Religion Beat: Colonial Church in Edina to Share Business Talents."

21. Ibid., 3.

22. Rivera, "Twin Cities Mobile Market," par. 4.

- *Creating*: Design thinking emphasizes not only the importance of creative design but also the importance of redesign. Leah and her husband and friends were able to launch this new social innovation because they not only imagined but actually created and introduced a viable new social enterprise on wheels that is meeting real human needs in their community. Predictably, they have had to do a bit of redesign, but the basic design is solid.

- *Reimagining the Church*: It was of course the leaders and members of Colonial Church who reimagined a way to become more of a church for others. They imagined their church as an incubator for new social enterprises, one that draws on the creativity of the young, which provided Leah and all the others the opportunity to discover the surprising ways God could use their mustard seeds to make a difference in the lives of their neighbors. Doesn't this stir your desire to discover the creative ways God might use your life and the lives of the young in your community and church to become a more active part of this changemaking celebration?

In chapter 8 we will show you how you, your friends, and your church can likewise collaborate with Gen Y and Gen Z to create new ways to empower your neighbors as well as new ways of living and being church that more authentically reflect the radical way of Jesus.

Don't Miss Out on Being a Part of This Changemaking Celebration

Many good people, particularly people of faith, could miss out on being an active part of this new changemaking celebration. We could miss out on joining those who are creating their best communities, their best world, and often their best lives as well. We could miss out on the satisfaction many people like Leah and her mentors are experiencing as they make a real difference in the lives of their neighbors in the Twin Cities.

In the important book *Imagination First: Unlocking the Power of Possibility*, the authors lobby for a "bottom-up" rather than a top-down approach to innovation in all our institutions. They invite us to view imagination as a "virus," insisting that "the goal for a healthy organization is an epidemic of imagination."[23] Wouldn't you like to join those who are

23. Liu and Noppe-Brandon, *Imagination First*, 202–4.

enjoying being a part of this "epidemic of imagination"? Wouldn't you like to join those who are dreaming, scheming, creating, and launching new ways to make a lasting difference in the lives of others? In the next chapter we will take you on a tour of some of the new opportunities and challenges that are likely to be a part of our world as we gallop into the 2020s.

Dreaming, Scheming, and Creating

Wouldn't you like to discover creative new ways the Creator God can use your mustard seed to join those creating their best community, their best world, and their best lives as we enter what will surely be a decade of rapid change and great challenge? Get out your iPads and notebooks again and connect with your friends. It is time not only to dream and scheme—it is time to become much more a part of the epidemic of imagination.

- If all of life for followers of Jesus is a design opportunity, what are some creative ways you could reinvent your life to live with more intentionality, more compassion, and much more festivity (including throwing better parties)? Be sure to share with a friend and ask him to join you in this process.

- Get together with one or two friends and explore new approaches to prayer that are more experiential, involving everything from prayer walks to painting spiritual images on stones and shells or drawing images of hope in a sketch pad.

- How might those over 35 in your church enable the under 35, not only those in your congregation but also in your community, to unleash their creativity—to imagine new ways to create new innovations? (Think of the contest sponsored by Innové.)

- How might you and your friends collaborate with people in your neighborhood to enable your community to begin welcoming strangers and empowering the vulnerable?

3

Anticipating New Opportunities to Create
Our Best Tomorrows Today

The Alarm Is Going Off!

THE GLACIERS ARE CRUMBLING, the shorelines are eroding, and the seas are rising at an alarming rate. The giant Chinese economy, as I write, seems to be sending all our economies on a roller coaster ride that could impact all our lives and particularly those of our most vulnerable neighbors. We are witnessing the largest migration of refugees, primarily from the Middle East and Africa, since the end of World War II.

The image of one three-year-old lad named Alan Kurdi, wearing a red T-shirt, black shorts and sneakers, lying face down in the surf, drowned off the coast of Turkey, has arrested the attention and stirred the compassion of people all over the world. I believe that the Spirit of God is using this kind of tragic image to evaporate our sense of place, space, and distance. For one brief moment, many of us viewed this small boy as our child or grandchild or our neighbor's son.

The message of this chapter is simple. Not only is the clock ticking, as I mentioned in chapter 1, but now the alarm is going off—all over the planet. We no longer have the luxury of living our lives, raising our young, operating our businesses, and leading our churches as though the context in which we live is stable and predictable. It isn't. As I will show, the rate of global change seems to be accelerating. As a consequence we all need to imagine new ways to live and join the changmaking celebration and discover the difference it will make not only in the lives of our neighbors but our lives too.

However, to live responsively in a world that seems to be changing at warp speed, we need to learn from urban planners, business leaders, and social innovators how to develop the skills not only to anticipate some of the approaching waves of change but also how to creatively respond to them before they hammer the shores of our lives and those of our neighbors. So keep your iPad or notebook handy and identify some of the possible waves of change and opportunity that could break on the beaches of our lives and those of your neighbors, near or far.

To the extent that we can anticipate some of the waves of change coming our way, we have lead time to work with our neighbors to create our best communities, our best world, and our best lives. We will have lead time to collaborate with others to create new forms of changemaking that engage some of tomorrow's challenges today. I suspect you will be surprised by how God might use your mustard seed to create responses to some of the new challenges that have not fully arrived. Remember, all of these incoming waves of change are really opportunities for compassionate and creative response.

Join me as I share a moment when, as a younger man, the alarm of changing times first went off in my life. Even though it shook me to my core, I discovered it presented me a stunning new opportunity.

CONVERSATION 1—ANTICIPATING NEW OPPORTUNITIES IN ALL OUR TOMORROWS

My Earth Day Alarm Going Off

"For those who say we can't power our future let them come to the Bullitt Center!" declared Governor Jay Inslee on a brilliant Seattle Earth Day, April 22, 2013. As a crowd of several hundred gathered to listen to the governor and other speakers, we learned that many people consider the new six-story Bullitt Center to be "the greenest office building on the planet."

We also learned that this innovative structure provides its own energy from solar panels on its roof. Its water supply consists solely of rainwater, stored in tanks in the basement. City ordinances were actually changed to make it possible to add the first self-composting toilets in any office building in Seattle. And it even has a garage . . . for bikes.

The Bullitt Center houses the Bullitt Foundation, a leading environmental foundation that provides grants for urban environmental projects in Portland, Seattle, and Vancouver. Denis Hayes, the head of the foundation, is one of the leading environmental voices in the United States. A college dropout, he organized the first Earth Day on April 22, 1970, and can now witness its celebration in over 180 different countries.

As I was heading to the sixth floor, on the final tour, Denis came up behind me. I turned and said to him, "That first Earth Day radically changed my life." He responded, "I hope for the better." "It did," I replied, "and I'll tell you about it sometime."

Three weeks later Denis was kind enough to invite me back to the sixth floor for a cup of coffee. As we sat down, I sipped my coffee and began to relate my story of that first Earth Day on April 22, 1970. "I was thirty-four and Dean of Students at Maui Community College," I began. "I prided myself on keeping up on what we used to call 'current events.' However, frankly, like many in 1970, I had no idea that our world was rapidly changing and we were going to face a specter of daunting new environmental, economic, and social challenges as we careened toward the twenty-first century.

"My most vivid memories of that first Earth Day in Hawaii was the presentation by Dr. James Dator, from the University of Hawaii. He declared, 'We are putting the future of our planet and its people at extreme risk with the thoughtless ways we dump our garbage into the atmosphere, the land and the water!' He shared, in convincing detail, the destruction we are inflicting on the rain forests, reefs surrounding the Hawaiian Islands, and the atmosphere that supports all life." I added, "I will never forget one of the student's responses."

"Ed Yamamoto, a student leader, organized a handful of other students to act on what they had just heard. Ed said, 'On the way to classes this morning I spotted two of the staff at the Kahalui Motel dumping an enormous mountain of garbage on the beach, behind the motel, for the ocean to take away.' Ed held up a stack of black plastic bags and asked, 'Who wants to do something about it?' Fifteen students joined him and headed to the motel. Out of interest I tagged along."

Denis listened intently as I drank the rest of my coffee. "An hour later Ed and the other students brought over fifty large black plastic bags they had filled with garbage and stacked the mountain of garbage right in the lobby of the Kahalui Motel. The manager came roaring out of his of-fice, shouting, 'Put that garbage back on the beach!' However, he was ab-solutely dumbfounded when the typically compliant island students did not comply. Late in the afternoon, the manager finally caved in. Ed and his friends, with a sense of satisfaction, took the garbage back outside, but this time stacked it on the sidewalk in front of the motel for a proper pickup." Denis responded, "There was a lot of spontaneous activism on that first Earth Day, but I had never heard this story before."

During the seventies there were thousands of young people like Ed and his friends who, like millennials today, not only took direct action but also demonstrated publicly and influenced both Republicans and Demo-crats to pass new laws to clean up our air, water, and land. Influenced by the vision of Dr. Martin Luther King and others, these young people were also leaders in the civil rights and antiwar movements of that era.

I told Denis, "That first Earth Day was not only a wake-up call for me but also became an unexpected vocational call. I sensed God calling me to learn more about tomorrow's new challenges and opportunities to enable people of faith to create new ways to live and make a difference in response to these waves of change."

In fact, after much prayer and many discussions with family and friends, I moved to Seattle three months later to embark on a doctoral program at the University of Washington to pursue a degree in American intellectual history and educational policy studies. I also persuaded my advisor, Charles Burgess, to allow me to create my own minor in futures planning and innovation. It was one of the best decisions of my life.

Waking Up to a World Exploding with New Opportunities!

Strategic foresight is an essential element of strategic planning for urban planning, the world of business, and economic and social entrepreneur-ship. One of the first steps in social innovation is to use strategic foresight to identify new opportunities for changemaking. Tim Brown, the CEO of IDEO, states that effective innovators are always watching the hori-zon to spot everything from new "threats and new opportunities to new forms of technological innovation."[1] Brown urges those who want to be

---

1. Brown, *Change by Design*, 73.

more innovative to start by becoming "more responsive to unexpected opportunities."[2]

One reason I am such a big fan of the millennial generation is that they seem to be hard-wired not only to identify "unexpected opportunities" but also to engage them. I agree with Neale Godfrey's assessment that millennials "see the social disparities and frightening global situations like climate change, gender inequality, resource scarcity, and terrorism that are all happening in their world. They care."[3] Millennials want to join those creating new ways to engage these urgent opportunities.

Our good friends who wrote *The New Parish*[4] are helping many of us listen more to places and the people in our communities. However, since our world is rapidly changing, it is increasingly essential that we research how our own communities are changing too.

In this chapter I will show you practical ways to identify how the contexts in our own community, country, and the larger world are likely to change. Then you will have lead time to imagine and create innovative ways to engage new waves of change instead of passively waiting to be hammered by them.

The three essential steps in the changemaking process that I am advocating include

1. identifying new opportunities in changing local and global contexts so that you have lead time to respond;

2. defining a sense of purpose that clearly describes what you want to accomplish as you engage the new opportunity; and

3. creating innovative ways to implement your purpose in ways that also effectively engage the new opportunities you have identified.

In this first conversation I will explain why it essential that we all learn to take the future seriously. I will show you how to begin doing a little contextual forecasting and give you a few concrete examples. Then, in the second conversation, I will take you on a whirlwind trip around the globe, inviting you to join me in attempting to identify some new challenges and opportunities that we are likely to face as we race into the 2020s. Keep your iPad or notebook handy and list not only new

2. Ibid., 37.

3. Godfrey, "Business Not as Usual," para. 4.

4. Sparks et al., *The New Parish*.

opportunities but also your initial ideas of innovative and compassionate ways you might respond.

Waking Up to a World Changing at Warp Speed

"We live in an age in which we have to reinvent many of our social industries like health, education, well-being, care and transport," states Josephine Green of the Philips Corporation. "We are living in a change of age rather than an age of change. Converging socio-demographic, technological and environmental forces are transforming and transfiguring our world so that in the space of approximately fifty years, from 1970s to the 2020s, the world will look and feel like a very different place."[5]

I am convinced that Green is right. We need to wake up to the new reality that we are heading into a future changing at warp speed. As a consequence, we all will need to create new forms of changemaking and reimagine how we steward our lives, raise the next generation, and reinvent our churches for rapidly changing times.

Without question, the major driving force for this accelerating rate of change is the digital revolution. However, a host of other factors come into play, from escalating violence in the Middle East and Africa to growing concerns about the volatile global economy and impending environmental crisis. These we will explore in more detail later.

Waking Up to Apocalyptic Fears as We Race into the Volatile World of the 2020s

"The Earth and its inhabitants are facing planetary catastrophe caused by 'six billion people, and every one of them trying to have it all,' which weirdly translates into a succession of blights, trashing the world's crops and sucking the oxygen out of the atmosphere."[6] As we view the implosion of our planet in the film *Interstellar*, we join space pioneers who have decided that their only hope is to find a new planet.

It is not hard to imagine why films like *Interstellar* and *Hunger Games* connect with so many viewers these days. It seems that growing numbers of those on both the left and the right view the future of our small planet in starkly apocalyptic terms. But as followers of Jesus, we must remind

5. Green, "Democratizing the Future," 5–7.

6. Monbiot, "*Interstellar*: Magnificent Film, Insane Fantasy," para. 3.

ourselves that the Creator God has not lost control. We should never react to changing times out of fear. We need to see all change as an opportunity for compassionate response.

Do you remember reading about the Y2K chaos we were supposed to experience as we crossed the threshold into this new millennium? This specter of possible technological meltdown motivated a number of American Christians to head to the hills with their guns and dehydrated food and with little apparent concern for the neighbors they left behind.

I happened to be flying from the US, during this time, to work with churches in the UK. I was surprised to discover that British Christians had a very different response to this time of transition. Rather than viewing Y2K and the arrival of the new millennium with fear, they viewed it as a time of opportunity to create and launch new ministries to make a difference in the lives of their neighbors.

Remember that Jesus started his ministry in an age that must have felt very apocalyptic, with his homeland under the control of the oppressive Roman Empire. When the Jewish rulers, in league with Imperial Rome, imprisoned his cousin John, Jesus did not retreat into survival mode. Instead, he hit the streets, preaching, "Time's up! God's kingdom is here. Change your life and believe the message."[7] Then Jesus started recruiting collaborators. He challenged Peter, Andrew, and others to take the huge risk of leaving their livelihood and joining him to create an insurgency of compassion and hope.

The people of God have often found themselves contending with powerful empires whether in Egypt, Babylon, or Rome. In our age it is no different. We also find ourselves dealing with an empire: the imperial global mall. This new global empire is seeking to not only control the flow of wealth but increasingly to define the aspirations and values of people everywhere.

Is it possible that many of us who profess to follow Christ are as caught-up in the self-interested lifestyles of the dominant culture as those outside the church? I sincerely believe that God is using the compassion and creativity of these young social innovators, most of whom are not Christians, to hopefully inspire more of us also to become agents of compassion and hope.

---

7. Mark 1:14 (The Message).

Waking Up to Anticipating New Opportunities Today to Create Our Best Tomorrows

In the second chapter, I expressed the concern that those of us in the church also seem to be facing a crisis of imagination. I argued that far too many of our communities, schools, and churches are often neglecting to invite creative ideas from all those involved—particularly young people.

In this chapter I am arguing that we are also facing a crisis of foresight because we don't take time in our lives, communities, and churches to anticipate new opportunities in our local, national, and global contexts. As a consequence, we are surprised by change much more often than we need to be.

For example, back in the nineties, I discovered that a number of mission executives continued to run up large international phone bills because they were unaware of a new digital opportunity called "e-mail." Resources are lost and opportunities missed when those of us who work in the human sector fail to anticipate change in the contexts in which we live and labor.

I have, in recent years, worked with a number of leaders in churches and Christian organizations that routinely do so-called long range or strategic planning. However, rarely have I found leaders who have taken the time to research how the context is likely to change in the next five to ten years, before they plan. Of course when we fail to anticipate change, we often wind up reacting to unexpected change instead of creating innovative responses!

I have also found a number of both Christian colleges and public universities that routinely do strategic foresight . . . for student recruiting. They use forecasting to identify how many of "their kind of students" are likely to be in the marketplace in the next five years as well how much money those students and their parents are likely to have. But I have yet to find a single college that does any foresight research on how the economic and social context is likely to be different for each new crop of grads.

I am concerned that student services have changed very little since I was a dean of students at George Fox University in 1967. In most schools the only help for life after graduation is simply to help students to try and find work, which is important. However, we need to do much more to prepare students for life after graduation in a world changing as rapidly as ours.

Don't those of us who are educators also have a responsibility to re-search how the economic and social contexts are likely to change for each group of grads? Don't we then have the responsibility to inform them of the new challenges and opportunities and also help them create new ways to launch their lives? Couldn't we enable students to create launch plans that engage these new opportunities by collaborating with other grads, reducing costs, and defining a clearer sense of life purpose?

Learning to Take the Future Seriously

Recently a group of "makers" at the *New York Times* created a way to spot important new directions in media innovation. "Their mission: to fore-cast game-changing technology trends that will unfold in the next three to five years. Then they build prototypes to envision how these ideas will impact media's future—and how these upend our notions of the com-municated word."[8]

It is not only social entrepreneurs who don't want to be surprised by change, but also businesses like Microsoft and Amazon. As a consequence, they not only monitor the changing economic and demographic context, they also monitor tech and business innovations. Remarkably, they tend to even view disruptions as opportunities for innovative response.

Superforecasting: The Art and Science of Prediction,[9] by Philip Tetlock and Dan Gardner, shows that some of these more sophisticated methods can have a relatively high degree of accuracy in predicting change. "This book shows that under the right conditions regular people are capable of improving their judgment enough to beat the professionals at their own game," write Tetlock and Gardner. Essentially the Wharton School of Business sponsored a forecasting project called the Good Judgment Project. They invited the participation of not only professional forecast-ers but also twenty thousand amateur forecasters. The amateurs, using some basic tools in probability forecasting, outperformed the experts.[10]

In *Mustard Seed vs. McWorld*[11] I outlined a range of sophisticated methods of strategic foresight that business leaders use to anticipate new challenges and opportunities; these range from scenario forecasting to

8. Lufkin, "New Tech Times," 24.

9. Tetlock and Gardner, *Superforecasting: The Art and Science of Prediction.*

10. Zweig, "The Trick to Making Better Forecasts."

11. Sine, *Mustard Seed vs. McWorld.*

demographic forecasting. However, in this book I want to offer a very simple direct form of contextual foresight that anyone should be able to use.

First of all, I want readers to learn how to do contextual foresight. It begins by researching how your local, national, and global context is likely to change in the next five to ten years. As you do so, it is important to try to identify both new opportunities and challenges that can impact your own life as well as those you want to help empower. Based on your research you need to define whether the new opportunity is highly probable or somewhat probable. Then it is time to imagine and create possible new responses. This could be creating new changemaking ventures or new ways to free up time or money to engage a new opportunity in your community.

Marina Gorbis, the executive director of the Institute for the Future in Silicon Valley, describes foresight research in her book *The Nature of the Future* in a way I find helpful: "We are indeed all migrating to a new land and should be looking at the new landscape emerging before us like immigrants: ready to learn a new language, a new way of doing things, anticipating new beginnings with a sense of excitement, if also with a bit of understandable trepidation."[12] In spite of our best efforts to identify new opportunities, we will still be surprised by change. Futurists call these "wild card" events. We need to see unexpected change as an opportunity for creative response too.

Tomorrow Watch: Local Communities
Taking Change Seriously

I suggest that you consider creating a Tomorrow Watch Group in your church, school, or community whose members come together to do research on the changing context in your own local community to identify new opportunities and challenges. Then you can begin exploring creative ways you might respond. I suggest you begin by talking to your neighbors and coworkers, and then reading the local news. Ask yourself, "How is my local community likely to change in the next five years?" With a little effort you should be able to harvest important information about places where you could create new forms of changemaking to engage emerging

---

12. Gorbis, *Nature of the Future*, 17.

areas of opportunity. Here are some of the questions you might ask as you do your research.

Dreaming and Scheming to Engage New Opportunities

- How is the demographic context of your community likely to change in the next five years in terms of age, race, and income, and what new opportunities do those changes offer?

- How is the natural environment in your locale likely to change in the next five years, and what new opportunities do these changes offer?

- How is the economic environment in your community likely to change in the next five years in terms of everything from new businesses to housing prices? What new opportunities and challenges do the possible changes bring?

- How are the social organizations, faith communities, as well as arts and sports and community celebrations likely to change, and what new opportunities do these changes present?

- How are rapidly developing new technologies likely to impact the lives of people of different ages in your community in the next five years and what are some of both the new opportunities and the new potential downsides?

By researching how some of these core areas of your community are likely to change, you will be able to "take the current when it serves," to borrow a line from Shakespeare. Anyone who has surfed knows the huge advantage of catching the right wave at its crest.

As you will see, paying attention to how our context is likely to change is an asset in changemaking and also a valuable opportunity for all of us to reimagine how to steward our lives, raise the young, and serve God in our rapidly changing world. Here are a few examples of people and churches we have worked with who have identified new opportunities and created new forms of changemaking and new possibilities for their own lives and churches.

Conversation 2. Futures Creativity Consulting: Creating New Responses to Tomorrow's Opportunities Today

Our team at Mustard Seed Associates has worked to enable local church-es, families, students, and mission organizations to anticipate new oppor-tunities and create innovative responses in the changing contexts where they live and serve. It is gratifying to see followers of Jesus create ways to *be* a difference and *make* a difference to engage some of these opportuni-ties. Here are some tasty samples of some of the dreaming and scheming that enabled many of them to become much more involved in innovative changemaking in their communities.

Japanese Presbyterian Futures/Creativity

In the early eighties our Mustard Seed Associates team[13] developed *Imagine That! A Futures Creativity Workshop* for local churches. Prior to a workshop, we ask churches to research how their local community context as well as the projected demographic profile of the congregation is likely to change in the next five years. We invite participants to work in small groups to create innovative responses to the new opportunities they identified.

One of the first churches where we offered the workshop was Japa-nese Presbyterian Church on Capitol Hill here in Seattle. It was a chal-lenging church to work with because most of their members had moved from Capitol Hill to the suburbs, yet they returned to Capitol Hill on Sundays to attend worship. Not surprisingly, they had little idea of the needs and challenges people in this inner-city neighborhood faced today or would face in the future. As they researched the Capitol Hill neigh-borhood they learned that a growing percentage of younger elementary students were having a difficult time getting started in school. During our *Imagine That!* workshop, they created a new tutoring initiative for those kids.

They also learned that a growing number of Indo-Chinese boat people would settle in Capitol Hill in the next three years, attracted there by low rents. They started working with one of the early responders, Cal Uomoto, an urban activist, to create a new refugee sponsorship program. Remarkably, in two months these good people transitioned from being

---

13. See www.msaimagine.org.

a detached commuter congregation to an involved community congregation making a real difference in the lives of both young children and Vietnamese families.

Baptist Futures/Creativity

A couple of years ago a graying Baptist church in Liberty, Missouri, researched both how the demographic profile of their community and their giving patterns were likely to change in the next five years. They had just hired a very effective young preacher and the church was growing again. They assumed that if they simply replaced one young couple for every older couple (who went on to their reward), their budget would also begin to grow again. However, their research revealed that they needed to replace each older couple with three young couples to simply sustain their present budget. Their creative response was to offer classes in whole-life stewardship for new members to create practical ways to free up more money and time to grow their ministry and increase their outreach into their community.

CCDA High School Futures/Creativity

One of my favorite memories was when Christine and I facilitated an *Imagine That!* workshop with an intercultural group of high school students at a Christian Community Development Association (CCDA) conference in Philadelphia several years ago. I told these students that research showed that they would be the first generation to grow up in an America that is no longer predominantly white. I asked them to create an innovative way to prepare for a richly intercultural future. The next day they presented their creative proposal to the entire conference.

Their innovative idea was to have high school students from a predominantly African American urban church and students from a predominantly white suburban church video a typical week in their lives in their respective communities. These two videos would capture scenes from their home life, school activities, sports, service projects, as well as their party lives. Then the two groups planned to meet to view and discuss one another's videos, and to continue to visit each other's youth groups, as one way to begin building a bridge to a new more inclusive future. The adults at CCDA gave these young innovators a standing ovation.

Goshen College Students Futures/Creativity

Four years ago Christine and I spoke in chapel at Goshen College on the theme "Is there life after Goshen?" We facilitated a pre-chapel two-hour creativity workshop for twenty juniors and seniors. During the workshop, I shared about how the economic context is likely to be much more challenging for their generation.

Then I invited them to stir their imaginations and come up with some ideas for life after Goshen. One creativity group imagined a way that five of them could settle in a neighborhood in Chicago that they were familiar with. They went online and quickly found a five-bedroom house for rent in the chosen neighborhood, within their budget. Then they envisioned life together. Two of them would take the IT jobs they had been training for and pay the lion's share of the rent. This meant the other three grads could support themselves on half-time jobs, freeing up time to mentor at-risk students in the neighborhood high school where they were already volunteering. When this group shared their idea in the final chapel, their fellow students, arrested by their creative ideas, approached them later to learn more.

Tearfund UK Futures/Creativity

Thankfully, there are some international Christian agencies that do lead with foresight—that do forecasting before they do long-range planning. Habitat for Humanity and World Vision are two examples. World Vision, for instance, is testing new vegetable seeds for farmers to use in Latin America to ensure that they will still be able to grow their most important crops if the menacing impact of climate change makes it impossible for huge populations to feed themselves.

Tearfund UK also instituted the Jordan Project a few years ago. They identified new opportunities in the coming decade in Africa and Asia such as accelerating birth rates, for which they created some innovative new responses in maternal and infant child care.

Then I encouraged them to look at the demographic profile of their donor base. They were surprised to discover that the median age of their donors was fifty-five. They immediately responded to this "opportunity" by hiring a young missional church planter named David Westlake. David and some younger staff designed an innovative way to engage teens and twenty-somethings to become involved in what they called "Art for

Mercy." Essentially they invited these young people to create artwork depicting the lives, celebrations and struggles of those associated with Tearfund in Africa and Asia. This program enabled them to begin growing a new and younger constituency again.

Seattle Churches Futures/Creativity for 2009 Recession Preparedness

On a chilly September Saturday evening in 2008, our team at Mustard Seed Associates invited fifty Christian leaders from the Seattle area to a local B & B—the Shafer Baillie Mansion. Our research in the previous two years led us to be deeply concerned that the US economy could take a serious nosedive. Frankly, I don't think anyone else in the room believed that a recession was possible. However, everyone fully participated in an idea-storming exercise to create new ways congregations might respond.

In an hour and a half these leaders came up with some very creative ideas. One person suggested developing a kind of Craigslist so that members could post underutilized resources such as an extra car in the driveway or available rooms in people's homes. Others suggested instituting courses on financial management and food processing. Later on, when it was clear that we were headed into a recession, Trinity Lutheran Church, in the Shoreline area, actually offered these courses to their members to help them prepare for the coming downturn.[14]

Even though we know that economic recessions occur on a somewhat regular basis, every six to eight years, the only ones I have found that have developed preparedness plans for the next recession are large corporations.

In contrast, churches—not only in New Orleans but all over the country—were a part of the process of the recovery of New Orleans following Hurricane Katrina. As I write, we are commemorating the tenth anniversary of Hurricane Katrina. *We're Still Here, Ya Bastards*[15] is a new book that celebrates the remarkable resilience of the people of New Orleans as they continue to rebuild their community. Another important historical study of how earlier communities collaborated with courage to

---

14. Sine, "Are You Recession Ready?"
15. Gratz, *We're Still Here, Ya Bastards.*

recover from other disasters in North America is *A Paradise Built in Hell: The Extraordinary Communities That Arise in Disaster.*[16]

One of the surprising outcomes of this response to Katrina is that churches all over the US followed up by developing sophisticated disaster response teams, collaborating with local governments in every flood, tornado, and earthquake since Katrina. Wouldn't it be a good idea to equip all our churches to develop disaster preparedness plans, in collaboration with our local municipalities, for the next economic recession, too? In 2007 I did scenario forecasting with World Concern regarding the potential impact of an Avian flu pandemic on the 22 countries they serve. As a consequence, they developed strategic response plans in those countries that included preparation before the pandemic, during the pandemic, and after it is over. In light of the emergence of the new Zika virus, I am sure that most Christian relief and devlopment agencies are already working with the UN and other agencies to prepare for this emerging crisis.

Lights Out: A Cyberattack, a Nation Unprepared, Surviving the Aftermath, by Ted Koppel, warns of yet another possible disaster that could rock all of our lives and devastate our poorest neighbors. He writes, "In October 2012, then-Defense Secretary Leon Panetta told an audience of security executives that a 'destructive cyber-terrorist attack could virtually paralyze the nation.'"[17] Koppel is not only urging national leaders to take action but also encouraging us all to be better prepared for any disaster.

In light of all these possible downturns, I encourage you to develop an economic buffer and to keep a one-month supply of food and water, at least, not only for sustaining your own families but for sharing with your most vulnerable neighbors. I urge all our churches to learn from the Mormon Church how to create a disaster-response capability—again, not just for our members but for our neighbors as well so that we are prepared to be Christ's compassion in times of widespread crisis.

Creating a Center for Christian Imagination and Innovation

Our team at Mustard Seed Associates are in the process of pulling all of our futures consulting services together into a single Christian incubator,

---

16. Solnit, *A Paradise Built in Hell.*

17. Koppel, "Where Is America's Cyberdefense Plan?," para. 4.

a center for imagination and innovation. The mission of this center will be to enable Christian organizations, congregations, families, and students to create innovative ways to engage tomorrow's opportunities and challenges that also advance something of God's loving purposes for a people and a planet. We are fortunate to have Forrest Inslee, who is on our team, to lead the creation of this center.

After I came back from my first pilgrimage to Iona in 1982, I started looking for land as a site for a possible Celtic Christian Community. In 1989 we purchased a beautiful, wooded forty-acre parcel that we call the Mustard Seed Village. During the first week of August 2016 we will hold our 25th Annual Celtic Prayer Retreat. While we want to retain the Celtic Christian flavor in all that we do, we began developing the site to become an incubator for individuals, churches, and organizations to create innovative new responses to tomorrow's growing opportunities.

We have constructed a beautiful earth roof building designed by David Vandervort, one of the leading green architects in the Northwest. My son Wes, who lives nearby, has been a huge help in assisting us to maintain the property. We plan to start hosting futures/creativity sessions in this facility as well as traveling to our client's sites to imagine and create innovative new ways to both make a difference and be a difference in turbulent times like these.

As we consolidate our futures/creativity consulting services we invite your creativity. We welcome your ideas of how best to enable followers of Jesus of all ages, as well as churches and Christian organizations, to more fully anticipate new opportunities and creatively engage these in ways that reflect God's loving purposes.

A Tour of Accelerating Global Change in the 2020s: Identifying New Opportunities and Challenges

In this second conversation of chapter 3, I will take you on a very quick tour of some of the expressions of rapid global change that seem likely to impact both our world and many of our lives and communities as well. I invite you to join me in not only identifying some of the new opportunities but also in imagining possible new responses for our neighbors near and far as well as for our own lives, communities, and churches.

I need to make clear that these forecasts are a product of my own research and analysis and others would likely frame them differently.

However, I hope they offer readers a helpful starting point from which to explore how the larger global context is likely to change.

The Coming of New Digital Innovation as We Race into the 2020s

Eric Schmidt and Jared Cohen, two high-level Google executives, predict that "by 2025, the majority of the world's population will, in one generation, have gone from having virtually no access to unfiltered information to accessing all the world's information through a device that fits in the palm of one hand. If the current pace of technological innovation is maintained most of the projected eight billion people on Earth will be online."[18]

The day I worked on this section, I heard Elon Musk, the CEO of SpaceX here in Seattle, interviewed on NPR. Musk said he plans to build, in collaboration with Google, a network of communications satellites that will orbit Earth and provide Internet access to every remote village on the planet. He also has some very good news for those getting ready for an apocalyptic future. "Musk said SpaceX's ultimate goal is to build a settlement on Mars . . ."[19]

In *Mustard Seed vs. McWorld,* circa 1999, I observed that "we are hardwiring our planet electronically into a single global system of satellites, fax machines, and Internet communications. Borders are melting, distance is dying. One and one-half trillion dollars flashes around the planet every day as we witness the creation of a new world economic order."[20] However, I never imagined a future where virtually everyone on the planet would be connected via a single global electronic nervous system.

The film *Enemy of the State,* released in 1998, offered a chilling fictional portrayal of life in a high-surveillance society. Every time I see the movie, it reminds me of the high-surveillance society we live in today. Julian Assange, the founder of WikiLeaks, states, "We live not only in a surveillance state, but in a surveillance society. Totalitarian surveillance is not only embodied in our governments; it is embedded in our economy, in our mundane uses of technology and in our everyday interactions . . .

---

18. Schmidt and Cohen, *New Digital Age,* 4.
19. Calamur, "Google's Stake in SpaceX," par. 6.
20. Sine, *Mustard Seed vs. McWorld,* 18.

It is too early to say whether the 'democratizing' or the 'tyrannical' side of the Internet will eventually win out."[21]

A number of challenges accompany this breathtaking digital revolution, with issues ranging from privacy to radical alterations of what it means to be human. One of the most obvious opportunities is how to use digital technology both to continue to democratize access to information and to increase our capacity to work for the common good.

"Rise of the Machines: The Future Has Lots of Robots, Few Jobs for Humans" is more than a provocative title for an article in *Wired* magazine. It is also a very troubling prediction for the future that could put many people on this planet at risk in the next ten to fifteen years. Author Marguerite McNeal begins with this claim: "The robots haven't just landed in the workplace—they are expanding their skills, moving up the corporate ladder, showing awesome productivity and retention rates, and increasingly shoving aside their human counterparts."[22] Of course, others predict that new jobs for humans will be created. However, this remains a concerning challenge on the horizon. Bots are already being used as caregivers in Japan, and some are reportedly being designed as both alternative companions and even sex partners. It is only a question of time until they are used for military purposes as well.

Where Are the Opportunities?

How might we use the range of these new technologies to raise awareness about everything from the climate change crisis to growing income inequality? How might colleges, high schools, and even church youth groups design creative ways to use everything from virtual reality to 3D printing to create new forms of social innovation that have both social and environmental impacts? How might we create new ways to use everything from synthetic resources to YouTube and holographic design in new forms of art? How might we create new ways to use gaming and social media in order to draw the young into becoming participants in the changemaking celebration in their own communities? Finally, what are ways to increase the democratizing character of the internet while decreasing the capability of both governments and corporations to use

---

21. Assange, "Who Should Own the Internet?," par. 9.
22. McNeal, "Rise of the Machines," para. 1.

data about our lives and communities for purposes that undermine the common good?

With our young in the US reportedly on their screens nine hours a day, we are facing a very tough challenge in how to help parents, educators, and youth workers enable young people to steward these technologies wisely so they don't miss out on the formation of face-to-face relationships and the value of seclusion from all our technologies. I suspect we could be on the threshold of a crisis of formation as well, since parents, churches, and schools increasingly have less to do with shaping the values of coming generations. These too are emerging opportunities.

The Coming of New Environmental Opportunities as We Race into the 2020s

After 20 years of difficult meetings, on December 12, 2015, in Paris, France, some 200 nations signed a historic legal agreement that set ambitious goals to cut greenhouse gas admissions, limit temperature rises, and hold governments accountable for reaching those targets. *The Guardian* reported that "Jennifer Morgan of the environmental thinktank, The World Resources Institute, said the long term goal was 'transformational' and 'sends signals to the heart of the markets.' The deal set a high aspirational goal to limit warming below 2C and strive to keep temperatures at 1.5C above pre-industrial levels—a far more ambitious target than expected, and a key demand for vulnerable countries."[23]

Shortly after my Earth Day wake-up call in 1970, I read a book that arrested the attention of thoughtful people all over the planet: *The Limits to Growth*.[24] It awakened us to the new reality that "we can't continue to grow like this!" I sincerely believe the Creator God is using global leaders, like those at the Paris Climate Summit, to slow the enormous risks not only to our oceans, our air, and our entire climate, but also to the well being of future generations. Most importantly, this historic agreement is an opportunity for all of us to become more actively involved in limiting climate change and in joining those changemakers that are committed to restoring our natural world.

23. Goldenberg et al., "Paris Climate Deal."
24. Meadows et al., *The Limits to Growth*.

Where Are the Opportunities?

In light of this historic accord, what creative possibilities are stirring for you? Many of us could learn from Gen Y and Gen Z to adopt more sustainable lifestyles, shop locally, and learn where products are made. On the first Earth Day in 1970, when environmental activism was born, it was fiercely optimistic. It tapped into a deep concern for our future and the future of the next generations.

Alex Laskey, writing in the *Christian Science Monitor*, identified some intriguing new ways to work to improve the environment in spite of widespread resistance. "I'm hopeful . . . . If the public and private sectors can work together and seize this moment, millions of Americans will soon have powerful new tools to reduce their energy consumption and curb our carbon emissions."[25]

Laskey urges us not to focus on contentious differences in defining the daunting environmental challenges we face. Rather, he urges us to find new opportunities where we are much more likely to agree. He cites four areas where looking for innovative solutions might actually bring people together.

1. He suggests, for example, that focusing on saving energy instead of carbon reduction might have a greater immediate payoff. Businesses understand that operating in a way that reduces energy consumption saves them money. As a consequence, in the last five years we have seen a surprising upturn in the number of corporations that are leading the charge in energy reduction, including the use of waste products and alternative energy. While the federal government in the US is at loggerheads, states like North Carolina, Texas, and California are finding sound value in also creating innovative ways to reduce energy costs.

2. Laskey also argues that what seems to be most effective is for consumers to convince their neighbors who are finding ways to reduce energy consumption to save energy and reduce their own utility costs too.

3. One of the most hopeful signs in the social-innovation movement is a huge plus in environmental conservation—scaling up solutions to make huge levels of change possible. "For example, utilities are

---

25. Laskey, "Climate Change Is Divisive," 35.

using cloud-based analytics to inform families how much energy they are using compared with their neighbors. This tiny behavioral cue, given to millions, is yielding massive energy savings."[26]

4. US automakers are finding a growing market for hybrids and plug-ins. A range of other businesses are also discovering that investments in clean energy and energy efficiency are creating jobs and pouring money back into their businesses.[27]

Given the host of other environmental challenges facing us in the 2020s, social innovators are also creating an array of brilliant ways not only to conserve energy but also to turn pollution into products. For example, The Plastic Bank has created a way to transform waste plastic collected from ocean beaches and urban waste into a source of income for the poor as a valuable feedstock for 3D printers. David Katz, an entrepreneur, developed this startup with the help of engineers at the University of British Columbia.[28]

What are some innovative new ways you, your family, community, and congregation could find to respond to these escalating environmental opportunities, to help us head off a climate-change catastrophe for the well-being of generations to come?

The Coming of a Turbulent Political Future

The so-called Arab Spring seems to be giving way to a prolonged winter of Arab discontent. The Russian military action in the region is making a complex international crisis even more complex. We are also witnessing the spread of violent extremist groups like ISIS that are destabilizing regions in the Middle East and Africa.

Through their effective online marketing activity, ISIS organizers are attracting thousands, largely from the millennial generation, with the fraudulent message that joining this brutal organization is an opportunity to make a positive difference in the world. Muslims all over the world repudiate this movement. For example, 70,000 Muslim clerics recently gathered in India to issue a Fatwa condemning the kind of terrorism that

26. Ibid.

27. Ibid.

28. Field, "Social Entrepreneurs Create 3D Printed Wrench from Recycled Ocean Plastic."

ISIS is promoting, insisting that this is not consistent with the Islamic faith.[29]

Recent terrorist attacks in Paris and San Bernardino, California, make clear that this type of terrorism is no longer just a Middle Eastern crisis but an emerging global crisis as well. Thankfully, there are also counter forces from our Muslim neighbors who are opposed to this violence. Muslim Americans have already raised $150,000 and the contributions are still coming in for the victims of the mass shooting in San Bernardino.[30] Also, young Muslims in Oslo organized a "ring of peace" to surround and protect a Jewish synagogue from anti-Semitic attacks.[31]

In the United States we are seeing people not only concerned about terrorist activities; we are also seeing increasing alarm about the anti-Muslim and anti-immigrant rhetoric that strikes at the very heart of both our Christian faith and our national identity. Jim Wallis declares that "Stopping this hateful spread of Islamophobia and racism must become a bi-partisan and trans-partisan issue—because it is now a *moral* issue."[32]

Many American Christians are not aware of a remarkable three-year journey of reconciliation (1996 to 1999) that was undertaken primarily by European Christians. They traveled the old crusader trail asking Muslims for forgiveness for the slaughter of tens of thousands of innocents. In April 1096, the Crusaders left the cathedral in Cologne, Germany. They killed thousands of Jews before they left Europe. As the Crusades swept through the Middle East, they not only killed tens of thousands of Muslims but unwittingly thousands of Orthodox Christians as well.

Lynn Green, who headed the YWAM base in Harpenden in Britain, led a group of 150 Christians leaving the same cathedral in Cologne on Easter Sunday 1996, exactly 900 years later. Their first stop was a Turkish Mosque where Green read the same letter of apology that they would read at every stop on their three-year journey. "We deeply regret the atrocities in the name of Christ by our predecessors. We renounce greed, hatred and fear, and condemn all violence done in the name of Jesus Christ."[33] Muslims broke into spontaneous applause and embraced these pilgrims of reconciliation, a response that happened repeatedly during the journey.

29. Schewitz, "70,000 Muslim Clerics."

30. Chan, "American Muslims are Raising $1,000 an Hour."

31. "Muslims Form 'Ring of Peace' to Protect Oslo Synagogue." *The Telegraph*, February 22, 2015.

32. Wallis, "America's Flirtation with Fascism."

33. Fox, "Reconciliation of Christians and Muslims."

Almost 500 pilgrims of peace arrived in Jerusalem on July 15, 1999, on the 900th anniversary of the killing of 60,000 residents and the destruction of Jerusalem.[34] Nothing can do more to undermine the propaganda of terrorists than this urgently important work of reconciliation.

These days, Mennonites are the strongest Christian force for the work of reconciliation in the Middle East, offering compassionate projects for the vulnerable from Iran to the West Bank and also bridge-building with Muslims throughout the region. I would encourage other Christians to not only support their initiatives but also learn from them how to build bridges with Muslim neighbors in our own countries as well as in the Middle East and throughout the world. Contact the Center for Justice and Peacemaking at Eastern Mennonite University to discover how your organization can join those building bridges.[35]

The Coming of a New Period of Economic Volatility

Keep your seatbelts buckled as we all get a free ride on China's roller coaster.[36] The dramatic ups and downs of the Chinese economy have been dramatically unsettling for both established and emerging economies— and no one seems to know where the ride will end. The only thing that seems relatively certain, according to economists' predictions, is that we are headed into a future of continuing volatility. "Flat is the new up" heralds an article on the future of the US economy in 2016—Goldman Sachs has cut its economic growth forecast from 2.8 percent to 2.4 percent.[37]

As I write, the economies of Russia and Japan are also showing serious signs of stress. Currently, concern is still being expressed that the Eurozone could face another disabling crisis. Recent reports about the weakening of a number of the emerging economies, from Argentina to Turkey, caused by falling commodity prices, are concerning too.[38] Any financial crisis in China, the Eurozone, or the emerging economies could plunge us all into a new recession that could be worse than the last one. *The Economist* stated, "If the world economy does stumble, restoring

34. Ibid.

35. Center for Justice and Peacemaking, Eastern Mennonite University. See www.emu.edu/cjp.

36. Eavis and Jolly, "Stock Markets Dive," par. 1.

37. Sherter, "Goldman Sachs: 2016 Looks Like a Dud," paras. 1–2.

38. Schuman, "The BRICs Have Hit a Wall."

stability will be harder than the last time round because policy makers have so little room to maneuver."[39]

As nationalism, divisiveness, and violence increase, the political and economic influence of the Atlantic alliance of North America and Europe is likely to decrease. We will probably see other countries such as China, India, and Brazil grow in economic power and political influence as well, in the coming decade.

Cybercrime is also likely to become a growing threat to political stability, as well as to all of us who are connected to the digital global mall. International crime, and particularly human trafficking, will be a continuing threat to both the vulnerable among us, and to our common future. There could be growing distrust of those who are involved in co-ordinating international finance in ways that seem to increase the wealth of a few at the expense of both the poor and the middle class.

These changes are likely to have an increasing impact on the middle class in all our countries. Many middle-class families in the US are still recovering from the 2008–9 recession. Many more are settling into a new normal where personal debt and college debt are rising, while salaries have remained more or less stagnant since the beginning of the millennium. Many Americans have not placed enough in savings for retirement. I encourage readers to view all these pressures as an opportunity to increase savings while reducing debt and the cost of living so that we have the means to help empower our vulnerable neighbors and to minimize our own economic vulnerability.

The UN recently reported that our planet has the largest youth population in the history of the world—1.8 billion between the ages of ten and twenty-four.[40] Many of these youths are from the poorer parts of the Middle East, Africa, and Latin America. By the end of the decade, we are likely to see a future with millions of unemployed young people, which would likely add to the global sense of volatility.

There is also some important good news as we look at the global economy. We have seen a dramatic rise in the numbers of the poor joining the middle class—not only in China, but in emerging economies all over the planet. In fact, extreme poverty has decreased for the first time in history. But there are still over one billion people living on about a

---

39. *The Economist*, "Past and Future Tense," 13.

40. Sengupta, "Global Populations of Youths Is Highest Ever, U.N. Reports," A6.

dollar a day.[41] This rise in the middle class represents a real opportunity to create still other forms of social entrepreneurship and community empowerment innovation to make poverty history for all the world's people.

China is developing a beginning safety net for its large and growing population. India's population is likely to surpass that of China, with nearly a billion and a half residents projected by 2028. India has also begun creating a beginning safety net for many of their citizens who are benefitting from India's economic lift-off over the past decade. However, it is not clear that either country or the emerging economies will be able to provide for those left behind. This is why it is urgent for followers of Christ to join those creating innovative ways not only to grow the middle class but also to enable all our communities to become more resilient and to create mutual-care networks to care for those who can no longer care for themselves.

Where Are the Opportunities?

In light of both accelerating change and growing economic, political, and environmental volatility, this new changemaking celebration—and the remarkable number of those in Generations Y and Z who want to use their lives to have a social and environmental impact—could not come at a better time. Thanks be to God. Why don't you join those of all generations who are committed to creating more resilient and flourishing local communities for the good times and the tough times as well as those who are seeking to address larger global problems?

I was so impacted by the changemakers I had met at SOCAP 13 that I went back to SOCAP 14. I was surprised and delighted when I learned that even USAID had joined the changemaking celebration. They began funding ventures in social enterprise, with the goal of empowering some of the poorest communities in Africa and of strengthening their local economies, thus making them less dependent on shrinking global aid. This is important innovation, since it addresses yet another opportunity, a likely decrease in foreign aid from Western nations as we become increasingly aging societies.

A volatile future is an opportunity for all of us who are a part of the middle class to decrease our costs and our debt and to increase our margins so that we have both more time and resources to invest in the

41. Moore, "'Extreme Poverty' Cut by Half," 30.

changemaking celebration. Reducing our debt and increasing our margins will make it possible to better weather the coming downturns and to be something of God's compassion to our most vulnerable neighbors.

"Where you spend your money reflects what is most important to you," observed Mark Scandrette during a provocative conversation he led at a gathering at our home in January 2014 after the publication of his *Free: Spending Your Time and Money on What Matters Most*, which he co-wrote with his wife, Lisa.[42] In the next chapter I will invite you to do something unusual; I'm going to invite you to think much more carefully about what matters most. In fact, I'm going to give you the opportunity to use scripture to do something that Christians seem to do very rarely—to redefine the good life for both good times and tough times.

One of our most urgent issues is the need to re-imagine and reinvent how we raise and educate the young to live and navigate their lives in light of some of the formidable challenges and stunning new opportunities for both Gen Y and Gen Z. Since there is a growing awareness that jobs may be harder to find in the 2020s, I urge parents, educators, and youth workers to collaborate in enabling the young to become much more entrepreneurial. We need to strongly affirm the desire among many members of these generations to invest their lives in working to make a social and environmental impact.

I believe this also means enabling the young to develop problem-solving skills, as Kayra demonstrated in the last chapter. I am sure it also requires training the young to become much more responsible much earlier. We had a young couple living with us for seven years who had three kids, all born as wild things. This couple spent two summers as camp counselors with other people's kids and became masterful at setting and maintaining boundaries. And they are brilliant with their own kids. They set boundaries and never give in, and now have three very responsible kids. Camp counseling anyone?

I am personally grateful for the strong voice of Pope Francis, who not only condemns the growing economic inequity and the seduction of global consumerism but also serves as a diplomatic influence at a time in which trust between major players seems to be diminishing. Pope Francis has restored a sense of "diplomatic boldness, a willingness to take risks" in diplomatic disputes where he can serve as an independent broker in regions like the Middle East.[43]

42. Scandrette and Scandrette, *Free*.
43. Yardley, "Under Francis, a Bolder Vision," A18.

The Coming of a New Season of Urban Opportunity

As we look forward to a new global political future, there are some hopeful possibilities as we anticipate the urbanization of our planet. By 2025 the United Nations predicts that 8.1 billion people will live on this shrinking globe. That number could reach 9.6 billion by 2050.[44] More than 70 percent of the world's populations will live in cities, it is predicted.[45] This presents wonderful design opportunities to all those involved in the creation of more sustainable communities—remarkable new opportunities for collaboration in addressing environmental, social, and political challenges. Incredibly, nearly forty cities will host populations of ten million people. A number of cities are creating new forms of agricultural innovation. Singapore, for example, is producing impressive new forms of vertical gardening, and Havana reportedly has become the world's leader in urban agricultural self-reliance.

According to Benjamin Barber, "as nations grow more dysfunctional," cities alone offer the best alternative for creating a democratic future that is both environmentally and economically sustainable. He envisions the influence of nations declining relative to the influence of twenty-first-century "metro city regions," which could become central for achieving positive change. Cities are already having remarkable influence in reducing emissions and promoting energy efficiency.[46]

Where Are the Opportunities?

Global networks of cities are working together to promote best urban practices in ways that seems to elude national governments and even states. For instance, these networks have raised insulation standards for buildings, promoting the use of sensors to distribute energy more efficiently. Barber advocates a "glocal cyber commons" where urban leaders can regularly share best practices, and also collaborate in creating social innovations to engage more of tomorrow's challenges today.[47] This affords a remarkable opportunity for those creating both new forms of community empowerment and social enterprise to provide innovative leadership

44. Associated Press, "U.N.: World Population to Reach 8.1B in 2025."
45. Kjaer, "Urbanisation and the Smart Society," para. 1.
46. Barber, *If Mayors Ruled the World*, 358.
47. Ibid., xi–xix.

in designing new forms of sustainable, flourishing urban communities for the 2020s and beyond.

Dreaming and Scheming as We Race into the 2020s— Conversation 2

I have taken you on a very quick tour of some of the challenges that might comprise the landscape of tomorrow's world. This is one person's effort to make sense of our rapidly changing world; others will have a different take. As you look ahead, what are some of the possible new opportunities in your community, your own life, and the larger world that attract your attention?

It is time for you and your friends to get out your iPads or notebooks and do some innovative dreaming and scheming. There has never been a better time to join those changemakers who are discovering the joy of the life Jesus called us to—the life given away in service to God and others.

Dreaming and Scheming to Engage New Opportunities in the 2020s

- What are one, two, or three possible new opportunities for change-making in your community in the next five years?

- Share these with a couple of friends in your community and imagine some creative new forms of community empowerment or social enterprise that might effectively engage these emerging opportunities.

- What are one or two new challenges facing your church in the next five years, and what are some creative ways your church might respond?

- What are one or two new challenges that you or your family could face in the next five years and what are some creative ways you might respond?

4

Choosing a Changemaking Purpose Today
for All Our Tomorrows

USA, Here I Come!

"USA, HERE I COME!" bellows Meng as he receives his visa to travel to the United States in the Chinese comedy *American Dreams in China*, the number one film in the box office in China when it was released there in 2013. It takes Meng's two college friends, Chang and Wang, a little longer to obtain their visas and join Meng in America. The three young entrepreneurs head to the US because they sense a huge economic opportunity. As they look into the future, they see a rapidly growing market of young people in China who want to learn English.

These three young innovators come to the United States with a strong sense of purpose to engage this opportunity: to launch an online school to teach Chinese students English. The venture begins with the trio brainstorming in a KFC restaurant. However, it rapidly grows into a massive online educational empire called New Dream.

This comedy is a takeoff on the American film *The Social Network*. Both films display young entrepreneurs driven by a singular quest for money and power. David Wiegel compared the two films in an article for *Slate*: "*The Social Network* ended with the squib about Facebook's future valuation. *American Dreams in China* ends with an inspiring montage of countrymen who studied in the States and then came home to conquer, people like Alibaba's Jack Ma and Google's Kai-Fu Lee.[1]

1. Weigel, "American Dreams in China Storms the Box Office," par. 12.

Garbage Dumps, Here I Come!

Now I want to introduce you to Albina Ruiz, from Peru, who like the young men in both films is an entrepreneur. She also begins her entrepreneurial dreaming by identifying a compelling opportunity. However, she is motivated by a very different sense of aspirations.

"Every time I go to a waste dump, whether it's in Brazil, Colombia, Guatemala, Peru, or India, my heart breaks when I see human beings, like you and me, who are working, many accompanied by their children, and deplorable risky conditions,"[2] reflected Ruiz.

When Albina was a child, her parents moved from the rain forest to a poor neighborhood in Lima, Peru. She grew up in a community in which entire families waded through hills of garbage, often in the middle of the street, to find a few bottles they could sell. Her personal experience gave her empathy for those living in this kind of extreme poverty, and a sense of purpose in helping them.

Conversation 1—Taking Purpose-Focused Changemaking Seriously

In the last chapter we argued that both business innovators and social innovators begin by identifying new opportunities in our communities today and tomorrow. For both business and social entrepreneurs, the second step is to define a clear sense of purpose. Tim Brown, who heads IDEO, insists that entrepreneurs must have "an overarching sense of purpose" to successfully launch their ventures.[3]

The three young Chinese entrepreneurs in the film identified a huge and growing opportunity—a rapidly growing clientele of Chinese young people who want to learn to speak English. Their purpose couldn't have been clearer. These three enterprising young men wanted to create an educational empire to respond to this opportunity in ways that also enriched their lives.

Albina did not have to look very far to find an opportunity that engaged her life. Where many see a problem in garbage, she sees an opportunity. Albina saw garbage as gold. She started her entrepreneurial dreaming by defining "an overarching sense of purpose": to create jobs,

2. Schwartz, "The Road From Garbage to Gold."
3. Brown, *Change by Design*, 74.

improve the environment, improve public health, and create more social entrepreneurs.[4]

While pursuing a university degree in industrial engineering in Lima, Albina began collaborating with others to create innovative ways to implement her clear sense of purpose. "Albina came up with an idea for local enterprises to collect and process garbage: charging affordable fees, reducing waste volume and municipal landfills and generating more income by separating recyclables, spinning off additional microenterprises to produce compost and other marketable by-products."[5]

In 2001, Albina founded the nonprofit organization Ciudad Saludable (Healthy City). This nonprofit has organized over fifteen hundred waste collectors, creating employment and improving health and living conditions for more than six million people in Peru and in urban areas of Bolivia, Brazil, Colombia, Mexico, Venezuela, and India.[6]

As these two different entrepreneurial ventures illustrate, all innovators derive their sense of purpose from very different narratives. The purposes selected for these two different ventures also reflect different views of what is important and what is of value. At core, most forms of social entrepreneurship usually define a sense of purpose that is committed to working for social well-being and the well-being of the natural order. As you can see, Albina's innovation addresses both. Although the entrepreneurs in *American Dreams in China* and *The Social Network* created useful online services, ultimately they seemed to be highly motivated by a quest for "money and power," which of course isn't unusual in our global economic order.

However, if we who are followers of Jesus want to join those who are creating their best communities, their best world, and their best lives, then isn't it essential that we begin by doing the extremely difficult work of identifying the different narratives that are at work in our lives that often define our personal sense of purpose?

Doesn't it make sense, if we choose to join this changemaking celebration, that we develop "an overarching purpose" not only for creating new social innovations but also for our own lives? However, this is hard work because it begins by first identifying the ways that different cultural narratives shape all our aspirations and our values.

4. Schwartz, "The Road From Garbage to Gold."

5. See www.ashoka.org/fellow/albina-ruiz.

6. Ibid.

Waking Up to a World of Competing Narratives

We live in a world filled with many competing narratives, from pre-modern Islamic tribalism in parts of Pakistan to off-the-grid anarchist communities in some regions of North America. However, for the sake of this conversation I will narrow it down to two of the dominant narratives that shape the aspirations and values of many readers. The first is the American dream narrative, which often tends to influence us to lead more acquisitive, self-interested lives. The second narrative is the narrative of the in-breaking of God's new creation that challenges us to refocus our lives and to aspire to advance the love of God and work for the well-being of neighbor. In this second narrative, we are invited to discover how we can invest our lives more fully in advancing something of God's loving purposes for a people and a world.

Kerry Dearborn, in *Drinking from the Wells of New Creation*, urges us not to miss this feast we are invited to share with those from every tongue, tribe, and nation, to celebrate the in-breaking of God's new creation narrative. She also invites us, out of gratitude for all we have received from God, not to become "like those described by Jesus, who were too pre-occupied with other things in their lives to join in the feast."[7] Since we are all people who are often preoccupied with countless things, it is essential that we discover how the dominant culture defines the direction of our lives. We need to do the hard work of identifying how the aspirations and values of the culture tend to influence how we steward our time and resources as well as what we raise our children for.

For three decades I enjoyed teaching a course on Christian worldview at Fuller Northwest, a regional campus of Fuller Theological Seminary, here in Seattle. My students always taught me a great deal. I always began the course by confessing some of the ways in which I had unconsciously embraced values from American culture. For example, I often confessed that I am not a person of great faith. I believe one of the reasons is that I grew up in the world of the movie actor John Wayne. I seemed to succumb to the strong cultural message about rugged American individualism: "It is always up to the individual male to kill the bear, save the day and overcome every obstacle!" Even now I find myself contending with the sense that it is my responsibility to try to solve every problem. Only recently have I started inviting others to join me in prayer to seek God's good help and wisdom.

7. Dearborn, *Drinking from the Wells*, 147.

What are the cultural messages you struggle with in terms of the aspirations and values of American or Eurocentric Western culture? A number of millennials tell us that they want to see a more authentic whole-life faith from those who follow Jesus. They are less interested in how much we know about the Bible. They are more interested in seeing those who "walk the talk." How many of us in our churches seem to be caught up in quietly endorsing notions of the good life that reflect the aspirations and values of the American dream more than the aspirations of the servant Jesus! Is it possible that many of our churches have indeed become chaplains to the dominant culture? Isn't it possible that some of us have settled for a largely private, compartmentalized faith, so that our following Jesus has become little more than a devotional add-on to our "real lives"?

Remember, in chapter 1, I raised a provocative question: "Does the future have a church?" I expressed concern at the declining levels of attendance in many of our churches in Western countries. I also expressed my concern about declining levels of participation and giving. Is it possible that our declining levels of participation and giving reflect a change in our aspirations and values too?

I wrote this book because, as I mentioned earlier, I sincerely believe that the Spirit of God is using young changemakers, largely outside the tent, to help us recover a sense of purpose for our lives that calls us beyond ourselves. Wouldn't it be a shame if we missed being a part of this changemaking celebration—and the satisfaction of making a difference in the lives of others—because we are too preoccupied with other things?

I find that many authors write convincingly about the importance of taking scripture seriously. Many of my evangelical friends emphasize bringing scripture to bear on our spiritual and moral values as well as on our relationships, all of which is important. My mainline friends tend to bring scripture to bear on their concerns for social justice, racial justice, environmental justice, and creating inclusive communities—concerns that are important as well.

However, I find that few authors of any stripe bring scripture to bear on our cultural values—particularly our notions of what constitutes the good life and a better future. Given the daunting challenges that we are likely to face in the coming decade, the growing cultural influence of the imperial global mall, and the declining levels of participation in the church and its mission, wouldn't this be a great time to start a conversation about how to bring scripture to bear on our cultural aspirations and values too?

The author of Romans already started this important conversation: "Brothers and sisters, in light of *all I have shared with you* about God's mercies, I urge you to offer your bodies as a living and holy sacrifice *to God*, a sacred offering that brings Him pleasure; this is your reasonable, essential worship. Do not allow this world to mold you in its own image. Instead, be transformed *from the inside out* by renewing your mind. As a result, you will be able to discern what God wills and whatever God finds good, pleasing, and complete" (Rom 12:1–2 The Voice).

I will take you on a brief excursion of my experiences of growing up with the American Dream—both in terms of its positive concern for the common good as well as its strong narrative that promotes a very acquisitive, self-interested way of life. Then I will invite us, as followers of Jesus, to revisit scripture to hopefully discover a more compelling sense of purpose that I believe calls us beyond ourselves. We will start with a very important question: What seems to be God's loving purposes for a people and a world?

I am convinced that if we can begin to discern something of God's purposes for a people and a world we can find innovative ways as followers of Jesus to more fully join those working for the common good. We can discover how God can use our lives to join those who are creating their best communities and their best world. We can also discern, as followers of Jesus, a clearer and more compelling sense of purpose for our own lives and a new notion of the good life of Jesus. This can enable us to join a growing Christian minority that is taking more time to be present to both God and neighbor—as well as taking more time to celebrate.

Growing Up with the America Dream during World War II

I can still remember when my mother, Katherine, pulled me up on her bed in Twin Falls, Idaho, on a cold December day when I was five. She turned on our small family radio, which we kept on a nearby nightstand. Then she said, "I want you to listen to the following announcement by our president, Franklin Delano Roosevelt." The radio crackled a bit. Then I heard: "Yesterday, December 7th, 1941—a date that will live in infamy—the United States of America was suddenly and violently attacked by the naval and air force of the Empire of Japan."

My mother patiently explained what this announcement meant. She also took the time to share a bit of how people were suffering in parts of Europe. While I didn't begin to grasp what it meant for our country to go to war, I do remember being deeply moved by her descriptions of the suffering that families and kids my age were dealing with in countries far away.

As I mentioned earlier, in June 1942, my dad, Tom, took a job as a laborer helping construct troop ships in Alameda, California, and my parents moved to San Francisco. I stayed with my grandparents at their farm in Blackfoot, Idaho, a place that I loved, for that summer. In late August, my parents arranged for an older woman, Mrs. Johansen, to take me on the train to join them in San Francisco. I loved riding trains. (They are still still by far my favorite way to travel!) As the train slowly pulled out of the station in Pocatello, I looked around and made a surprising discovery: Mrs. Johansen and I were the only civilians on board.

Everywhere I looked there were soldiers. About an hour into the trip a young soldier asked Mrs. Johansen if he could take me to the snack car. She agreed. To my amazement, for the rest of the trip soldiers took turns taking me to the snack car. While I enjoyed the soda pop and comic books, I realized what this was about. I understood that I was a stand-in for their own kids, whom many of these soldiers might never see again.

My folks rented a one-bedroom apartment on Nob Hill and set up an army cot in the living room for me each night. As you can imagine, World War II became the backdrop of my childhood, with frequent air raid alerts at school, and during many evenings everyone had to turn their lights out. We never knew if they were real alerts or not, until we heard the all-clear signal.

One of the highlights of my young life was going with my friends to the six or seven parades held every year on Market Street. I remember saluting the military bands and being swept up in the patriotism of the moment. I was convinced then, as I am today, that a totalitarian conquest of all nations would have been devastating. Through these experiences, I developed a deep sense of gratitude for the freedoms we enjoy and the narratives that shaped them.

I still remember when our war with Germany finally ended in May 1945. People in San Francisco went absolutely crazy. Some jubilant servicemen turned over cars and even one streetcar. Others scaled office buildings. Though I was only eight years old at the time, I remember the overwhelming sense of relief that my fears of a fascist future were over.

At the end of the war I also saw the first newsreels from Auschwitz and other concentration camps and the survivors who had been liberated. Frankly, the images of piles of human bodies, stacked like cordwood, were the most devastating images I experienced as a child. I have never forgotten the horror of those images. Then, in the late nineties I read an important book reflecting on World War II: *Snow Falling on Cedars*, by David Guterson. As I read about the battle scenes, I visualized images of shocking violence: young men being disemboweled and crapping their pants. I had to keep putting the book down because of the sheer horror of the images. It was only then, as an adult, that I realized that this was not the war I grew up with. I grew up with John Wayne's version of that war, which glorified combat, patriotism, and nationalism while minimizing the enormous human costs.

I still can't begin to imagine the enormous human cost of World War II—between fifty and sixty million people killed in six years of unbelievable violence, and huge refugee flows. God have mercy.

Some months before the end of the war, I had taken my first job: I delivered a daily called the *San Francisco News* to my neighbors in the apartment houses on Pine Street on Nob Hill. After I finished my deliveries I often went exploring. This time I decided to check out the roof of the last of the five story apartment houses on my route.

To my surprise, I found six soldiers camping on the roof with their pup tents set up. I learned that leaders from a number of countries, including the United States, were convening at the Fairmont Hotel just one block from where I lived. The soldiers explained that their mission was to start a new form of international collaboration called the "United Nations" in the hope of creating a lasting peace. They added that since we were still at war with Japan, the entire area around the Fairmont Hotel had been made a high-security zone during this gathering.

So every day after that discovery, as soon as I delivered my papers, I raced one block up the steep hill to California Street to watch the parade of national leaders drive up to the Fairmont in their black limos. The only two leaders I recognized from the newsreels were President Harry Truman and Russia's diplomat Vyacheslav Molotov. Even though I was young, this experience made me very aware of a growing sense of hopefulness that filled those important days.

The preamble to the Charter of the United Nations drafted in San Francisco in 1945 reads, "We the peoples of the United Nations are determined to save succeeding generations free from the scourge of war, which twice in our lifetime has brought untold sorrow to mankind."[8] This led to the UN drafting the Universal Declaration of Human Rights in 1948, which "for the first time unequivocally proclaims the inherent rights of all human beings.[9]" This document inspired the growth of global advocacy for human rights, and a growing grassroots collaboration to work for the common good. One of the most significant expressions of this was the US Marshall Plan, which enabled people in Europe devastated most by the war to rebuild their communities and their lives. While the first Earth Day in 1970 ignited a growing advocacy focused on the well-being of the natural world, the Universal Declaration of Human Rights in 1948 ignited a growing global commitment to work for the well-being of humankind and working for the common good.

Frank Laubach celebrated this Declaration of Human Rights, and the growing global concern for our most vulnerable neighbors, in a watershed book titled *The World Is Learning Compassion*. Laubach was one of the leading Christian social innovators of the twentieth century and the creator of a literacy program that served more than sixty million people. In his book, Laubach asserted that the compassion of Jesus was no longer confined to the walls of the church. He argued convincingly that this growing sense of compassion was increasingly reflected not only by those advocating for human rights and humanitarian initiatives but also by marketplace initiatives to empower those struggling to build or rebuild their lives and communities.[10]

We saw these important beginnings give rise to a dramatic increase of philanthropy initiated by many groups outside the church. However, in the fifties, sixties, and seventies, we also witnessed a dramatic increase in Christian philanthropy with the creation of agencies like Tearfund UK, Habitat for Humanity, Bread for the World, World Vision, and World Concern.

Since the end of World War II we have seen God stir up many people outside the church, to set aside their personal aspirations, to work for the common good like those involved today in the chagemaking celebration. Is it possible that God is again using people outside the tent to remind us that we, as followers of Jesus, are called beyond our own personal pursuits, to be agents of God's compassion in these turbulent times?

8. United Nations, "Charter of the United Nations," Preamble.

9. Ibid.

10. Huddleston, "Beyond the Walls of the Church," 13.

Growing Up with the Suburban American Dream

In 1948, my folks packed me and my younger brother Jack into the first car our family ever owned—an old Nash Rambler. We moved to a two-bedroom rental in a new suburban neighborhood in San Mateo. We saw miles of orchards disappear overnight to make way for these huge new tract developments. In the fifties there was no concern about environmental impacts. Through my dad's work in the shipyards, he had learned to read blueprints, so he took a job as an estimator with a suburban tract developer named Williams and Burroughs.

My brother and I enjoyed the adventure of relocating to the suburbs and having a yard to play in with our pup named Inky. However, I had no idea as a young teen how radically this new social invention called the suburbs would redefine the aspirations and values not only of Americans but, increasingly, of people all over the planet.

Coming out of both the Great Recession of the late thirties and WWII, people had a very different experience of the American Dream than we do today. Back then, the dream had very little to do with consumerism. It had much more to do with valuing extended family, place, community, and caring for one another. The words of Wendell Berry's poem "A Vision" capture something of that simpler dream: "The abundance of this place, / the songs of its people and birds, / will be health and wisdom and indwelling / light. This is no piratical dream. / Its hardship is its possibility."[11]

However, back then America was also much more divided by race and class than today, with many being denied basic political freedoms and economic opportunities. People of color were also subject to widespread discrimination and often violence as well. With the explosive growth of the suburbs in the fifties, the American Dream narrative and the images that constituted the good life began to radically change.

Government funding for the GI Bill for returning service personnel made it possible for many vets to go back to school and buy a home. This investment began to create a future of opportunity. It enabled millions of predominately young white Americans to overcome some of the boundaries of class that existed at the time. However, that huge suburban boom had some equally huge environmental impacts, which few seemed to note. Today, of course, the costs of the McMansion gated communities are well publicized (especially their huge energy costs).

11. Quoted in Collum, "Cultivating a Better America," 42.

Back in the fifties, sixties, and seventies, few seemed to recognize that this rapid suburban development was also creating a more racially segregated society. I can remember when huge numbers of white Christian couples living in Seattle started moving their kids to the "safe" (and largely all-white) suburbs.

Finally, the rapid growth of suburbs was also a major factor in creating a more age-segregated society. Most of those first suburban house buyers were not only white, they were also young. The extended family rapidly gave way to these nuclear family settlements. We lost the stories, the wisdom and community support of our seniors, many of whom were settled in retirement homes. I am convinced that this age segregation has impoverished recent generations of Americans.

However, my greatest concern regarding the suburbanization of America was the remarkable way it began to radically alter the aspirations and values of Americans. "Historically, suburban development was characterized by a utopian idealism of progress, modernity, cheap land and abundant access to resources . . ." This also included the development of a new American identity where we learned to increasingly define ourselves by what we owned or acquired. "Consequently, the new identity was shaped by symbols of material acquisition and excessive lifestyles."[12] In recent years this new suburban model of the "goods life" has gone global. In Australia it is called "the house on a quarter acre"—though these days, few Aussies can afford the quarter acre.

Bringing the American Dream Home to China

Remember the three young Chinese entrepreneurs in the film *American Dreams in China*? The premise of the film was right on target. A growing number of Chinese students are not only interested in learning to speak English; they are also interested in being educated in the US to get a taste of the dream. According to a recent report from the *Chronicle of Higher Education*, 886,052 students from abroad came to the US to attend our colleges and universities. Remarkably, Chinese students constitute 60 percent of all international students coming to the US.[13]

I suspect that many international students don't just receive a good education for their careers. They also receive an informal education in US

12. Islam et al., "Negative Environmental Impacts of Suburban Sprawl."
13. Fischer, "Chinese Students Lead Foreign Surge," pars. 2–3.

culture. It certainly did for Annie Liu, who had been a student in the US. When she returned to China, she and her husband bought a $300,000 home for weekend escapes in a very unusual location: Jackson Hole, China! Believe it or not, the Chinese Jackson Hole is comprised of some one thousand homes outside of Beijing that look surprisingly like rustic lodges you might find in Wyoming. Annie even chose a broad range of US consumer products to furnish this weekend getaway. They include everything from American country and western furniture to old American license plates hung on the walls, completing the illusion.[14]

What isn't an illusion is that people all over the planet are consciously, like Annie Liu, and many of the rest of us, being drawn into a new global culture of acquisition, consumption, and waste. Don't you find it highly ironic that Communist leaders feel the need to promote a Chinese version of the American dream to sustain the growth of the Chinese economy? "For many in the west, the Chinese dream looks remarkably like the expansionist nightmare many of our economies are already caught up in."[15]

Dreaming and Scheming

Time to get out your iPad or notebook again and find a friend to do the hard work of trying to discover what shapes your aspirations and values.

- What is your earliest memory of the cultural influences that began to shape your notions of what constitutes the good life?

- How has your notion of what is important and of value shaped how you spend your time and resources?

- Do you know any people in your church or community who seem to march to a different drumbeat, connecting their lives to biblical aspirations of compassion and generosity towards others?

- What are some ways you might use scripture, in concert with family or friends, to begin to redefine your sense of what is important or of value?

14. Jiang, "Living the American Dream in Jackson Hole, China."

15. Brown, "In Many Ways, the 'China Dream' Is Not Different from the American One."

Conversation 2—Waking Up to the Accelerating Influence of the Imperial Global Mall

While this version of the American dream often finds its fullest expression in suburban communities in North America, the UK, Australia, and even Jackson Hole China its reach is much broader than that. However, before we discuss its growing reach, I think it is important to briefly consider its origins.

The American Dream, I believe, is largely a product of the Enlightenment that began in Europe in the seventeenth and eighteenth centuries. A transcendent view of a better future, shaped largely by the influence of the church, gave way to a view of a better future focused exclusively on this world. Increasingly, the better future was almost exclusively defined in terms of growing materialism and economic progress.

Doesn't it seem that many of us have learned to view the Creator God as showing up in our churches and prayer meetings, but having little to do with the "real" world? Hasn't the so-called "invisible hand of the marketplace" become something of a secular providence, arbitrarily determining winners and losers? Haven't we also increasingly defined the ultimate in human experience almost exclusively in economic terms as well? Don't we also often seem to hold a very utilitarian view of God's good creation as just the place where we dig our oil and set up our campers? Haven't we also, unlike many of our First Nations' friends, lost some sense of a more community-based view of knowledge and the sacredness of God's good creation?

Randy Woodley, in *Shalom and the Community of Creation*, reminds us that for "indigenous Americans knowledge is not abstract or neutral; it is directly related to life experience, stories, songs, ceremonies, and traditions."[16] By contrast, the Enlightenment, and a more Eurocentric view of knowledge, has meant that many of us tend to view persons primarily in economic terms—striving to become ever more acquisitive consumers. It follows, of course, that many of us view the good life as the endless effort to scale the mountain of economic success. Remarkably, an incredible number of people (including professing Christians) also seem to believe the Enlightenment fiction that the best way to help the poor is to pursue our own economic self-interest, believing that somehow this will raise all boats.

---

16. Woodley. *Shalom and the Community of Creation*, 98.

While the United States slowly loses its high level of political and economic influence in the world, I am convinced that the aspirations of the American Dream are, through the digital revolution, reaching new "converts" all over the planet at a rate never seen before. However, once people connect to the Internet, several important changes take place. First, corporations start keeping records of our personal lives in ways they have never before been able to do. The Center for Digital Democracy reports that the marketers of the global mall capture personal information about us every time we use a laptop, mobile phone, gaming device, or credit card. They create detailed files of personal data about our lives, addictions, and consumption patterns. They then sell these files to other marketers, who use the data to narrow-cast ads back to us. They are also using "stealth forms of social media surveillance and behavioral advertising" to target our young people in ways that were never before possible.[17]

One of the creepiest tools in their arsenal of surveillance may be "Hello Barbie," Mattel's Eavesdropping Barbie Doll and a specialist in child surveillance. "In Mattel's demo, Barbie asks many questions that would elicit a great deal of information about a child, her interests, and her family. This information could be of great value to advertisers and used unfairly to market to children."[18]

Sarah Nicole Prickett, writing for the *New York Times Magazine*, explains one new way that social media is also used to seduce consumers of all ages through Instagram:

> If Twitter is the street, Facebook the suburban-sprawl mall, and Pinterest some kind of mail-order catalog, Instagram is the many-windowed splendor of a younger Bergdorf's, showing all we possess or wish for, under squares of filtered glass, each photographic pane backlit 24/7. Each pane is, or intimates, an entire landscape or room. Follow enough of the international lifestyle-setters, and you'll see: women's fashion, men's fashion, home or apartment décor, beautiful food, art, color-coordinated books and magazines.
>
> All elements must be carefully staged to look happenstance. Only the crassest Instagrammer snaps a new pair of shoes in a box, or plainly on a floor. The cannier, cinematic one will instead

17. "Promoting Consumer Rights, Protecting Privacy, Ensuring Transparency, and Empowering the Public in the Digital Era." See www.democraticmedia.org/about/history.

18. Campaign for a Commercial-Free Childhood, "Stop Matell's 'Hello Barbie' Eavesdropping Doll."

make a display of the shoes, arranging her feet on a shabby-chic desk . . . What each [image] says is not "this is a good shoe" or "these shoes look good on me," but "these shoes look good in my life" . . .[19]

What a remarkable way to instill a little covetousness. "There's a term for this. Social psychologists, journalists and social-media users call it 'lifestyle envy,' or 'Instagram envy,' and savvy Smartphone users are well acquainted with its tell-tale sign: the little pang you get when a friend posts photos from his or her swanky vacation in Istanbul."[20] Hey, honestly: Have you ever noticed a little "lifestyle envy" creeping into your life? Many of our youth are on screen and online six or seven hours a day. How much impact can we hope to have as we share about the servant Jesus in forty-five minutes of Sunday school once a week? How is concern for neighbor ever going to trump "lifestyle envy"?

Four years ago I presented a paper at a conference of First Nations leaders at Trinity Western University in Langley, British Columbia. I observed that the first wave of European colonization came with boats and guns. I added I believe that the newest wave of colonization is coming through smartphones and the Internet, promoting the widespread creation of a more individualistic, acquisitive, and self-interested lifestyle. Aren't these aspirations and values likely to pose an increasing threat not only to a more vital Christian faith, traditional cultures, and all our families, but even to values of mutual care that are so important to the integrity of our neighborhoods?

As others have argued, there is something about this new global economy that reflects some of the aspects of empire and that increasingly defines for people everywhere what is important and what is of value. However, this new imperial global mall is much larger and really more influential than most former empires. I share Cynthia Moe-Lobeda's concern that "for the global market to continue in its purpose of maximizing growth and accumulating wealth, it must convince people to consume as much as possible."[21] Beyond the simple fact that this acquisitive way of life is not good for us, not to mention our children and grandchildren, it is also clear that our finite planet simply can't sustain this kind of growth.

19. Prickett, "Look Out, It's Instagram Envy," pars. 4–5.

20. Anderson, "Instagram Effect," par. 5.

21. Moe-Lobeda, *Resisting Structural Evil*, 59.

However, I also see a few encouraging signs of hope in this new global economy. I am increasingly discovering corporations that realize it is not in their interest to ignore the costs of growth. I am impressed by the number of corporations that are making significant investments in reducing environmental impacts and incorporating a social mission into their corporate mission. "Social change becomes a part of the equation—companies have to compete around their ability to improve social conditions and achieve social outcomes."[22]

I am increasingly concerned by how politically divided followers of Jesus are in the United States these days. There are Christians on the left who share the concern I raise about the imperial quality of the new global economy. However, a number in this camp are categorical in their denunciation of global capitalism. They can't bring themselves to acknowledge the millions of our neighbors who have been delivered from extreme poverty by the global economy or the power of social entrepreneurship to help solve major global problems.

I am even more concerned by some on the right who use fearmongering about the threat of big government taking away their liberties and their guns and collectivizing people in a totalitarian state. Evangelical Christians in other countries read some end-time writings. However, I have only found this literature being used as a tool to arouse a deep sense of fear among a number of sincere Christians living in more conservative communities in the US.

In *Cease Fire: Searching for Sanity in America's Culture Wars*, I wrote, "If we are going to be a biblical people, we must recognize that God's agenda transcends liberal and conservative agendas . . . We need to be involved in the public square—not in the contentious, adversarial spirit of partisan politics but in the reconciling spirit of Jesus Christ."[23] However, we must begin this journey by finding another reason for being and by getting back in touch with our ancient narrative and identifying God's loving purposes for a people and a world. It will become immediately clear that God's purpose isn't just about personal change but societal change as well. Don't we as followers of Jesus need to join those in every age working for the well-being of the human and natural orders? Doesn't it all begin not with the biblical imagery of being rescued from this world

22. Eggers and Macmillan, *Solution Revolution*, 35.
23. Sine, *Cease Fire*, 277–78.

but with being a part of the transformation of this world through the risen Christ?

Rediscovering God's Purposes for a People and a World

What are God's loving purposes for a people and a world? Join me at a faculty lunch at Seattle Pacific University in 2005 with New Testament theologian N. T. Wright, who offered a surprising opening statement. He arrested the attention of everyone in the room when he declared, "Heaven is not my home! Heaven is where the future of God is kept, but it is not my home!"

As Wright explained in *Surprised by Hope*, "Jesus' resurrection is the beginning of God's new project not to snatch people away from earth to heaven but to colonize the earth with the life of heaven. That, after all, is what the Lord's Prayer is all about."[24] He explains that what we are looking forward to is coming home as a great multicultural, bodily resurrected community—not to the clouds, but to a new heaven and a new earth.

Relatedly, Walter Brueggemann reminds us that this vision of a restored creation begins with the prophets and the recovery of prophetic imagination. "The prophets dismiss the pursuit of commodities and the practice of 'the good life' of endless consumption." The prophetic imagination challenges us to de-legitimize the dominant images of power and wealth, including those promoted by the imperial global economy of our time.[25]

The prophets also offer us a hope of "a new social possibility, namely a return to homeland and the restoration of a flourishing Jerusalem."[26] Again, this is not imagery of escape from this troubled world but of restoration of this good creation. My imagination is always ignited by the powerful poetry of Isaiah, who invites us to envision a new homecoming for all the world's people to a new heaven and a new earth where all things are made new (Isa 65:17–19).

He offers us astonishing imagery of people from all nations coming home, ascending a new transcendent mountain and entering a new flourishing city, where weapons of war are transformed into implements of

24. Wright, *Surprised by Hope*, 293.
25. Brueggemann, *Practice of Prophetic Imagination*, 30–33.
26. Ibid., 37.

peace (Isa 2:1–4). He invites us to imagine a restored and abundant creation where the blind see, the broken are healed, and the disabled come running up that mountain (Isa 35:17–19). Of course, it is also imagery of all of us being welcomed home to a celebration of feasting and reconciliation, "the best of food and the finest of wine" (Isa 25:6–9).

Josh Garrels, a singer-songwriter, invites us to join in this great homecoming celebration now in his stirring song "Zion & Babylon": "On your way to Mount Zion / All you slaves set free / Come on out child, and come on home to me / We will dance, we will rejoice / If you can hear me then follow my voice."

In *A New Heaven and a New Earth*, J. Richard Middleton also affirms his view of a resurrected future where we come home to a world in which all things are made new. He reminds us that Jesus came announcing his sense of God's purpose for his life, drawn from the compelling imagery of Isaiah 61: "The Spirit of the Lord is upon me, because he has anointed me to bring good news to the poor. He has sent me to proclaim release to the captives and recovery of sight to the blind, to let the oppressed go free, to proclaim the year of the Lord's favor" (Luke 4:18–19).

Middleton convincingly argues that this passage was never intended to be spiritualized, as is often done: "God in Christ was actually concerned about real flesh and blood poor people, or captives or those oppressed by societal injustice . . ."[27] In Luke 4:18–19, the servant Jesus makes clear that to embrace God's purpose for his life is to devote himself to embodying God's compassion to the flesh-and-blood lives of people around him.

Walter Brueggemann, in his classic *The Prophetic Imagination*, states that Christ's compassion not only "penetrates the numbness" of his world and ours, but also stands as a critique of the system that causes the pain in his time and ours. "Jesus enters into the hurt and finally comes to embody it."[28] Isn't this a part of God's call on all of our lives to become more of the compassion of Christ in the times in which we live? Isn't this also an invitation to free-up more time to become actively invested in the changemaking celebration today?

Shane Claiborne has long been an advocate of a more radical whole-life faith committed to a very different sense of purpose than the aspirations of the imperial mall. He encourages all followers of Jesus everywhere not to accept the world as it is, but to join creative "troublemakers,

---

27. Middleton, *New Heaven and a New Earth*, 250–51.
28. Brueggmann, *Prophetic Imagination*, 86.

rabble-rousers and mischief-makers" in changing the world into what it needs to be.[29] I invite you to join those who are already discovering that the good life of God is more than a devotional add-on to our "real lives." Isn't the invitation to follow Jesus an invitation to dream and scheme—to join those creating new forms of changemaking, and even to join those who sometimes become "troublemakers, rabble-rousers and mischief-makers"?

It is an invitation to follow Jesus by more intentionally connecting one's life to the compassionate purposes of God. It is an invitation to join or create small mustard seed groups where one can discover, with others, how to create more compassionate, festive lives than anything the imperial mall can offer. Shane calls us to "live into, serve into, and celebrate into that new world that is already here!"

It is also an invitation to join with all those in the changemaking celebration who are outside the tent, who often seem to invest more in caring for neighbor and God's good creation than many of us who claim to be disciples of the servant Jesus. Jim Wallis puts it succinctly: "Our life together can be better. Ours is a shallow and selfish age, and we are in need of conversion—from looking out just for ourselves to looking out for one another. It is time to hear and heed a call to a different way of life, to reclaim a very old idea called the common good."[30] This call to work for the common good, which began with the calling of Abraham and Sarah, has found expression in the call to promote human rights after World War II and the call to work for the well-being of the natural world that has found growing support since that first Earth Day. This call is strongly supported in that ancient narrative from which we derive our faith and our lives.

Rediscovering the Surprising Influence of the Mustard Seed Empire of Jesus

If we want to find a biblical alternative to the American dream that calls us beyond ourselves, we need to find an answer to a question our Australian friends ask: "What is God on about?" What are God's purposes for a people and world?

29. Claiborne, "Imagine a New World."
30. Wallis, (Un)Common Good, 3.

Remember, Jesus came not only inviting us to a vital personal faith in the Creator God. He also came announcing the in-breaking of a new order that is clearly counter to not only the Roman empire, but to all human empires, including the imperial global mall, of our world today. Jesus came announcing the in-breaking of the kingdom of God. However, I find that "kingdom of God" language has come to symbolize so many different things to believers today that it has lost much of its meaning.

Here is my struggling attempt to offer some fresh imagery for the mustard seed empire of Jesus. From Jesus' first announcement that God's new order was breaking into this one, few people have recognized God's unlikely alternative to empire, in his time or ours. In *The New Conspirators*, I wrote:

> Remember that Jesus' empire was not ushered in with pomp and circumstance . . . It came on donkey's back. Its 'imperial council' was comprised of a handful of unemployed fishermen, a couple of I.R.S. agents, a prostitute and some other hangers-on. Jesus demonstrated how to wield his imperial power by washing feet, telling stories and playing with kids. Jesus' empire is based on the absurd values that the last should be first, losers are winners and the most influential in this empire should clean the toilets.
>
> Members of this empire are instructed to love their enemies, forgive their friends, always give twice as much as people ask of them and never pursue power or position. Jesus insisted that those who are a part of this empire shouldn't worry about their finances, but simply trust God. The resources to run this empire were basins, towels and leftover lunches. This empire developed the reputation for endlessly partying—almost always with the wrong kind of people.[31]

Clearly, one of the most compelling characteristics of the leader of this unlikely imperial order was how generously he shared his life with others—healing lepers, feeding the hungry, and always reaching out to those in need. Even as Jesus was called to be a man for others, aren't we called to be people for others? Reflect on the enormous impact this new mustard seed empire of Jesus has had on the lives of millions, over the centuries, since Jesus called that first motley group of disciples to become part of his new way.

Isn't it clear that to be followers of this Jesus involves much more than showing up at church occasionally, giving out of our leftovers and

---

31. Sine, *New Conspirators*, 120–21.

staying out of trouble? Isn't it clear that to be a follower of this Jesus we need to consider joining those who are discovering creative ways that God can use our mustard seeds to advance God's compassionate purposes in times like these?

Recovering a Biblical View of the Good Life of God

This mustard seed empire of Jesus invites us not only to work for God's purposes but also to discover a new view of what constitutes the good life of God. I think it will become immediately clear that we are invited to discover a whole new way of being that is based on a very different set of aspirations from those promoted by the global mall.

I am very grateful for a best-selling book by David Platt titled *Radical: Taking Back Your Faith from the American Dream.*[32] David also battles with the seductions of our consumer culture. He calls his readers to live more sacrificially. However, if the way of Jesus shows us the good life, I suspect we will discover that reinventing our own lives after his example will lead to a more satisfying celebration of life, and not simply a sacrificial experience.

If we bring scripture to bear on redefining the good life of God, isn't it transparently clear that we can never find it by pursuing a self-interested life. *Doesn't Jesus make clear, in both his paradoxical teachings and in his life, that the good life of God will never be found in pursuing life? It will only be found in "losing life" in service to God and others.* Instead of our faith becoming little more than a devotional add-on to our "real life," now all of life becomes a design opportunity. We can join others following the mustard seed way of Jesus, designing new ways of living, new ways of raising our young, new ways of empowering our neighbors and, yes, new ways to party. We can make visible a more festive way of life than anything the imperial global mall can offer—and then perhaps people will take us more seriously again.

The question is, how can we help one another come out of hiding and begin to explore to what extent the messages from the global mall have shaped our sense of what is important and of value?

32. Platt, *Radical: Taking Back Your Faith From the American Dream.*

Discovering the Ingredients of the Good Life:
High Status and Extreme Cool!

Ten years ago, I created a little exercise for congregational groups. I called it "High Status/Extreme Cool" and offered it to people from different generations in order to uncover assumptions about what constitutes for them the good life and a better future.

Typically, I divide the group by age: the over forties and under forties. I ask those over forty, what constitutes an "extreme high-status lifestyle"; where would they live, holiday, and party? Likewise I asked the under forties, what constitutes an "extreme cool lifestyle" for their generation? As they share their two lists with the entire group, a generational divide emerges in their responses. The over forties tend to envision the good life as palatial suburban communities with huge homes, four-car garages, seaside condos, membership in the country club, and luxury cruise vacations.

For the under forties, the good life often seems to have a postmodern experiential quality. The under forties typically envision luxury lofts downtown, where they can experience the music scene, theaters, and a broad range of colorful ethnic restaurants. International travel is a big-ticket item too, often including extreme sports, but not cruises. Many of this age group seem to have a passion for fashion, but sometimes use repurposed materials to reflect their environmental credentials. Those in both groups invariably report that this is the first time they have ever talked about cultural aspirations and values at church.

The energy in the room always soars as participants start making their lists. When I ask, "What sparked all the energy?" there is usually an initial silence. Then someone always observes, "Even though we don't have all this stuff . . . we would really, really like to!" I then ask them what this might have to do with following Jesus. The observation "Doesn't the Bible have something to about where our hearts are?" usually follows. "Bingo!" I respond. This exercise makes it much easier to engage participants in a very honest conversation about our notions of the good life, and what we are on the planet for.

I am convinced that social innovators like Albina can motivate followers of Jesus to re-discover that the real good life of God is more likely to be found when we invest our lives to make a real difference in the lives of others. I am sure there are readers who are already discovering that the good life of God will never be found in seeking life but rather in losing life in service to God and others. Wouldn't you like to experience a little more of the good life of God? Wouldn't you like to discover creative new ways God might more fully use your mustard seed to make a difference in the lives of other? I find when people get to be my age they want to look back and feel their lives have counted for something. I love Kerry Dearborn's imagery of coming home to that feast where, I suspect, Jesus will not only welcome us but will wait at table as well.

In *Drinking from the Wells of New Creation*, Dearborn reminds us that

> Participation in God's work of new creation calls for deep prayer, reliance on the Holy Spirit, and the empowering vision that the table is set, the wine is poured, and all people are called to come to the feast. May God's people not be like those described by Jesus, who were too preoccupied with other things in their lives to join in the feast, so the host had to send his servants out to the streets and lanes to "bring in the poor, the crippled, the blind, and the lame" with the desire that his "house may be filled" (Luke 14:16–24). May God's people instead receive the vision of God's kingdom, be filled more fully with God's love, and share in the Spirit's purpose to draw all people in. May we live with deep gratitude for God's presence in our midst and the gift of being joined together in Christ with people from every tongue, tribe, and nation, celebrating the new creation.[33]

Dreaming and Scheming

It is time to get out your iPad or notebook once again, with the object of viewing discipleshp as an opportunity to discover a new reason for being—a new view of the good life of God.

- Invite some of your friends over. Ask the over forty to make a list of the elements that would likely be a part of a high-status lifestyle where they live. Then ask the under forty to list what they would imagine to be an extreme cool lifestyle where you live. Invite them to share their respective lists and to identify similarities and differences. Finally, ask them what the lists have to do with following Jesus.

33. Dearborn, *Drinking from the Wells*, 147.

- Now write down some of the imagery of the great homecoming future of God that we see in the societal change heralded by the prophets and reflected in the life and teachings of Jesus. Pick a couple of the themes that you and your friends find most compelling. Use these themes to plan a party with your friends to make those images of hope come alive.

- How did the biblical reflection begin to alter your own personal notions of the good life of God and how you might create a way of life where you make more time for being more present to God, a small faith community, and neighbors?

5

Imagine New Community Empowerment Today to Create Our Best Neighborhoods Tomorrow

Celebrating Justice Coming Down the Road to All Our Communities

As soon as I stepped off the plane in Port-au-Prince, Haiti, on a beautiful spring morning in 1977, I could have sworn I was back in Hawaii. The jacaranda trees, the tall palms, and the fragrance of the tropics reminded me of life on Maui. I was greeted warmly by Chavannes Jeunes, the assistant director of World Concern's first community development project in Haiti. Though I had been an urban social worker in my twenties, this was my first experience of coordinating involvement in a community empowerment project. I am grateful for all I learned from my Haitian collaborators, who had invited World Concern to partner with them in this project. However, I discovered that being involved in community empowerment in someone else's community was more challenging than I expected.

After a very bumpy two-hour ride south down a dirt road, we entered the small village of La Cayes. We took a right turn and headed north, up into the highlands, to the newly constructed Christian Hospital Lumiere operated by Mission Evangélique Baptiste du Sud d'Haiti (MEBSH). Our team had their living quarters and their offices at the hospital compound.

Chavannes asked me to join him in a hike up the mountains to a large, landlocked valley community of ten thousand people called Plaisance de Sud, or Pleasant Valley of the South. It took us two and a half hours to hike into the valley. Our hosts welcomed us with small cups of strong coffee.

One of the things these valley leaders made clear was that their highest priority was to build a road out of their landlocked valley. A road would, of course, help them get their goods to market in Port-au-Prince more easily. The leaders had an additional reason for wanting to build a road. They told us that they "wanted to see justice come down the road." I had no idea what that meant. Even Chavannes was baffled.

When Chavannes left a local doctor, Dr. Luke, took over the translation duties. Twenty of the valley leaders took me on a tour of some of their coffee and vegetable farms, the primary source of income for the ten thousand people living in this region. After the tour Dr. Luke explained that the valley leaders wanted to extend their hospitality to me by loaning me a small donkey for the trip back to the base at the hospital.

This brought me a couple of unexpected challenges. Number one: I had never ridden a donkey. Number two: this donkey was really too small for someone my size—6'2" and 185 pounds. However, my research into Haitian culture had clearly shown me that in Haiti you never turn down an offer of hospitality.

The valley leaders gave me clear directions back to the base as well their best wishes as the small donkey and I slowly started to ascend the narrow mountain trail. After traveling about a half an hour up the mountain, I suddenly realized that I had failed to listen carefully to the directions I had been given. Apparently, I took the wrong fork on the trail and was heading back to the village.

The donkey and I had traveled almost back to the village when we were suddenly engulfed in a tropical rainstorm that soaked me to the skin and almost sent us tumbling straight down the hill. Some twenty minutes later we found ourselves heading back into the village plaza. The trail had led us right back to where we started!

When our hosts saw me and the donkey—drenched, and with all six of our feet on the ground at the same time—they laughed so hard they almost fell over. (Unfortunately, this was not a new experience for me; I find that I often bring others the gift of light entertainment wherever I travel!) Thankfully, for the donkey's sake as well as my own, they allowed me to resume my trek on foot.

The major lesson I learned on my very first day of involvement in this community empowerment project is that it is essential to learn to listen with great care to all your collaborators. I hope you can find an easier way to learn about the importance of listening than I did. I will return below to share more about the Haiti project, "justice coming down the road," and the reward our team experienced because they had learned to listen with great care to the valley leaders.

Have you ever been involved in a community-empowerment project in your neighborhood or someone else's? Did you discover the importance of listening and of inviting the ideas and input of others? In the next chapter we will share how you can also join friends in the social entrepreneurship stream, which also requires careful listening as well as creative input from all those involved in the venture.

Inviting Followers of Jesus to Join the Community Empowerment Celebration

The Spirit of God does seem to be stirring people, largely outside the church, to become involved in a new movement—to create more sustainable, just, and flourishing local communities. Let me take you on a tour of some of the most interesting aspects of this stream of social innovation. You will see that it is very multifaceted and yet within reach of virtually all of us. I think you will also be as impressed, as I am, by the kind of change that is possible. I suspect you will also discover that this is a celebration you won't want to miss.

Let me start, however, by sounding a wake-up call again. As I mentioned in chapter 1, many churches in North America don't sponsor a single ministry in their own communities. Those that do tend to support ministries like food banks, which help a bit with immediate needs but also sustain people in their dependency. Very few churches become directly involved in initiatives that are designed to empower neighbors or create more resilient and just local communities.

It is even harder to find congregations that willingly collaborate in a community-wide empowerment venture where the church is not in charge. This is an invitation to church leaders in communities everywhere to discover creative changemaking ventures in your communities and join them. We can all learn something about new forms of community empowerment and community economics if we start dreaming and scheming with the creative leaders right in our own neighborhoods.

In this chapter I will show you some of the new ways the Creator God might use your mustard seed, in collaboration with others, to become more involved in creating our best communities, and in the process our best world, for both good times and tough times. I urge you to start today to find out what is already stirring in your community. Then discern whether this is an initiative you or your congregation might join. You may be surprised by the ways that the Creator God is already at work in your neighborhood.

In fact, I am convinced that the most effective way to influence the under forty to join you is to invite them to participate with you in creating innovative ways to make a difference in the lives of your own neighbors. Consider creating one new form of community empowerment with both the young in your community and those in your church.

CONVERSATION 1—CREATING COMMUNITIES OF JUSTICE, RESILIENCE, AND SUSTAINABILITY

Joining Hands to Bring Justice Down the Road in All Our Communities

As I write millions of Americans are praying, marching, and working to see racial and economic justice come down their roads, in communities form Ferguson to Baltimore. Groups like Black Lives Matter are becoming the voice for a new generation of activists. Lisa Sharon Harper, reporting for *Sojourners*, says that the leadership of these young activists has motivated older people in many of our communities and our congregations— not only black and mainline churches but also evangelical churches—to join this growing new movement for racial justice in America.[1]

On Labor Day 2015, the Sierra Club celebrated a "movement of movements" for equality, justice, and hope. "We recognize that the movement for a truly just society is much stronger when we join forces. The same interests that stand in the way of worker's struggles for economic justice are standing in the way of economic justice and a clean energy economy, and they are standing in the way of racial and immigrant justice."[2] This recent and growing integration of movements for economic, racial, and environmental justice will enable all our communities

---

1. Harper, "One Year Later."
2. Mair, "Labor Day 2015: Uniting Labor, Climate, and Racial Justice Movements."

to adopt a more integrated approach in working for the common good in our local communities.

There is a real possibility of growing economic uncertainty not only in the lives of the working poor but also for many in the middle class, as well as mounting challenges that are likely to impact all of our communities as we travel together into the 2020s. We are all likely to be increasingly impacted by climate change as well as the need to create stronger local economies.

For example, a recent conference focused on Shifting the Economy from Wall Street to Main Street was sponsored by SOCAP.[3] The presenters included Walter Brueggemann, Peter Block, and Amy Cotese. Attendees were encouraged to "invest . . . time, resources and imagination towards accelerating the flow of capital into our neighborhoods." They were also invited to "live into an alternative story"—a story that focuses on accelerating the growth of our local economies.[4]

Kevin Jones, a cofounder of SOCAP, was one of the presenters at the conference. Jones is one of the leading activists working for the creation of private financial resources designed to promote community-empowerment values, including loans, investments, and gifts. For example, Giving Circles[5] offer individuals or groups the opportunity to donate their money or time in community projects they care about. "This is giving that tees up local investing into businesses that deliver more value to the commons than they do to the market, but that still returns capital," Jones says.[6]

Let me share a few examples of how those involved in community empowerment are creating not only more resilient but also more just communities.

Sampling the Changemaking Celebration in Bellingham!

"Don't miss the roving garden party in downtown Bellingham!" reads a poster in this small city north of Seattle, where neighbors were invited to help plant some heirloom tomatoes, replant some raspberry bushes, plus

3. See www.socialcapitalmarkets.net.

4. See www.xavier.edu/campusuite25/public/calendar/graphical_get_event.cfm?grp_id=1&cal_id=39329.

5. See www.givingcirlcles.org.

6. Jones, "The Local Funding Kit Feeds Giving."

help with a bit of weeding. They enjoyed salmon and salads as part of this garden party, a neighborhood celebration sponsored by an organization called Sustainable Connections.

Bellingham was recently recognized as the number one small city in the nation in terms of creating resilient and sustainable local communities. It all began when a handful of people created Sustainable Connections in April 2002.[7] Since then, this network of nearly seven hundred Bellingham businesses has joined hands to promote a sustainable local economy. They also promote local sustainable agriculture, moving toward zero waste, and switching to green power, as well as working for a little economic justice by enabling workers in their communities to earn a living wage.[8]

Recently, Christine and I enjoyed having dinner with a new missional church plant in Bellingham called Fountain Parish. This Christian Reformed Church plant functions rather like a progressive dinner. The congregation meets in a different home every week to enjoy a meal, to hear one another's stories, and to share a time of worship. Sean and Julie Hall, who are the pastors of this youthful congregation, first introduced us to the Sustainable Bellingham movement.

Sean and Julie report that their church is actively involved in it. For example, the congregation participated in a citywide urban empowerment project. They worked with neighbors in a lower-income neighborhood to plant vegetable gardens in both their back and front yards. Couldn't you and your congregation find those who are already working to create a more sustainable, just, and resilient neighborhood where you live? Wouldn't you enjoy sitting down to a garden party with your neighbors after a good day's work, enjoying salmon, garden salads, and fresh raspberries and celebrating this kind of collaboration? Let's shift from small-city to big-city empowerment.

Transforming Crack Houses and the Imagination of the Young into a Just Community

Alexie Torres-Fleming, a presenter at the 2015 Inhabit Conference at the Seattle School of Theology and Psychology, shared how she grew up in a blighted neighborhood in the Bronx in the sixties and seventies. She

7. See www.sustainableconnections.org.

8. Jarvis, "Growing Local: Interview with BALLE's Michelle Long."

was one of the very few from her generation who made it up and out. In fact, she became a successful bank executive. Though living a very comfortable life in a more affluent neighborhood, Alexie would still visit her parents in the Bronx.

Then one day in 1992, God got her attention and she made a very radical decision. She quit her job and moved back into the run-down neighborhood where she grew up. One of the first things she did was to visit Father Mike Tyson, the Franciscan priest of the Catholic Church she had attended as a child. She simply asked if there was any way she could be of help in the neighborhood. Father Mike immediately invited her to join a small antidrug prayer group that was planning to march in front of crack houses in the neighborhood. She joined that march. Two days later the drug dealers retaliated by breaking into the church, setting fires and smashing statues, and threatening to kill Father Mike if the prayer marches didn't stop.

Determined not to let the drug dealers win the day, Alexie and Father Mike mobilized twelve hundred people for a second rally that received national attention. Over time these marches resulted in closing and taking back all those crack houses and rehabbing them for the community. Alexie made an important discovery about community empowerment during that first venture. Any new neighborhood venture must start with the people who live there.

She told us that the most important voices we need to listen to are those of the people who live in the neighborhood. She emphasized that it was particularly important to start with the voices, the imagination, and the activism of the young. Alexie explained that in 1994 the young people, older adults, and faith leaders in the neighborhood created a remarkable new form of neighborhood empowerment called Youth Ministries for Peace and Justice (YMPJ).[9] YMPJ has created a multidimensional strategy for creating a healthy, just, and sustainable community. Essentially, young leaders and adults in the neighborhood use community-organizing strategies to increase youth employment, workforce development, and access to health care. These local leaders also have become public advocates for tenant rights, education and tenant reform, police reform, environmental justice, and economic revitalization of the Bronx River waterfront. This model demonstrates that one way to effect far-reaching neighborhood transformation begins with inspiring and equipping young leaders to

9. See www.ympj.org.

become the agents of change, celebrating every single victory in creating healthy, just, and sustainable neighborhoods!

By the way, YMPJ ends their summer day camp for young leaders every August with a barbecue for the whole neighborhood. I can smell the barbecue grilling. Wouldn't you like to be part of a changemaking celebration that makes this kind of difference in our cities?

Inviting the Imagination of Gen Next in Placemaking

The young urban innovators in the Bronx are not unique. As we have already seen, Gen Y and Gen Z are hard-wired to make a difference in the lives of their neighbors; many of them care about the well-being of others. We need to invite their compassion and creativity in creating new forms of community empowerment. We also need to invite their imagination and leadership in creating new forms of placemaking and not miss all the innovation they have to offer.

"Young People and Placemaking: Engaging Youth to Create Community Places" is an article from Australia that describes a Youth Plaza designed by young adults from twelve to twenty-five years old in Fremantle, Western Australia. Cheryl Millard found that involving young people in this community to design and build a youth-friendly plaza had several immediate benefits. First, these young people used their creativity to imagine their own public space, including a skate park and a performance venue; the skate park, which is world-renowned, has become a tourist destination. Second, these young adults gained both a sense of investment in the place where they live and a sense of ownership in the artistic aspects of placemaking.[10]

Block by Block is another project sponsored by UN-Habitat, the United Nations Human Settlement Program. Essentially, the creators of Minecraft engage young people in a video game to redesign urban spaces by building whatever they wish. For example, seventy participants came together in the municipality of Prishtina in Kosovo to create a new public space—a neighborhood called Sunny Hills. Children as young as seven as well as young adults were involved in using Minecraft to design this new public space. What this group discovered is what others are discovering;

10. Millard, "Young People and Placemaking."

we need to start drawing on the imaginations and design capacity of children and young adult in the important work of placemaking.[11]

Transforming a Neighborhood Into a Connected Community in Alberta

Alberta, in Canada, is one of the first cities in North America to invite the Abundant Community Initiative to be field-tested as a way to create connected and empowered communities in the city of Alberta. The idea for this form of community empowerment is outlined by John McKnight and Peter Block in their book *The Abundant Community: Awakening the Power of Families and Neighborhoods.*[12]

Howard Lawrence, the coordinator of this Abundant Community Initiative and a former pastor, immediately saw the potential of this approach to connect people in a particular neighborhood in Alberta so that residents can both get to know one another and collaborate in creating a more connected, sustainable, and resilient community. The city of Alberta, which is funding this project, selected the Hamilton Community as a place to begin field-testing this process.

Lawrence started the process by enabling people on individual blocks to get to know each other. The second step was to have the twenty households on a single block identify one another's interests, passions, and gifts. Howard and his team believe that neighbors' interests, activities, skills, experiences, and passions are the glue that can hold neighborhoods together.

Data gathered block by block is being used not only to connect people but also to start fashioning concrete community resources webs—to build stronger mutual-care networks for both good times and challenging times. These could cover everything from community safety to caring for seniors. However, they can also become the basis for forming groups around common interests from gardening to crafting. For example, they can offer mentoring to teenagers in everything from food preservation and environmental stewardship to community arts.[13]

There are a few churches and Christian organizations that have already joined this celebration of creating more sustainable, resilient

11. See www.blockbyblock.org.

12. McKnight and Block, *The Abundant Community*.

13. Lawrence, "Gluing a Place Together, One Neighbor at a Time."

local communities where people create ways to care for one another. For example, Karen Wilk, who has planted a church called Neighborhood Life in Alberta to grow this kind of connectivity, encourages churches everywhere to shift from a "come and see" approach to a "go and be" approach in their neighborhood. On the Missio Alliance blog, she encourages readers to embrace and enter their place, their neighborhoods. One member of Neighborhood Life said, "I am passionate about neighborhood transformation because this is where I live, my friends and family live. It is where my child will grow up . . . it is home."[14]

Connecting to Neighborhoods in the UK
One Square Mile at a Time

The Evangelical Alliance in the UK started the Square Mile Project a few years ago as a way to connect neighbors to one another as well as address some of the needs in their neighborhood. Part of what motivated it was a concern for economic justice—in a number of neighborhoods, people at the margins tend to be victimized because they're unsure how to deal with those who would take advantage of them economically. Essentially, the Evangelical Alliance challenges churches to create innovative ways to empower these neighbors within one square mile of where their church is located. For example, Christ Church in Winchester seeks to help those struggling economically in their community by starting a debt counseling service. In the first year it has grown to five part-time volunteers who enable their neighbors to more effectively manage their financial resources.

Transforming Time into Money to Pay for
Health Care in Goshen

In Goshen, Indiana, a number of Mennonite churches collaborate with the Maple City Health Care Center, which was started by Dr. James Gingerich, to provide health care for low-income workers. In 2009, James and his team were concerned because many families didn't have even $10 to pay when they brought their sick child to see the doctor. So these innovative Christians created something called More Than Money. Essentially, if the unemployed volunteer for organizations like Habitat for Humanity or the Maple City Food Cooperative, they become participants in the More

14. Wilk, "Exiled to Discover God at Work," par. 4.

Than Money time-sharing plan. For every hour they volunteer, they earn $10 toward paying for health care costs—their own or those of their family members.

Transforming a Dirt Road into Property Justice

Let's head back to Pleasant Valley of the South in Haiti two years after my memorable donkey ride. Through a food-for-work program, the valley leaders and our World Concern team collaborated to construct a road connecting this valley community to the outside world. The first thing that the valley leaders did was to invite officials from the Haitian government to come down that road and visit their valley community for the first time. During this visit, the valley leaders explained how three wealthy landowners had, over the last ten years, appropriated property from twenty-two poor farmers in the community. Once the government officials from Port-au-Prince heard their concerns, they immediately began researching their claims. After confirming the farmers' stories, they took immediate action and returned all the property to the farmers.

Justice had finally come down the road! It was no longer a mystery to our World Concern team why this road was so important. In fact, our hosts invited us to a Haitian feast with them to celebrate their huge victory. The large tables in the community plaza were laden with a wonderful spread of roast goat, grio (spicy fried pork), fried plantains, sliced beets, rice and beans, freshly baked bread, and an array of sliced mangos, oranges, and bananas. The feast served as a reminder to us all to take the time to celebrate every step forward as we labor together for the common good.

Transforming Community Resources into
Community Empowerment in Tanzania

Savings cooperatives are starting to grow in countries where many people have no access to banks or credit unions. For example, Sara Mtui in Tanzania has found a new future for herself and her two young daughters through a village savings cooperative. Sara started a tree nursery and a vegetable garden to support her family. She began putting her savings into this cooperative, then realized that her income from selling tree seedlings and vegetables would not be enough to fund her daughter's schooling. She was able to borrow money from her cooperative to train as a tailor and buy a sewing machine. Sara's two daughters are now in school because her training enabled her to increase her family's income. Plant With Purpose is enabling small communities in a number of different countries to empower people through these local savings cooperative to become more self-reliant.[15]

Dreaming and Scheming

Time to get out those iPads and notebooks again and explore how you can do some dreaming and scheming with a few friends in your neighborhood or church.

- Who are the social innovators already at work in your neighborhood or region? Are any of these ventures that you or your congregation might join?

- What are some new opportunities for empowerment in your community that you and your friends have identified? What are your ideas for creating new forms of community empowerment, and who are the people or organizations that you or your congregation might partner with?

- Who are those who are advocating for economic, racial, and environmental justice where you live, and how might you join them?

CONVERSATION 2—CELEBRATING THE PAST, THE PURPOSE, AND THE STARTING PLACE

Community Empowerment Recalling the Past

Let me offer a brief history of a convergence of some of the streams that have led to the emergence of the community-empowerment movement. As I mentioned earlier, governments and NGOs launched a range of ventures that tended to be top-down in poorer communities beginning as early as the 1950s. Yet the current community-empowerment movement also has roots in the environmental movement.

---

15. See the website of Plant With Purpose: www.plantwithpurpose.org.

One of the earliest expressions of creating more participatory local communities is the Transition Town movement. It was started in 2005 in the UK by Rob Hopkins, an instructor in permaculture farming. Ordinary people have become a part of this movement not only in Britain but in more than one thousand communities in forty different countries. Transition Town proponents have discovered that they can empower their own local communities in places from Brisbane, Australia, to Palo Alto, California. These communities have created ways to increase the local food supply, enabled community members to buy solar panels wholesale, and even created alternative local currencies.[16]

Creating a stronger local economy is also a major theme for many in this new localist movement. In 2003, two businesswomen started a new organization called the Business Alliance for Local Living Economies (BALLE). BALLE is "building local economies by connecting leaders, spreading solutions and attracting investments toward local economies."[17] Studies show that in places where people support locally owned businesses, they are also more involved in community life and in caring for their communities.

In certain respects, what we are experiencing is the re-emergence of older forms of local community empowerment. First Nations peoples had strong mutually supportive communities before the Europeans arrived. Those first European settlers who came to North America would not have survived without developing their own mutual-care networks. Intergenerational families and collaborative rural and small-town communities where neighbors cared for one another were the norm for most of North America, even through the end of World War II.

Today we are witnessing a movement back toward the creation of forms of community collaboration and of more sustainable local communities. Some are awakening to the high costs and financial pressures of autonomous, suburban-living models. One of the surprising developments since the recession of 2009 is the growing demand for intergenerational housing for middle-class families. I encourage Christian colleges to shift from building ever more expensive luxury dorms to building cohousing communities with a mix of some retired residents, faculty, and students discovering the advantages of intergenerational living, from preparing food and gardening together to sharing their faith, dreams,

16. Comstock, "The 'Transition Town' Movement's Initial Genius."

17. See www.bealocalist.org.

and stories. This will enable all participants to become leaders in creating more community-based and less individualistic ways of living for the tougher times that are likely to await us in the 2020s.

In Silverdale, Washington, twenty-five households live in the Meadow Wood Cohousing Community, an intergenerational community comprised of largely Christian residents.[18] Their homes have no backyards. They garden together in a common garden, often cook together, and celebrate life together as well as with each other's relatives and friends. They share meals, pray, divvy up chores, and entertain in their common building several times a week. This intergenerational community is much better prepared to be mutually supportive during economic downturns or natural disasters than those that have adopted more autonomous lifestyles. Because of this strong community of mutual support, they are also likely to have much greater reserves to care for their neighbors in times of crisis.

In 2004, a large number of young people hungry for more authentic expressions of Christian community, including Shane Claiborne and Jonathan Wilson Hargrove, gathered in Raleigh, Durham, to give birth to the New Monasticism movement. Among those present were a number of academics as well some of us who were involved in the first Christian community movement in the early eighties. The New Monasticism movement has grown to have a global reach for those interested in a life devoted to contemplation, activism, and community.

> In the *New Monasticism as Fresh Expression of Church*, published in the UK, I asked, "What impact could these new expressions of embodied community have not only on those who share, life, faith and mission together but on the wider Church and even wider society? I have always believed that when we work together God can do more through our mustard seeds than we dare imagine. Living in the shadow of the empire we all have the opportunity to join this new wave, to design a spectrum of new communities that offer more than a simpler version of the Western dream with church on Sunday. We have the opportunity to imagine a spectrum of new communities where, as followers of Jesus, we can create new ways to be a difference and make a difference—ways that more authentically reflect something of God's loving purposes . . . in these turbulent times."[19]

18. See www.mwcondo.com and www.cohousing.org.

19. Sine, "Creating Communities of Celebration," 78.

Since we are racing into a new urban future where most of us will live in cities, designers are creating new urban environments all over the planet for life in the 2020s and 2030s. Many are designing more sustainable, mixed-used communities that are walkable and bike-friendly, with a strong sense of place, open spaces, and opportunities for urban farming, all of which encourages community collaboration. These urban centers also place a high value on energy creation and sustainability, from creative waste recycling to the repurposing of discarded possessions.

The Christian Community Development Association, founded by John Perkins, hosts the leading conference on urban empowerment in the US every year. Today, Noel Castellanos is the creative CEO who brings together an impressive array of urban innovators. For example, this year in Memphis they are beginning with a session on social entrepreneurship for the city.[20]

Andy Crouch, an editor at *Christianity Today*, points out that cities are increasingly the destinations of choice for the new millennial generation. He reminds us of our responsibility to be something of God's shalom in our cities. In 2011, he announced the commitment of *Christianity Today* to creating a multiyear project to report on how individuals, churches, and para-church organizations are joining with others in creating flourishing urban communities.[21] This venture is funded by the Murdock Charitable Trust and the Templeton Foundation. You can read their reports of urban innovation at This is Our City.[22]

The new sharing economy, which seems to have been started largely by innovators from the millennial generation, also plays a key role in both creating and sustaining more participatory communities. As political influence shifts back to cities, a decentralization of power tends to occur in many areas. Local citizens are beginning to secure greater influence in shaping their own lives and communities. For instance, some municipalities in California are actually inviting input from citizens on how a portion of county funds can be invested to make their local communities stronger.

Economic cooperatives are one of the oldest examples in this stream; they have been around for almost two hundred years.[23] Even though

20. See www.ccda.org.

21. Crouch, "A New Kind of Urban Ministry."

22. A good place to begin is Beaty, "The Top 10 *This Is Our City* Stories: Editors Choice."

23. Restakis, *Humanizing the Economy*.

many people are not aware of this form of community empowerment, it is among the most rapidly growing sectors within this stream of the changemaking celebration. I'm certain that one of the reasons cooperatives are growing so rapidly is that they give communities much more control over their lives, their economies, and their future. Worldwide, nearly one billion people are involved in cooperatives. In the United States, more than 130 million people belong to cooperatives or credit unions.[24]

Undoubtedly, the most recent addition to the community empowerment stream is the new Makers Movement that we mentioned earlier. Essentially, we are witnessing the re-emergence in our communities of an artisans movement. This is becoming an important income source for many local economies. The newly recovered cultural appreciation for handcrafted products has also resulted in more than $1 billion of handmade goods in the US being sold through Etsy, an online marketplace that connects craftspeople with individual buyers.[25]

Community Empowerment—Rediscovering Both the Commons and the Common Good

Jim Wallis invites us to rediscover the importance of our faith communities working for the common good. He writes, "Our life together can be better. Ours is a shallow and selfish age, and we are in need of conversion—from looking out just for ourselves to also looking out for one another. It's time to hear and heed a call to a different way of life, to reclaim a very old idea called the common good."[26]

Part of what makes this a selfish age is our buying into a narrative in which some corporate leaders in the global economy are committed to policies that privatize economic gain but socialize costs. In other words, our current economic model favors short-term economic growth, particularly for the wealthy and huge corporations, and leaves it to the rest of us (and our children and grandchildren) to pick up the tab—the costs of air and water pollution, depleted groundwater, acidic oceans, decreased biodiversity, and economic turmoil.

24. Kelly, "The Economy under New Ownership."
25. Stoll, "Too Much Stuff in Your Life?," par. 3.
26. Wallis, *(Un)Common Good*, 3.

The biblical narrative in Isaiah 58 makes clear that our healing and well-being are always linked to the healing and well-being of our neighbors. Scripture repeatedly reminds us that we must care for others, especially the vulnerable, as well as for ourselves; if we choose instead to pursue our own economic self-interest, it will not "raise all boats" but rather enrich a few elites, often at the expense of the many. This directly contradicts the biblical call to live justly.

In the important book *Our Common Wealth: The Hidden Economy That Makes Everything Else Work*, Jonathan Rowe urges us to recover a sense of the common good by recognizing that the commons, the shared resources of this good creation, belong to all humankind. Therefore he recommends, "Put commoners in charge of the air, let us charge polluters for using it, and we'll see a lot less pollution than we do now."[27] Today's commons are remarkably different from those of the Middle Ages, which consisted mainly of shared meadows. "Self-organized commons are undergoing a renaissance as one of the most robust alternatives to contemporary capitalism. They include such diverse endeavors as seed-sharing cooperatives in India, community gardening in major cities, open source software programming, D.I.Y. hackerspaces, FabLabs, scientific disciplines that publish their research in open-access journals, and local food initiatives such as community supported agriculture, Slow Food, and permaculture."[28]

As we work for the common good of our neighborhoods, it is essential that our overarching purpose be to work collaboratively and responsibly to steward the commons we share both with each other and with future generations. Recognizing that not everyone we work with in our communities is a person of faith, one key starting point is to find a sense of common purpose in order to create more sustainable and just local communities. I'm confident that if we listen with a sense of care and openness, we will find that common purpose and join with others in local community empowerment.

In their book *The Abundant Community*, John McKnight and Peter Block repeatedly remind readers that the individualistic way of life, which has become so highly valued in many Western cultures, is not the good life, nor is it sustainable in what are likely to be stormy times ahead. McKnight and Block remind us that together with our neighbors

27. Rowe, *Our Common Wealth*, 7.

28. Bollier, "Fab Labs, Time Banks and Other Hidden Treasures," 61.

we can discover a more satisfying way of life, which is always found in the abundance of our communities and neighborhoods. "A neighborhood can raise a child, provide security, sustain our health, secure our income, and care for our vulnerable people," they write. "Each of these is within the power of our community."[29] If we can begin to shift our focus from individualistic and often somewhat isolated lives, we can rediscover the enormous value of community as well as the great creative potential it holds for a better future with our neighbors.

I realize that this could be a tough one for some pastors and church leaders. Often, they have had very little experience planning with those in our neighborhoods, since many of us in the church are used to doing the planning without collaborating with others in our communities. If this is going to be a neighborhood venture, however, it is essential that we learn the art of creative collaboration so that our projects have strong neighborhood ownership.

Community Empowerment—Rediscovering the Importance of Listening

Listening to Place

We need to begin by learning to listen to the place where we live. Then, we need to listen to the stories that shaped that place and the ways in which God has been involved in those stories. In the process, we also need to learn to listen to one another much more attentively than we have ever done before.

The very first place to listen is where we are rooted. Wendell Berry urges us to find our "placedness," that spot in God's good creation that we call home. God's good creation does not exist simply as a utilitarian resource to be manipulated, fashioned into consumer products, and used to grow our economy. It is sacred—because God created it, Christ became a part of it, and the Creator God intends to redeem it. We need to join our First Nations sisters and brothers in rediscovering the stunning beauty of the place where we live.

An important way to "listen" to our "placedness" is to recognize that wherever our place may be—whether in a city, a suburb, or a rural area—we and our neighbors are sustained by a watershed, a water source

29. McKnight and Block, *Abundant Community*, xiii.

that makes our life possible.[30] Ched Myers, a Christian activist, reminds us that "our place is deeply intertwined within a larger system called a watershed, drained by a watercourse and its tributaries into a particular body of water such as a pond, a lake an ocean."[31]

Listening to Others

Ruth Padilla DeBorst, a theologian and author who grew up in Latin America, has observed that we Western Christians tend to be very individualistic. As a consequence, we don't always take as much time to be present to our neighbors as Christians from other parts of the world do.[32] Listening for all of us must start with taking time not only to listen but also to solicit our neighbors' stories.

I appreciate Paul Sparks, Tim Soerens, and Dwight Friesen, authors of *The New Parish*, for urging readers everywhere to rediscover our neighbors and our neighborhoods. I am so grateful for the way in which these authors teach us to listen, not only to the neighbors we are working with but also to the narrative of the neighborhood and the stories—past and present—that are shaping it.[33] They also encourage us to listen with care to what God is stirring up through scripture and prayer. Similarly, David Leong, in his book *Street Signs*, describes a neighborhood as being like a living text. He suggests that we need to learn how to read the signs, symbols, and codes where we live.[34] These could include everything from public art and graffiti to the ways in which our communities celebrate.

Christopher Smith and John Pattison also remind us to slow down a bit and be more present to our neighbors and our neighborhoods—and even to open our lives, homes, and churches to offer our neighbors hospitality. They write, "One of the most transformative, and intimate, forms of generosity is hospitality: sharing our homes, our tables and ourselves with others, particularly strangers."[35] One of the important benefits is the creation of trust between people who are going to work together in common cause.

30. McAnnally-Linz, "A Watershed Moment."

31. "What Is a Watershed?," par. 2.

32. Tomlinson, "An Interview with Ruth Padilla DeBorst."

33. Sparks et al., *New Parish*, 125.

34. Leong, *Street Signs*, 131.

35. Smith and Pattison, *Slow Church*, 194.

Christians Learning to Listen in Other People's Communities

One example of learning to listen began with a team of upper-middle-class volunteers from University Presbyterian Church in Seattle. They had made it their objective to be of some help to a poorer community called White Center. Mike McCormick, the urban minister there, developed a brilliant (if unusual) process to enable UPC volunteers to learn to listen first. Before they started trying to be of some help in the poorer community, McCormick had these volunteers become students of those with whom they would be working. He asked them to spend eight weeks learning about the community from the people who lived there—including those for whom life was a constant struggle. As you can imagine, when they finally did go to work with the people who had been teaching them, the dynamics of their work together changed.

World Concern Learning to Listen in Haiti

Let me share what we learned about the importance of listening in the project I coordinated in Haiti. Chavannes Jeunes, the co-director of the World Concern community empowerment project in Haiti, created a unique listening process to start this project back in 1977. He invited 120 leaders from different parts of the Pleasant Valley of the South for that first planning session to seek their input on what they wanted to see happen in their community. Many of them had not received even a third-grade education. However, over two days Chavannes did a brilliant job of using Haitian stories and parables to help them understand how to plan.

The valley leaders did a remarkable job of collaborating with the team to set goals for community empowerment. These goals included 1) constructing a road out of their landlocked valley; 2) increasing coffee production and creating an irrigation system that would provide water for their coffee crops and vegetable gardens; 3) planting trees for their children's future; 4) creating a basic health care capability; 5) finding resources for more children to go to school; and 6) working with church leaders to help restore broken relationships in the community.

When our team of three Americans came back home in 1984, the village leaders were able to take over leadership of each phase of the project, since Chavannes had made sure they were involved from the beginning. In fact, one of the first things they did was to start an economic cooperative; they pooled their money together to buy a truck to take their own coffee beans to market. By this innovative action they increased their profits 200 percent that first year. That increased the quality of life for many families and also made it possible to send more of their children to school.

As I mentioned in chapter 3, it's essential that we also listen and pay attention to how the global and national context is likely to change in the coming decade. It's especially important that we learn to listen to our own local context so that we are aware of how it is likely to change in the next five to ten years. This enables us to identify new opportunities and challenges before they have fully arrived. If we can identify even a few new challenges or opportunities in the future—from declining housing prices to the launching of new urban farming projects—then we have lead time to create innovative responses.

Learning to Listen in Communities that Create Character

In *The Vanishing Neighbor*,[36] Marc Dunkelman observes that people today have a close circle of family and immediate friends and an outer circle of online contacts but are much less involved in a middle circle of neighborhood and community organizations.[37] I suspect this condition is as true in most of our middle-class white churches as it is in the larger society. I would urge Christian leaders to introduce those in their churches to another way of being. Invite members to bring scripture to bear on transforming our cultural values to encourage aspirations to the values of compassion, empathy, and neighborly care over the values of individualistic achievement and acquisition.

David Brooks of the *New York Times* has stated that a growing number of secular schools are actually preparing their students to become stronger participants in creating more cooperative local communities. The students are given tremendous responsibility and placed in challenging social situations to draw forth their ability to work together in community for the common good.[38]

I am certain there are Christian schools that are also nurturing in their students the values of compassion, collaboration, and working for the common good. However, wouldn't it be encouraging if our local

36. Dunkelman, *The Vanaishing Neighbor*.
37. Brooks, "Communities of Character."
38. Ibid.

churches also nurtured parents and their youth in these values? Then we would all be more authentic witnesses to the way of Jesus instead of the driven individualism of the global mall, and also better prepared to be more a part of the kind of the collaborative, caring communities that we will need to create to weather tomorrow's turbulent times.

Steps to Creating New Forms of Community Empowerment

I believe one of the other big challenges facing us and our churches is to learn to choose to move from a dependency model of assistance to creating new models of mutual care and local empowerment, drawing on the creative input of all our neighbors—particularly the young. I suggest that our first step involve learning more about what motivates those in our communities to invest their lives in creating networks of mutual care and stronger local capacity, resilience, and celebration. Our second step will entail learning from both business and social entrepreneurs to research the best practices of those who have successfully launched new ventures with their neighbors. Then it is time to embark on a creativity process that invites community members to collaborate in creating innovative responses:

- Seeking to engage some of these new opportunities in your community, today and tomorrow;
- Researching best practices in other communities;
- Defining your common sense of purpose and your goals;
- Identifying some of the resources available in your community;
- Creating innovative strategies that use local resources to achieve your intended goals;
- Evaluating each step of the process and reinventing your process as you go;
- Celebrating both every advance and every setback.

Find a group of people who are willing to explore collaborating with each other and sharing their lives and gifts in common cause. In most neighborhoods such groups will be comprised of people who are not faith-based. Therefore, those of us who are Christian need to collaborate as learners and listeners, seeking to identify purposes we can pursue together that clearly work for the common good. These might include creating innovative programs in educational empowerment for struggling students, creating jobs, establishing community gardens, and even planning celebrations to bring your neighborhood together.

What is essential is that we start by getting to know our neighbors and discovering what God is already stirring up in our neighborhoods—so we can join in. It might begin with painting a crosswalk, or enabling immigrants to start a small business, or joining others in your neighborhood to implement more sustainable environmental practices. In the next chapter I will invite you to consider doing some dreaming and scheming with those in the social entrepreneurship stream.

Dreaming and Scheming

It's time to get out your iPads or notebooks, join your friends and perhaps a neighbor or two, and take several important steps toward becoming a part of the community empowerment celebration:

- Talk to people in your community and try to identify one to three new challenges or opportunities that could be facing you and your neighbors in the next five years.

- Select the easiest opportunity to engage from your list. Seek to define with your neighbors a sense of common purpose in engaging that opportunity.

- Put on your design thinking cap and create some innovative ways to implement your purpose that engages your new opportunity (be sure to draw on best practices).

- Identify people and resources within your community that you might draw on to make a beginning in community empowerment.

6

Imagine New Social Enterprises Today to Create Our Best Tomorrows

Welcome to the Social Entrepreneurship Changemaking Celebration!

Soaring up! Quietly we rose fifty . . . one hundred . . . two hundred feet above Queen Anne High School on a very clear blue-sky afternoon in Seattle on Friday, November 16, 1972. We could see the Cascade Mountains to our east, the Olympic Mountains to our west, and Seattle spread out below us.

The only thing the pilot, Tony Rossi, and I could hear was the rhythmic swooshing sound as helium filled the gigantic balloon above our heads. Tony was kind enough to contribute both his time and his balloon to make this day possible. This was my first ride in a tethered balloon and it was absolutely breathtaking. Tony's balloon had been up five times that day; this was the sixth and last ascent. As I looked across the playing field to the three-story classroom building, I saw hundreds of high-school kids—they were hanging out of every window. I learned later from my son Wes, who was a freshman there, that the students loved the disruption and the teachers were having a hard time regaining control. A small team of a dozen collaborators and I had gotten permission from the principal to use the field for this hot-air balloon launch, but none of us had anticipated how distracting it might be.

"Watch *The Class of 84 Has Their Dreams* Saturday King 5 at 4!" was emblazoned on huge signs on both sides of the balloon. This eccentric promotional stunt proved to be more successful than we had hoped. People could see the signs not only from central Seattle but also from the I-5 highway as they were coming home from work. We even had a couple other TV stations film our stunt—which was welcome publicity. Our small team celebrated this successful launch with a pizza party right there on the field.

Remember that first Earth Day in Hawaii that turned my life upside down? Soon after, I moved to Seattle to start a doctoral program at the University of Washington to learn more about how people could create new ways to live and to respond to changing times. The first class I took, in 1971, was "Utopias and Dystopias," which was taught by science-fiction writer Frank Herbert, author of *Dune* and numerous other books. He was a brilliant teacher and became both a mentor and a good friend.

In 1972, I asked Frank to lunch to solicit his fertile ideas on how to offer people in Seattle an opportunity to explore new ways to live and raise the young in changing times. This conversation led to recruiting two students from Seattle Pacific University, as well as Robert Rushmer and Murray Meld, professors from the University of Washington, to join us in creating the Evergreen Chapter of the World Future Society (WFS). WFS publishes a monthly magazine called *The Futurist*.[1] We were also fortunate to secure the participation of Ed Lindaman, who in 1970 had arrived to be the new president of Whitworth College. Not surprisingly, he was a frequent lecturer on the future, since in his former position he had overseen the Apollo spacecraft project for North American Rockwell.

Our small group was intrigued that a handful of states had created innovative statewide futures processes, including *A Maine Manifest*, California Tomorrow, and Hawaii 2000. As we studied these documents, Frank called our attention to the fact that all of these groups seemed to be headed by elite citizens who didn't invite the voices of ordinary citizens. We wanted to create a civil-society experiment that invited citizen input on public issues. So we decided to create a small demonstration project on the future of education where we invited broad citizen input in Seattle. We were fortunate to secure six months of funding from the Washington State Commission for the Humanities and the participation of King 5 television to produce our experimental broadcast, *The Class of 84 Has Their Dreams*.

---

1. See the website of the World Future Society: www.wfs.org.

We wrote a script where a mom and dad and their seven-year-old son visit four schools with four different approaches to preparing students to live in a changing world as they headed toward a new millennium. We recruited actors from the local repertory theater group and created a television presentation about a fictional family. One private-school model focused on preparing the young through an emphasis on a highly disciplined traditional model of education. A second offered a behavioral approach that focused on reinforcing desired behavioral change. The third model focused on enabling students not only to learn their subject matter but also to become creative problem-solvers in both their studies and their own lives. The final group was an open-classroom learning model in which students were given the freedom to learn at their own pace. After the TV dramatization of *The Class of 84 Has Their Dreams*, we invited viewers to respond by using newspaper response ballots. We also hosted community discussion groups with citizens in one neighborhood, which convened immediately following the viewing of *The Class of '84 Has Their Dreams*.

Our team was gratified by the widespread community response. However, we were even more gratified by the apparent success of this innovative venture to secure informed citizen discussion and input. Citizen response favored the option of placing more emphasis on enabling students to develop their problem-solving skills in order to be able to live more creatively in changing times. My son Wes reported that the high school teachers at Queen Anne also gave us two thumbs up for the broadcast (and forgave us for our hot-air balloon disruption the week before). Our first venture turned out better than I had hoped. It reminded us of that great ascending feeling in the hot-air balloon.

CONVERSATION 1—DISCOVERING THE POTENTIAL OF SOCIAL ENTERPRISE PROBLEM-SOLVING

In this chapter I want to give you a fuller sense of the potential of launching entrepreneurial ventures whose mission is to significantly increase our capacity to solve large problems and to work for the common good, in our own countries and all over the world.

While most of you can imagine becoming more involved in the community empowerment stream we just explored, I suspect that few of you can imagine starting a new business with a social or environmental mission. Of course, most of us do not have a business background or entrepreneurial gifts. It is important to realize, however, that all of us can be on support teams that assist those who do have these gifts, helping them as they prepare to launch their ventures.

Remember Katie Metzger, a member of our MSA team who collaborated with two of her friends to launch Same Thread?[2] They sell garments made in northern Thailand from natural fabrics and dyes, and provide a living wage to vulnerable women. Christine and I have neither the education nor the experience to become social entrepreneurs. We are delighted to be a real part of Katie's team, however, providing encouragement, counsel, prayers, and financial support that helped make Same Thread's liftoff possible. So I am encouraging every reader, as you read this chapter, to view yourself as a possible participant in social entrepreneurship so that you don't miss the opportunity to be a part of this stream of the changemaking celebration.

Are We Settling for Less and Missing the Best?

Is it possible that many of us in the church have settled for giving a little token charity and seldom ask the question that many entrepreneurs do: how can we create processes to solve some of the most daunting challenges facing our most vulnerable neighbors? With the likely reduction of both government assistance and Christian philanthropy in the next ten years, wouldn't it make sense to use the power of free enterprise, the Internet, and social media to empower our most vulnerable neighbors to solve some of the challenges that families and communities face all over the world?

As I read her book *From the Other Side of the World: Extraordinary Entrepreneurs, Unlikely Places*, Elmira Bayrasli convinced me that "the new millennium entrepreneurship" has the potential not only to produce new products and increase prosperity but also to enable our neighbors to overcome these challenges and create a whole new future of opportunity for their children and grandchildren. She persuasively argues that a new generation of innovators will use both entrepreneurship and social entrepreneurship to overcome obstacles that have kept people locked in poverty for generations. Why do we who are followers of Jesus seem to invest so little of our time and money in collaborating with others to

2. See www.samethread.com.

create innovative ways to have a social or environmental impact in times like these? Why don't we live like we give a damn?

I sincerely believe, as I said before, that God is trying to use social entrepreneurs, who are largely outside the tent, to show those of us who profess to be followers of Jesus how to live with more compassion and with a greater investment in creative new forms of changemaking. I believe God is showing us innovative ways we can join others in moving from simply sustaining people in their dependency to using the power of social enterprise to enable them and their communities to achieve a greater measure of self-reliance.

Most importantly, I also urge you to pay attention to the possibility that you could be missing out on the good life of God. You could miss out on discovering how God might use your mustard seeds to make a lasting difference in the lives of others. Again, I invite you to consider joining those who are creating their best neighborhoods, their best world, and their best lives—and so discover how you too can create your best life as a follower of Jesus.

My Brief Excursion into the World of Business Innovation

Two months after our TV broadcast in 1972 inviting viewers to explore new alternatives for the future of education in Seattle, I received an unexpected call from the Weyerhauser Corporation. Ed Soule, the director of the New Business Division for Weyerhaeuser, asked me to meet with him. Three days later I met Ed in his office. He wanted to learn more about my interest in strategic forecasting. After a forty-five minute interview, he invited me to work as a part-time consultant with him and his team of six business entrepreneurs. I was surprised by his invitation, since I had no experience in business, although I had taken courses in strategic planning and in forecasting at the University of Washington.

I immediately called Frank Herbert and told him my good news. "Frank, Weyerhaeuser has started a New Business Division to give birth to new startups. They intend to create new businesses that draw on their corporate strengths—abundant land and water, experience in growing things and a strong cash flow." I added, "I could really use your help with both forecasting and the creativity aspects of what I have been asked to do." Frank replied, "Sure, I'm between projects right now and I would be glad to help. Let's get together at the Faculty Club at the UW and you can tell me more about it."

As I consulted with Ed, he encouraged me to lead his new business startup team in a little scenario forecasting regarding how the demographic and economic environments were likely to change in the next five years. I went to work on my research. I gave Frank my data on demographic and economic trends, from which he drafted three different scenarios to share with the new business startup team.

Three weeks later, Frank Herbert and I did our first presentation. To be honest, I was more than a little apprehensive. As soon as Frank began sharing about innovations in his science fiction novels that the US government had already developed, I could see he had everyone's attention. Then he shared a bit about his personal innovations: "My wife Beverly and I recently purchased a lovely home on five acres about four miles outside of Port Townsend. My goal in the next three years is to be innovative and totally redesign my property to achieve a high level of 'techno-peasantry.'" He added, "I have already planted a large vegetable garden as a step toward becoming highly self-reliant. I have also constructed a duck pond and populated it to provide a little protein." Then, as a big smile spread across his full-bearded face, he said, "My next project is to build a windmill to catch the strong trade winds at my site. Then I plan to purchase a small electric car and plug it into my windmill for my four-mile drive into Port Townsend. I will never go back to Exxon again!" (Believe it or not, back in the seventies an electric car would have worked for that task.) After that we shared our scenarios and discussed the implications for different forms of new business startups. This first session couldn't have gone better.

I am not sure I made much of a contribution to this team of business entrepreneurs, but I certainly learned a great deal by watching the remarkable way Ed assisted each person on his team to find creative solutions every time their new ventures began to come apart. He always enabled members of the team to get their projects back on the launch pad. Just before I left, I witnessed two entrepreneurial ventures soar from the launch pads, including one of the earliest salmon-farming ventures and a startup that would grow nursery stock for the retail market.

Back in the seventies, social entrepreneurship really was not yet a visible form of changemaking. As I mentioned in the introduction, however, in the last ten years it has become widely visible all over our planet.

Even more importantly, social enterprise offers an array of innovative ways to address some of the most daunting challenges of the 2020s.

Why Is Social Entrepreneurship Important in Times Like These?

Judith Rodin, who heads the Rockefeller Foundation, has observed that the "blending of business ideas with theories of social change [has] opened the doors to the possibility of accelerating human development and more effectively conserving natural resources, all at a greater scale than government or philanthropy alone could provide."[3] While those in the community-empowerment stream rely primarily on the resources of their regions and their own lives to create sustainable and resilient local communities, those in the social-entrepreneurship stream can utilize the power of economic enterprise to solve large societal problems and create a future with a broader range of new possibilities.

The Bill and Melinda Gates Foundation, the Rockefeller Foundation, and a number of other philanthropic organizations are increasingly investing in social entrepreneurship because of its remarkable potential to achieve major social and environmental change. We have also seen the surprising growth of crowdfunding and Kickstarter campaigns that have helped launch a number of new ventures. Likewise, in the past ten years, "impact investing" has developed rapidly. Growing numbers of individuals, pension funds, and credit unions are choosing to invest in forms of social enterprise that reflect their values.

Judith Rodin explains that "the rise of impact investing comes at a critical moment. Catastrophic environmental trends have created an imperative to mitigate the effects of climate change. Alarming levels of global youth unemployment—with young people three times more likely to be jobless than older people—demand heavy investment to help vulnerable individuals launch careers or become entrepreneurs. Seismic shifts in the global economy have left insufficient public funding to tackle the world's social and environmental challenges."[4]

One of the surprising side effects of the dramatic growth in social entrepreneurship and impact investing has been the growing number of corporations that have likewise been influenced to embrace a sense of

3. Rodin and Brandenburg, *Power of Impact Investing*, 4.
4. Ibid., vi.

mission broader than simply returning dividends to their stockholders. The *Harvard Business Review* reports that a growing number of corporations are placing a greater emphasis on contributing to the well-being of communities and the environment as well as shareholders. IKEA, for example, has developed a People & Planet initiative; its goal is for its entire supply chain to be 100 percent sustainable by 2020.[5]

Another factor in the United States that makes the social entrepreneurship stream distinctive is the growing number of states that are creating an alternative way to both start and register "benefit corporations," or B Corps. The specific intent of B Corps is to change their registration to place the interests of the community, environment, employees, and consumers ahead of profits. This is accelerating the growth of social enterprise in the US.

T. J. Cook, the CEO of CauseLabs, writes that four of his "B Corp friends" learned that the "unexpected benefits" of B corporations "go beyond the obvious ones listed on the B Corp site. They ranged from leveraging B Corp certification to spark change in suppliers, to fellow B Corp leaders giving time freely to plot one company's next venture, to job applicants willing to pass on bigger offers to work for an entrepreneur out of her kitchen."[6]

Let me introduce you to a few more of these innovative changemakers who are, in a range of ways, improving the well-being of people and the natural world that sustains us all.

Touring the Social Entrepreneurship Changemaking Celebration

Creating Change in the Lives of People in Emerging Economies

"The clock is ticking" was, as you may remember, the opening line of the book. The clock is ticking not only for the tomato but for all garden produce in markets all over Nigeria. The entrepreneurial innovation of using solar panels on cargo containers to provide inexpensive refrigeration for produce has the potential to have an enormous impact in those places in Nigeria where people have no access to electricity. And it could

---

5. Rangan et al., "The Truth about CSR," par. 11.

6. Cook, "4 Benefits That 4 B Corps Didn't See Coming," par. 4.

have a similarly dramatic impact on communities without electricity in Asia and the Middle East.

Let's head from Nigeria to Benin, Africa, and look at a social entrepreneurial business that has already been scaled up to improve the lives of millions of people in these kinds of regions who are without electricity. I'd like you to meet another young innovator named Sam Goldman. When he was a Peace Corps volunteer in Benin, a neighbor's son was badly burned by a kerosene lamp that tipped over in their home. Sam learned of the accident and helped care for the boy. This experience motivated Sam to do some research and also unleash his creativity. He discovered that over 2.3 billion people in the developing world do not have access to reliable electricity. When Sam returned to the States, he attended classes at Stanford University on innovative design. There he and a colleague, Ned Tozon, designed a new product, called d.light, to address this major challenge.[7] This product collects solar energy in the daytime and provides families with light in the evenings. Not only is d.light less expensive than kerosene lamps, but there is no fire risk and it doesn't add carbon to the atmosphere.

And it is not only families and school kids who value having safe, reliable light in the evenings. An older woman we will call Premila is a street vendor. For the first time, she says, she is able to stay open in the evenings. In fact, business is so good that she has added a sweets table. I can imagine sampling my favorite, payasam—a creamy rice-and-milk South-Indian pudding with raisins, cardamom and cashews. D.light currently serves more than seventeen million people. Their goal is to scale the business up to serve fifty million people all over the planet by 2015 and one hundred million by 2020.

Elmira Bayrasli introduces us to another young Nigerian entrepreneur named Tayo Oviosu, who has used his creativity to overcome another major obstacle to progress in many emerging economies—no access to banks or financial services. Nigeria is the largest economy in Africa, but of the 182 million people living there, 136 million have no access to banking. To address this unmet need, in 2009, Tayo launched Paga Tech.[8] Paga uses the Internet to offer the closest thing to one-stop shopping for financial services in Nigeria. It now provides an invaluable

---

7. See www.dlight.com.
8. See www.mypaga.com.

service for people all over the country, enabling them to pay bills and save money electronically.[9]

Now let's travel from emerging economies to established economies to see the potential of social entrepreneurship to bring important change. Our first stop: Britain.

Creating Change in the Lives of People in Established Economies

Transforming Vacant Lots into Sustainable Produce and Jobs in London

"It has taken over my life and I love it!" declares Sean. For six months he has been working as an apprentice gardener with an innovative urban garden project. The formerly unemployed nineteen-year-old beams with delight and says, "I used to just stay at home watching TV and playing Xbox. Now I am not only gardening every day, but I have started an herb garden at home and my blood sugar has dropped 20 percent since I joined Cultivate London."

Cultivate London is a social enterprise launched in 2011 with the mission of growing local organic vegetables on vacant urban land. This not only enables the provision of local produce in London, but it also reduces the greenhouse gas emissions that would be a byproduct of transporting vegetables from rural Britain and from other countries. The second aspect of Cultivate London's mission is to offer a six-month apprenticeship training program in horticulture for sixteen- to twenty-five-year-olds who, like Sean, are in critical need of job training and employment. This creative social innovation is now providing jobs for young people and supplying quality organic herbs and vegetables to London's top restaurants, to Whole Foods stores, and to local vendors throughout the city. You can be sure that Londoners are enjoying the rich feast that Cultivate London is contributing to in their homes and restaurants as they savor a bit of the changemaking celebration.

General manager Adrienne Attrop, head grower Ben Simpkins, and their team of gardeners created Cultivate London in direct response to two new opportunities they identified in their context: first, the growing preference of London residents for locally produced food, and second,

---

9. Bayrasli, *From The Other Side of The World*, 47–51.

the concerning rise of unemployment among UK young adults (over 20 percent!).

Recently, Prime Minister David Cameron and celebrity chef Jamie Oliver spoke at an event held in London called "Social Saturday" to recognize a handful of social enterprises, including Cultivate London. "This is the day to celebrate and buy from social enterprises—businesses that put people and planet first," David Cameron told *The Telegraph*. "In villages, towns and cities up and down the country there are increasing number of shops, cafes, cinemas and nurseries that are run for the benefit of local communities. Every purchase we make has an impact on the world we live in."[10]

Now I'd like you to meet a creative social and business entrepreneur in the US who is using all he does to advance the cause of global political, racial, and religious reconciliation.

Transforming Spreads and Snacks into Reconciliation and Acts of Kindness

Daniel Lubetzky grew up as the son of a Holocaust survivor in a Jewish family in Mexico. His family later moved to the US, where he became an attorney with a passion for building bridges bringing between people. He is both a social and business entrepreneur. His first social enterprise began in the Middle East, where Daniel became convinced that one of the best ways to bring together people who have been divided politically was to help them start a joint economic venture. So in 1994 Daniel began an initiative to bring Palestinians and Israelis together through a political advocacy group called PeaceWorks.[11] Daniel's dad, after surviving a Nazi concentration camp as a child, was not embittered by his experiences. Instead, he demonstrated kindness to everyone he encounterered. Daniel credits his father's kindness with shaping the passion and purpose that motivates him.

Through PeaceWorks, Daniel actually tested his idea of bringing neighbors in conflict regions together in a common economic venture. Their first product: a delicious sun-dried tomato spread. Daniel decided to have a little fun creating a brand for this line of speciality sauces and spreads, which became very popular in Middle Eastern markets. He

10. Burn-Callander, "Jamie Oliver and David Cameron Join Forces," par. 3.

11. See www.peaceworks.com.

invented a fictional Jewish chef named Moshe and an Arab magician named Ali. The story was that Moshe and Ali had concocted a Mediterranean spread that was so delicious that it hypnotized rival armies and put them in a friendly trance instead of fighting. On each jar the slogan read, "Moshe and Ali's Spreads: Cooperation never tasted so good!" His product line of spreads grew to include basil pesto, green olive tapenade, roasted eggplant tapenade, and a roasted red pepper tapenade.

Then, in 1996, Daniel decided to do a launch event for his spreads in New York. Even though he himself lived in New York, he had no idea how to get the attention of busy New Yorkers. He decided to start by renting a restaurant and inviting one hundred food industry elites to his launch. He had just hired two recent college grads; he asked them to help him come up with some arresting new ideas of how to capture people's attention. These college grads came up with a much more captivating stunt than my hot-air balloon launch decades earlier. They were attracted to the charming story of Moshe and Ali and the kind of Middle Eastern imagery they evoked. They suggested renting a camel and creating a Middle Eastern "event" right in the front of the restaurant where food elites were gathered. It seemed like a preposterous idea, but to his amazement, Daniel found that you could actually rent a camel in Manhattan for $1,000 a day. He then hired two guys from the Dominican Republic to dress up like Moshe and Ali.

Daniel actually persuaded Ben Cohen, of Ben & Jerry's fame and a member of his advisory board, to lead the camel with Moshe and Ali back and forth in front of the restaurant where the food specialists were gathered. Every time Ben tried to give someone a sample of pita bread with the luscious tomato spread, the camel snatched it from his hands, causing an uproar of laughter.

Their stunt won them a mountain of press coverage, including local and national TV and a story in the *New York Times*. Daniel observed that this would not have happened had he not given one of his recent grads' crazy ideas a try.[12] Successful social innovators like Daniel are smart enough to draw on the ideas of others.

Daniel also created the OneVoice Movement in 2002 to provide another way to give voice to the concerns and aspirations of moderate Israelis and Palestinians working toward a reconciled peaceful future.[13]

12. Lubetzky, *Do the Kind Thing*, 159–60.

13. See the website of OneVoice: www.onevoicemovement.org.

OneVoice creates innovative ways to use media to promote civic engagement to work for the common good. Today, Daniel Lubetzky is founder and CEO of KIND, makers of healthy and delicious snacks, which he launched in 2004. Daniel continues to invest his time and resources not only in producing healthy snack products and inspiring consumers to practice acts of kindness but, outside of KIND, also working for reconciliation in the Middle East and other places where race, politics, or religion cause division.[14]

Transforming Feasting in Oz into Human Empowerment Locally and Globally

Young people in Australia seem to be having a better time of launching businesses intended to have a social impact than any groups I have heard of. One of these launching groups is Y Generation Against Poverty, or YGAP. Elliott Costello, son of World Vision Australian chief Tim Costello, left a corporate position to join with some friends in starting this organization. Their mission statement is quite simply to "inspire impact entrepreneurs to end poverty." Reportedly, this is the largest ever movement of young people in Australia seeking to bring serious social change.

Here's how they're doing it: YGAP has started two restaurants as social businesses. The first is the Kinfolk Cafe in Melbourne. Here you can have a great cup of coffee, delicious desserts, or lovely salads made with locally grown greens and tomatoes. What makes this café truly distinctive, however, is that it trains a team of volunteers to help run the restaurant so that YGAP can channel the profits into empowering their neighbors in their own community, as well as communities in Ghana and Cambodia, to become economically self-sufficient. Now, thirteen different cafes with this kind of social mission have been opened in Melbourne. Good on these young innovators.

Recently, YGAP opened its second restaurant, called Feast of Merit, in the city of Richmond, VA. Here, too, all the profits go to empowering people locally and globally. The inspiration for Feast of Merit was drawn from the culture of the Naga people in northeast India. In that culture, if an individual becomes a person of wealth, then they can choose to hold a festival—a feast of merit. The entire community, including the poor, are invited to gather and to share not only in the feast but also in the

14. Lubetzky, *Do the Kind Thing*, 33.

wealth of the person being honored, who returns to their life without their wealth but with the respect and gratitude of the entire village. YGAP likewise affirms that merit is found not in what we accumulate but rather in what we give away.

Picture yourself at one of their evening feasts in a communal dining house, enjoying locally sourced food and a main course of either braised eggplant, smoked yogurt, and pine nuts and parsley, or a shank of lamb cooked for twelve hours with harissa sauce and roast onions. Spiced chocolate cake and grilled pears are offered for dessert.

Are you ready to join this feast with those both inside and outside of the church and rediscover that the good life of God is never found in seeking life but in joining those who are investing their lives in making a difference in our troubled world? Has this brief tour of successful social enterprise projects helped you see why it is essential that followers of Jesus and Christian organizations join others in using the power of social entrepreneurship to address both large challenges and local opportunity to bring lasting change?

Dreaming and Scheming

It is time to get out your iPad or notebook again and find a couple of innovative friends as we explore the potential of social entrepreneurship to make a difference in the lives of our neighbors locally and globally.

- What did you find most promising about the potential of social entrepreneurship in the lives of neighbors in emerging economies?

- What did you find most promising about the potential of social entrepreneurship in the lives of our neighbors in established economies in the West?

- What are some social enterprises you would like to consider joining?

- What are your ideas for creating new forms of social entrepreneurship that engage some of the new opportunities you identified earlier and who might join you in exploring these forms of changemaking?

CONVERSATION 2—DISCOVERING HOW YOU CAN JOIN A SOCIAL ENTREPRENEURSHIP TEAM

How can people, who are not entrepreneurs, become involved in this stream of changemaking? Who are some of the participants, and what might be some of the benefits and the costs of this form of changemaking? Let's visit a few more examples of social enterprise and forms of investing in this form of changemaking.

Christian Organizations Joining the Social Entrepreneurship Stream

- World Vision Australia's Social Entrepreneurship & Economic Development (SEED) program has been facilitating social entrepreneurial startups as well as savings groups, business facilitation, and microfranchising for more than a decade.[15] Tearfund UK also has started encouraging those they work with to use social enterprise to increase community empowerment.[16]

- Inhabit,[17] sponsored by the Seattle School of Theology and Psychology[18] and the Parish Collective,[19] is a cutting-edge conference that focuses on both community empowerment and social entrepreneurship. At last year's Inhabit, the founders of SOCAP[20]—Rosa Lee Harden and her husband, Kevin Jones—gave presentations; Rosa Lee spoke about the Meaning of Money and Kevin about Innovative new forms of Financial Investment in Social Innovation in local communities.

- Hack4Missions is an opportunity for students attending Urbana 15 to prototype new ideas on using cutting-edge technology in order to create real-time solutions for missions organizations and those they work with.[21] The Christian Community Development Association

---

15. See www.worldvision.com.au/get-involved/partner-with-us/seed.
16. See www.tearfund.org.
17. See www.inhabitconference.com.
18. See www.theseattleschool.edu.
19. See www.parishcollective.org.
20. See www.socialcapitalmarkets.net.
21. See www.urbana.org/hack4missions.

is starting with a pre-conference this year with Market Solutions for Community Transformation.[22]

- My favorite Christian festival, the Greenbelt Festival, takes place every August north of London and often hosts up to thirty thousand primarily younger participants. The festival includes a strong focus on advocacy for both social and environmental justice. It is also the "mothership" that gave birth to the Wild Goose Festival in the US. I was delighted to learn that this is one of the first Christian conferences to host an annual social entrepreneurship competition. Last year, the winning idea was called Clean Living. Miriam Goodacre conceived of developing a new social enterprise employing people who are without work to become city cleaners in London, paying them a living wage of $8.80 per hour.[23]

- Virtually all of the graduate business programs in our Christian colleges in the US are leading this parade. The graduate business programs at Seattle Pacific University, Seattle University, Houghton College, and Asbury University offer courses in preparing their students to become an innovative part of this stream of changemaking. Every year in April, Seattle Pacific University has an annual Social Venture Plan Competition for college students, who create entrepreneurial projects that can make a difference in the world.[24] Professor Randy Franz at SPU reported that the 2015 winner was the team behind Brio Pak, a container designed to keep medical supplies cool while being transported in areas without electricity; Brio Pak works entirely on solar power.

- Praxis Labs offers a rich range of resources to enable both business entrepreneurs and social entrepreneurs to make a strong beginning. For example, the mission of Sinapis Group is to empower early-stage entrepreneurs working in emerging economies to develop innovative business skills and scalable business ideas that strive to create sustainable employment and an improved quality of life for people in ways that reflect Christian compassion.[25] The online magazine

22. See www.ccda.org/mksolutions.
23. See www.greenbelt.org.uk.
24. See www.spu.edu/acad/school-of-business-and-economics/SVPC2015.html.
25. See www.praxislabs.org.

Faith & Leadership is one of the few Christian publications I have seen that regularly has articles on social entrepreneurship.[26]

- There are a few churches in the US that are actively sponsoring social entrepreneurship, including Colonial Church in Edina, Wisconsin, which we mentioned earlier, and Redeemer Presbyterian Church in New York City, which has funded twenty startups in recent years as part of its annual small business competition.[27]

Clearly, there is an enormous opportunity for followers of Jesus, for churches, and for Christian organizations in all our countries both to discover the social-entrepreneurship stream and to start collaborating with changemakers. Again, why would any of us want to miss being a part of this changemaking celebration, which has so much potential to make a lasting difference in our world?

Defining the Social Entrepreneurship Changemaking Stream

In looking at the community-empowerment changemaking stream, I hope it was immediately clear that all of us can find ways to be involved with our neighbors in making a difference in our own neighborhoods and communities. As we begin this conversation on social entrepreneurship, I'm certain that a number of readers can't imagine themselves creating a new social enterprise. However, I would encourage every reader who finds the possibility of being on a social-enterprise team to see if there are aspiring entrepreneurs in your community or church and to gauge whether their social or environmental mission aligns with your senses of purpose.

Social Entrepreneurship: Steps for Getting Started

The social-entrepreneurship stream is, by its very nature, often more complex than the community-empowerment stream. As a consequence you need to find the necessary resources to launch your new venture. Michelle Goodman, writing in *Entrepreneur*, offers some excellent advice: "Don't quit your day job . . . The lessons you learn while working for someone else can mean the difference between a successful

26. See www.faithandleadership.com.
27. Smith, "Christian Tech Entrepreneurs Find Funds, Support," par. 10.

entrepreneurial enterprise and one that fizzles." She adds, "Holding down a day job means having only so many waking hours to devote to your side venture. That's why validating your idea will work—and that people will pay for it—should be priority No. 1."[28]

Now let me outline the steps of successful social entrepreneurs for getting started. This list also includes the major components of design thinking we discussed earlier.

1. **Start with friends and mentors.**

If you aspire to be a social entrepreneur, one of the first things you need to do is to gather friends and supporters who believe in what you're trying to accomplish. Don't recruit based on friendship alone. Search for people who might bring needed expertise, gifts, or resources that could be critical to launching a successful social enterprise. Seek out a coach or mentor who has had experience enabling other entrepreneurs to launch their projects. As I mentioned before, most of us don't have the ability or the tenacity to become a social entrepreneur. However, virtually all of us can be on teams that support entrepreneurs in their work for a social or environmental venture that captures our passions and imaginations too. Your participation could be key to helping an entrepreneur get her venture off the ground. I would encourage readers who would like to be involved in this changemaking stream to find social entrepreneurs who are already at work to assist them in launching their ventures. Particularly, look for those ventures that connect most directly to your concerns and calling. I suggest you start with the business school at virtually any Christian or public college. You will undoubtedly find students who might value your support in launching their social enterprises. Finally, also look for incubators, like Impact Hubs,[29] that can be found in many major cities.

2. **Connect with conveners.**

"SOCAP, the Social Capital Markets conference, has grown to likely be the largest annual conference connecting social entrepreneurs with impact investors," writes Devin Thorpe, a contributor to *Forbes*. Thorpe interviewed Kevin Jones, the cofounder of SOCAP, who had this to say about the conference: "A lot of what goes on at SOCAP is

28. Goodman, "Don't Quit Your Day Job," 89–90.
29. See www.impacthub.net.

relational—prospective mentors and angels meeting and forming relationships with entrepreneurs."[30] The Skoll World Forum hosts a gathering of social entrepreneurs and impact investors at Oxford every April.[31]
Forbes hosts the Change the World competition for entrepreneurs under
thirty; reportedly, it is the largest competition for young entrepreneurs,
with a million-dollar prize pool this year.[32] Social Enterprise Awards have
competition for entrepreneurs in Australia every year.[33] The UK Social
Enterprise Awards are held in London every fall as well.[34] One of the
major global conferences that is devoted "to building sustainable solutions to poverty" is the Social Impact Conference.[35] The Global Shapers
Community, sponsored by the World Economic Forum, brings together
a network of young leaders from all over the planet who are committed to
making a difference in the lives of their neighbors locally and globally.[36]
Of course, there are other groups like the Clinton Global Initiative, the
TED Talks, as well as a number of universities that are likewise convening
social entrepreneurship conferences and competitions. Finally, Ashoka
Changemakers has been working for more than three decades to build a
global network that embodies a vision of everyone learning how he or she
can be a changemaker. They have built a network of ten thousand innovators, hundreds of partners, and tens of thousands of changemakers in 125
countries, as well as running online competitions.[37]

3. Research the changing context, best practices, and major players.

As we mentioned in chapter 3, all design thinking needs to begin by
identifying new opportunities in our rapidly changing contexts today
and tomorrow. David Bornstein and Susan Davis write, "Because of the
size of the global population, the pace of change, the spread of technology, the urgency of financial, health, and environmental crises . . . we
must anticipate problems and attack them at their sources before they
grow and multiply. And we must continually invent new solutions as

30. Thorpe, "SOCAP Adds Gratitude Awards," par. 4.

31. See www.skollworldforum.org.

32. "Forbes Announces $1 Million Global Change the World Social Entrepre-
neurs Competition."

33. See www.socialenterpriseawards.com.au.

34. See www.socialenterprise.org.uk/events.

35. See www.opportunitycollaboration.net.

36. See www.globalshapers.org.

37. See www.changemakers.com/futureforward.

conditions change."[38] Above all, social entrepreneurs must constantly monitor the horizon to spot new opportunities and challenges, as well as new technologies, so that there is adequate lead time to create innovative entrepreneurial responses. Social entrepreneurship at its core is problem-solving. It is also essential, with any form of entrepreneurship, that you carefully research the major players in the arena you're choosing to work in so that you have a clear idea of how to position your new venture.

4. Define the purpose.

As design thinking recommends, all social innovation needs to begin with an overarching purpose that directly engages the new opportunity you identified. Bornstein and Davis remind us that for business entrepreneurs, maximizing profits or shareholder wealth is the defining purpose. For social entrepreneurs, however, the defining purpose is to maximize some form of social or environmental change that promotes the common good. Both Gens Y and Z are increasingly asking the question, what kind of an enterprise is worth devoting your life to build?[39] Again, is it possible that people who make no profession of faith could teach us followers of Jesus about what is worth devoting our lives to? In any case, for people of faith, it is essential to provide a very clear sense of purpose for what you intend to achieve and how you seek to advance a sense of God's purposes for a people and a world.

5. Idea-storm.

Design thinking always values drawing on the imagination of not only all those on the team but also those who will benefit from this innovation. This means increasing our capacity not only to listen, as we discussed in the last chapter on community empowerment, but to actually invite the creative input of all those involved. Tim Brown, who invented design thinking, urges those who want to be entrepreneurial to join others who are creating a culture of innovation. In other words, you need to create an environment of collaboration with everyone on your team, an environment that invites creativity.[40] In addition to that, it is vital that you have regular idea-storming sessions to specifically imagine and create new

---

38. Bornstein and Davis, *Social Entrepreneurship*, xviii.

39. Ibid., 30–34.

40. Brown, *Change by Design*, 31–32.

ways to implement your social or environmental mission in ways that engages the new opportunities you identify.

6. Invite input from far and near.

In the community-empowerment stream we emphasize how important it is not only to listen but also to invite the input and ideas of all those with whom you work. This is particularly important when you are directly involved in someone else's community or culture. In fact, those working in this kind of context should take the time to read Paulo Freire's classic, *Pedagogy of the Oppressed*.[41] Freire is very critical of the kind of the benefactor-recipient relationship that has characterized too many Western development initiatives. He encourages outsiders not only to become better listeners but to actually incorporate in the empowerment process an educational initiative to enable those who are seen as disadvantaged to learn how structures have been designed to keep them in a subservient position.[42]

7. Seek resources.

"Social investment opportunities are flourishing. Investors find it increasingly easy to use their funds to earn returns and reward socially conscious, publicly traded businesses, which account for 10 percent of all managed assets," write William Eggers and Paul Macmillan.[43] Large sums of money for social ventures are also being raised through Kickstarter campaigns and crowdfunding. Having said that, most entrepreneurs are likely to find that securing funding for new ventures is never easy. Therefore, it is essential for you and your team to both develop broad networks as well as a strong marketing platform, and even creative stunts to make your new venture as attractive as possible to funders large and small.

8. Evaluate progress.

It is difficult to overestimate how important it is to develop convincing evidence that your new business is achieving both its social and economic goals. It is essential that you develop ways to chart your progress as well as design sophisticated tools to evaluate your success in achieving your goals. More and more funding organizations, including large foundations,

41. Freire, *Pedagogy of the Oppressed*.
42. Mehr, "Why Every Social Entrepreneur Needs to Read This Book."
43. Eggers and Macmillan, *Solution Revolution*, 151.

are raising the bar for both nonprofit organizations and social ventures to make sure they are achieving outcomes by being able to articulate clear metrics, in order to retain their support. I would urge every innovator and her team to celebrate every advance and view every setback as an opportunity to find a better way forward. Do you remember my meeting Ed Soule, head of the New Business Division of Weyerhaeuser, at the beginning of this chapter? He enabled his six team members to use every setback as an opportunity to find a better way forward to the launch pad.

A Quick Trip "Back to the Past"

One of the most promising ways to use our global Internet to advance the common good is to create a forum for an informed grassroots discussion of how to build a more civil society locally, nationally, and globally. This timely topic deserves a broader conversation.

Remember the launching of that hot-air balloon to promote the dramatization of a new way to invite citizens in Seattle to be a part of a new form of civil-society experiment on the future of public education? President Edward Lindaman from Whitworth College and several of our team were invited to meet with Republican Governor Daniel Evans to both share a bit about our small demonstration project and some of the recent statewide futures projects in Hawaii, California, and Maine.

Governor Evans, wanting to test a broader statewide civil-society experiment, launched the Alternative for Washington process in 1974. He decided to create the first state futures process that didn't rely on the work of a select committee. Governor Evans asked Edward Lindaman to chair the Alternatives for Washington process. He also invited the Brookings Institution to work together to create a process for a statewide citizen participation process utilizing PBS television.

The Brookings team designed the content and invited citizens to consider the costs and benefits of nine different options for the future of the state. Sixty percent of citizens favored the top three options to work for a more sustainable approach to both agricultural growth and growth in international trade, while also seeking to enhance the unique quality of life that Washington residents value.[44] This kind of project could still be a prototype for creating similar civil-society experiments using the potential of the Internet in this new millennium.

44. Baker, "The States Experiment with 'Anticipatory Democracy.'"

A Quick Look Back at Social Entrepreneurship

As you toured the diverse spectrum of examples of new forms of social enterprise we presented in this chapter, which of the entrepreneurial ventures attracted your interest and ignited your imagination? Are you one who feels you might like to discover whether you could, with the help of others, launch a new entrepreneurial venture? Or are you one who feels drawn to be a part of this kind of social innovation as a member of the support team on the launch pad? Or perhaps you find that more direct involvement in some new forms of community empowerment in your neighborhood is where God could best use your mustard seed.

In any case, I urge you to join me in leaving the bleachers and getting back down on the field of play. Let's all discover how we can be a much more vital part of this changemaking celebration. The people we have met in the last two chapters are relishing discovering the difference they can make in the lives of others. Why would anyone want to miss out on being a part of this celebration? In the next chapter, I'm going to show you creative ways you can begin to reinvent your life so that you will have more time to be present to both God and neighbor—and discover firsthand that the good life of God is indeed the life given away!

Dreaming and Scheming

Get out your iPad or notebook and write down:

1. As you consider the social entrepreneurship stream of changemaking, do you sense you have the abilities, background, and energy it would take to be a social innovator? Do you sense that God might be able to use your gifts as a support-team member on the launch pad? Or would your gifts find better expression in your own community or in a community overseas?

2. What is a possibile starting point for you to become a team member or a social entrepreneur in this kind of changemaking?

3. Make a list of steps to further research this form of changemaking, to join social enterprises that are already underway, or to create a project and share your ideas with friends or colleagues that could be of support in moving forward—and making a beginning.

7

Imagine Living on Purpose Today to Create
Your Best Life Tomorrow

Reaching for Our Best

I DANGLED A SMALL stick on a string just high enough so that the five newborn kittens could barely reach up and bat it. After another twenty minutes of play, however, I found I had to raise the stick quite a bit higher because two of the kittens learned by practice that they could jump higher and bring the stick to the ground.

It was a warm, blue-sky June morning in my favorite place in the world—my grandparents' five-acre farm in Blackfoot, Idaho. The year was 1941. My grandfather, Norman, had constructed this small two-bedroom house with a basement back in 1915. My mother, Katherine, and her two sisters, Virginia and Mildred, grew up sharing one bedroom, my grandparents the other. My two uncles, Bob and John, grew up sharing a bed in the dank, unfinished basement.

That's where my grandmother, Sarah, kept my summer treasure—a ten-year collection of *National Geographic* magazines stacked high against one wall. I spent hours traveling around the world, meeting intriguing people and seeing faraway places.

I was down to my last stack of magazines, and I was frustrated. Try as I might I couldn't reach the top of the stack, even standing on my tiptoes. I searched the entire basement for something to stand on. Then I spotted a huge bucket of eggs that my grandmother had harvested earlier that morning. I found that by standing on the rim of the bucket I was able to reach the top three copies I wanted. Then something happened . . . You guessed it: my magazines went flying and I came crashing down.

I immediately ran upstairs and confessed. "Grandma, I'm sorry, I used your bucket of eggs to stand on the edge to reach some of those magazines and I had an accident." I paused and added, "But Grandma . . . I only stepped on the top ones!" (All the way to the bottom, of course.)

She swept me up in her big arms and took me into her lap. Though I had egg dripping down both of my legs, she gave me a huge kiss, told me it would be all right, and reminded me of how much she loved me.

As a young boy I was deeply grateful for my grandparents' love and care. When I joined my parents in San Francisco, in 1942, I wanted to express my appreciation for my grandparents and find some way to honor them. I remembered that they were deeply committed Methodists and discovered Glide Memorial Methodist Church was located on Market Street about a mile and a half from our apartment on Nob Hill. Although my parents weren't churchgoers, they supported my decision to take myself to Sunday school when I was seven. I let my grandparents know and began to enjoy learning about Jesus.

As you reflect back on your own story, what are your earliest memories of being motivated to reach as high as you could? What stirred your aspirations—a speaker at church camp, an experience on a family vacation, a special time at school, or perhaps treasured moments on your grandparent's farm? Are you reaching high for your very best life today?

Conversation 1

Are Our Churches Enabling Us to Reach High for Our Best Lives?

In chapter 1 I posed this question: Does the future have a church? I expressed a growing concern regarding the graying and declining of both mainline and evangelical churches in Western countries. Another question asked even less often is, how many of us who are part of the church are reaching high for our best lives as followers of Jesus? I am convinced that we are facing a much more serious crisis than declining numbers, and that is the decline in participation of many of our core members.

Regular church attendance in many congregations, not only in North America but also in the UK and Australia, has declined to once or twice a month. Pastors tell me that their members have less time to be involved in service in their churches and communities. For example, I recently learned of one evangelical church that is no longer able to find volunteers to teach their elementary Sunday school class for six consecutive weeks. So they have settled for a different set of parents volunteering every week just to keep one class going.

Research also reveals that members are spending less time in service to others and less time in prayer and scripture study. Ed Stetzer, in his blog *The Exchange*, reports that "only 19 percent of churchgoers personally (not as part of a church worship service) read the Bible every day."[1]

The Empty Tomb, Inc. reports in a 2015 publication that per capital giving in American and Canadian congregations has declined from 3.02 percent of per-capita income in 1968 to 2.17 percent in 2013—during a period in which most North Americans experienced a dramatic increase in their discretionary income. Per-capita benevolence income, to reach out to our neighbors in need, during that same time period decreased by almost 50 percent, from 64 percent of per-capita giving to the church in 1968 to 33 percent of their per-capita giving to their churches in 2013.[2]

Shouldn't we all feel a little more urgency knowing that this trend of declining participation could seriously undermine the vitality of apparently healthy congregations? Shouldn't we all call our congregations to promote a more serious approach to whole-life discipleship and stewardship? Finally, shouldn't our congregations actually offer small classes that both challenge and enable members to "up our game"? Imagine the difference it might make in your life and church if we learned to reach for our best lives by connecting more directly to God's purposes, and if we reinvented our timestyles to make time each day to be present to God and weekly time to be more involved in reaching out to neighbors.

Too often, I suspect, we are all distracted from seeking to live our best lives not only by the pressures of daily life but also by the aspirations and values of the dominant culture. Don't these aspirations and values often define how we use our time and money?

I'm aware that many readers may feel as if it's all they can do to make it through the week, given the pressures we all face at work, in our finances, and in finding time. The last thing I want to do is to add more stress to people's already stressful daily lives. I know that pastors are also

1. Stetzer, "New Research: Less than 20% of Christians Read the Bible Daily," par. 5.

2. Ronsvalle and Ronsvalle, *State of Church Giving through 2013*, 10.

under great pressure to serve their congregations and help them deal with a host of issues. It is essential, however, that we wake up to what I believe is a crisis in discipleship and stewardship education.

Many evangelical churches offer courses on discipleship, and mainline, Mennonite, and Catholic churches offer courses on spiritual formation, yet I find that while they all provide valuable help with people's spiritual journeys and their relationships with family and friends, few seem to challenge members to really change their priorities and live with greater intentionality and discipline. I am personally indebted to the Anabaptist call to a more radical whole-life faith, which challenged me to change my timestyle and lifestyle in order to refocus and more authentically serve God and neighbor. Shouldn't courses on biblical formation include practical ways to reinvent our priorities to put first things first?

Creating Our Best Lives and Refusing to Settle for Less

Isn't following Jesus more than a devotional add-on to our "real" lives as we dance to the seductive songs of the imperial global mall? Following this Jesus is an invitation to become whole-life disciples and stewards to discover that all of life is an opportunity to reach for our best. We invite you to "dream and scheme" about innovative ways to translate the aspirations and values of the mustard seed empire of Jesus into whole new ways of living, empowering, and celebrating.

Michael Frost, in his book *Incarnate*, suggests a very original organic image for the church and for all of us who wish to see our mustard seeds flourish. "Like the gardens at Honolulu International Airport, the church is to be . . . dirt and worms and compost compared to the sterility of the departure lounges of the excarnate life. We are to embody faith and life in the company of those who've fallen for rootlessness . . . [and] for screen culture and virtual reality."[3]

We invite you to discover that all of life is an opportunity to grow in the garden of God. The Creator God invites us all to imagine new ways to raise kids with compassion and creativity, to design sustainable communities, to dream up new forms of changemaking, and to throw (by far!) the best parties. If we discover that following Jesus is actually a design opportunity, then all of us "gardeners" will invite people both in the church

3. Frost, *Incarnate*, 28.

and society to flourish in rich soil and to discover a more festive way of being. Why would anyone ever want to settle for less and miss the best?

Reaching for Your Best: Coaching for Disciplined Living

I just finished reading a book on life coaching, ironically titled *Creating Your Best Life*,[4] which shows how life coaching enables both social and business entrepreneurs to develop the personal focus and disciplines necessary to create and launch new social enterprises and businesses. It also illustrates how entrepreneurs, like athletes and artists, can actually create new disciplined life practices to reach for their highest. This and other books like it provide much practical help in enabling not only entrepreneurs but all of us to sharpen our sense of purpose for our lives as well as design a disciplined pathway to live into that purpose.

What seems to motivate these entrepreneurs is the realization that they have a great deal riding on their attempt to launch risky new ventures, and as a consequence they often want to do everything they can to be on top of their game in their own personal lives. I sincerely believe the Spirit of God can use these entrepreneurs and much that is offered by life coaching to enable followers of Jesus to create more purpose-focused and disciplined lives too. I believe if we did, it might help those outside the church—particularly Gen Y and Gen Z—to take us a little more seriously.

After reading this book on coaching, I realized I couldn't remember ever reading a single Christian book that draws on current behavioral research, as this book does, to learn what works best for people trying not only to set new goals for their lives but to actually attain them. Let's learn more about the positive consequences of living on purpose instead of succumbing to the seductions of the culture. I bet you have some friends and people in your church you could add to this short list.

Reaching for Your Highest by Living on Purpose

Remember Alexie Torres-Fleming, whom we met in chapter 5? We learned about her making a radical vocational change when she moved back to her neighborhood in the Bronx. She reached for her best life as an agent of compassionate change. It all began when she embraced a new sense of purpose for her life. And remember the story of social and

4. Miller and Frisch, *Creating Your Best Life.*

business entrepreneur Daniel Lubetzky? Do you remember what motivated him to live on purpose and reach for his best? He was motivated to work for reconciliation, in part, because of his dad's experience of surviving the concentration camps of World War II.

Join me as we travel back to the horror and hope of World War II one last time. I want to introduce you to one of my heroes, a man who redefined, for himself and millions of others, what is important and what it means to live on purpose. His name is Viktor Frankl. In 1941, while the chief of neurology at Vienna's Rothschild Hospital, he faced a horrific life decision. He had just been granted a visa to continue his psychological work in the United States; his parents, however, would have to remain in Austria. Facing an excruciating, life-changing decision, he went to St. Stephen's Cathedral to grapple with the question of whether to go. He repeatedly asked himself, "Should I leave my parents behind? Should I say goodbye and leave them to their fate?" When he got home that day he found a marble fragment of one of the Ten Commandments, which, his father explained, had been rescued from the rubble of a synagogue the Nazis had destroyed—it was the commandment to honor your father and mother.

That tipped the scales. Viktor Frankl chose to put aside his personal safety and vocational pursuits in the US to stay with his parents. In September 1942, Frankl, along with his wife and parents, were sent to Theresienstadt; his father, Gabriel, died there. Two years later, Frankl and his wife were sent to Auschwitz. Emily Esfahani Smith observes that "the wisdom that Frankl derived from his experiences there, in the middle of unimaginable human suffering, is just as relevant now as it was then. 'Being human always points, and is directed, to something, or someone, other than oneself—be it a meaning to fulfill or another human being to encounter. The more one forgets himself—by giving himself to a cause or to serve another person to love—the more human he is.'"[5]

Frankl was liberated with many others when the war with Germany ended in 1945. Among the first things he did was to write the book *Man's Search for Meaning*,[6] which reflected what he had learned. According to Smith, he learned that "what sets human beings apart from animals is not the pursuit of happiness, which occurs all across the natural world, but the pursuit of meaning, which is unique to humans." He discovered

---

5. Smith, "There's More to Life than Being Happy."

6. Frankl, *Man's Search for Meaning*.

that those who found meaning in the midst of their suffering, even in horrendous circumstances, were far more resilient than those who did not.[7]

Doesn't this example directly contradict one of the fundamental tenets of the American dream—that the way to achieve happiness is always to pursue it? Why do we not realize that we can only find a deep sense of happiness by giving our lives to a purpose that calls us beyond ourselves?

Cal Uomoto, a friend of mine and of many others here in Seattle, was a remarkable example of someone who as a young man discovered a purpose for his life that called him beyond himself. In the early 1980s, Cal's heart was stirred by the growing plight of Indochinese refugees who were just starting to arrive in Seattle. One day, as we were having lunch at Uwajimaya Food Court, Cal told me that he was particularly concerned for the well-being of the Hmong refugees arriving from Laos. "Many Vietnamese refugees are used to living and working in an urban environment like Seattle," he said. "But the Hmong refugees are from an agricultural society in Laos, and I have no idea of how they will be able to make it in Seattle."

As I stayed in touch with Cal during the next six months, I watched his concern grow and evolve into his sense of purpose for his life. Like many others I've introduced you to in this book, Cal and his new friends from Laos became collaborative innovators, with the support of friends from Bethany Presbyterian Church. When Cal asked the newly arrived families what they wanted to do to become established, they responded, "We want to farm."

I'm sure that in the months that followed Cal used most of his free time to help his friends lease twenty-two acres of farmland in King County. He also helped them lease a booth at Pike Place Market so that they could sell their produce. I know he wasn't sure if this venture would work. In a relatively short period of time, however, a number of Hmong families became economically self-reliant through this venture. Cal and his wife, Annie, and their growing family found that God's purpose for their lives was enabling refugee families from literally all over the world to resettle here. Often, many of them would stay in Cal and Annie's home—sometimes for weeks—while looking for work. Not surprisingly, World Relief was smart enough to employ Cal to head up their refugee

7. Smith, "There's More to Life than Being Happy,"

resettlement program in the greater Seattle area for more than twenty years.

Cal was a servant leader who avoided the limelight. We lost him much too soon to cancer. The memorial service was held at First Presbyterian Church in Seattle on November 15, 2012. More than a thousand people attended. It was like a meeting of the UN, with people from many different nations expressing their deep admiration for Cal, Annie, and their children, who demonstrated that the good life of God is found in providing hospitality to strangers. By the way, if you ever have the opportunity to come to Seattle, be sure to visit Pike Place Market. At least half the booths are filled with the most beautiful flowers you have ever seen, all produced by the thriving Hmong community that calls Seattle home.

Reaching for Your Best: Remembering Followers of Jesus Who Decided to Live on Purpose

Cal and I became good friends shortly after I arrived in Seattle in the early 1970s. We would go out for lunch periodically. He surprised me one day in 1973 with a subscription to a magazine called *The Post-American* (now *Sojourners*). I relished this magazine because it directly engaged many of the most difficult and challenging issues of racial, economic, and environmental justice of the day.

This magazine introduced me to a Christian world I didn't know existed. First, most of the writers back then seemed to be Mennonites. I had never heard about the Anabaptist branch of the church. As I tell my Mennonite friends, "I immediately went to the library at Seattle Pacific University and found three books about Anabaptism—and two of them were against it." In spite of that, I became a convinced Anabaptist through the way that Mennonite writers brought Scripture to bear on all of life and a broad range of social issues well.

Without doubt, the most important Christian book of the 1970s for me was *Rich Christians in an Age of Hunger*,[8] written by Mennonite author Ron Sider. It was the first time I had read a call to a more serious whole-life faith; it was a call to live simply that others might simply live, as they say. I was so affected by the book that I immediately started simplifying my life. The first thing I did was to head to my closet and take

8. Sider, *Rich Christians in an Age of Hunger*. The book was first published in 1977.

out my three suits. I left myself with one sports coat and pair of slacks. I came back from the Salvation Army feeling very good about this first step toward simplifying my life.

Because of my occasional tendency toward disorientation, when I got back I checked my closet—and discovered that I had inadvertently donated not only my suits but also my last pair of slacks as well. I immediately called the Salvation Army. The coordinator "helpfully" responded that the slacks would be on display at one of their four outlets in the next two days and they would be happy to sell them back to me.

In spite of how frustrating that moment was, not only did I continue simplifying my life, I also began seeking other books on what used to be called "radical biblical discipleship." In the process, throughout the late seventies and early eighties I discovered that there was a robust and growing network of Christian communities springing up across North America and Down Under, and even a few in the UK.

The remarkable gift was that in most of these communities a large number of Christians were intentionally living together in order to free up time and resources to invest in changemaking ventures in their neighborhoods. At the high point, there were several hundred Christian communities around the US that would gather at Christian campgrounds in different states every summer. David and Neta Jackson tell the story of this remarkable movement in their book *Living Together in a World Falling Apart.*[9]

Reba Place Fellowship and Jesus People USA, both in the Chicago area, are two such communities that are still making a difference in the lives of their neighbors. In 2004, they were joined by friends in the New Monasticism movement, which has given rise to communities like The Simple Way in Philly and Rutba House in Raleigh-Durham.

What was particularly remarkable to me was the widespread impact of *Rich Christians in an Age of Hunger.* I remember that at least three mainline denominations were motivated by the book to create educational resources for adult study groups on specific ways to live more simply. I was surprised at how many evangelicals in Great Britain, Australia, and New Zealand began to publish books and articles that echoed the important message of Ron's book. The book didn't do as well among many evangelicals in the US, however, because of its criticism that our current

9. Jackson and Jackson, *Living Together in a World Falling Apart.*

form of capitalism seemed to favor the wealthy, often at the expense of the poor.

My friend Graham Kerr showed me a place in his memoir, *Flash of Silver,* that reminded me of when he attended the Lausanne Conference on "An Evangelical Commitment to Simple Life-style," hosted by John Stott in Britain in 1980.[10] I told Graham that I am increasingly concerned at how little emphasis there seems to be by leaders in evangelical or in mainline churches in the West on challenging followers of Jesus to live more simply that our neighbors might simply live. I am concerned that so few of our churches seem to be helping us reach high for our best lives.

Dreaming and Scheming

Time to get out your iPads or notebooks again and find a few friends to explore how all of us can reach a little higher to create our best lives.

- As you reflect back on your own journey, when did your faith seem to motivate you to live with a clearer sense of purpose, and in what ways did you live into that sense of purpose?

- In what ways could you orchestrate how you steward your life to more fully live into that sense of purpose so you are able to free up some time and resources to make a little difference in the lives of others?

- If all of life really is a design opportunity, what are ways you can create not only a more purpose-focused and disciplined life but also a way of life, with others, that is more festive?

- If you were to decide to join those who are reaching as high as they can to create their best lives, what three steps might you take to get started?

10. Kerr, *Flash of Silver,* 342.

CONVERSATION 2—DO YOU WANT TO JOIN THOSE REACHING FOR THEIR HIGHEST?

Reaching for Your Highest in a Post-9/11 World

Immediately after the devastating attack and loss of life on 9/11, many life coaches found that they had more clients than they could handle— people whose world had suddenly been turned upside down. They were no longer satisfied to simply to make it through the week. Many Americans were strongly motivated by this crisis to find a new way to live with a much greater sense of intentionality. Reportedly, some of these new clients were Christians, but many were not; they were people who made a decision no longer to wait for "someday."[11]

People were looking for a clearer, more focused reason for being. Many were seeking to create a mission statement for their lives going forward. "A mission statement becomes the North Star for people," says Dr. Jack Groppel, cofounder of the Johnson & Johnson Human Performance Institute. "It becomes how you make decisions, how you lead, and how you create boundaries."[12] As a secular life coach, he begins with questions such as, "Who do you want to be? How do you want to be remembered? What are your deepest values? What makes your life really worth living?"[13]—all good questions to begin with.

David Brooks, a columnist for the *New York Times*, reflects on people he knows who are searching for and finding a purpose for their lives. He introduces us to Greg Sunter from Brisbane, Australia, whose quest for purpose was also birthed by unexpected crisis. Greg lost his wife of twenty-one years to brain cancer. He then began a journey over four years to find a new reason for being.

Greg writes, "In his book *A Hidden Wholeness*,[14] Parker Palmer wrote about the two ways in which our hearts can be broken: the first imagining the heart as shattered and scattered; the second imagining the heart broken open into new capacity, holding more of both our own and the world's suffering and joy, despair and hope. The image of a heart

---

11. Miller and Frisch, *Creating Your Best Life*, 127.

12. Parker-Pope, "In with the New Mission Statement," D4.

13. Ibid.

14. Palmer, *A Hidden Wholeness: The Journey Towards an Undivided Life.*

broken open has become the driving force of my life in the years since my wife's death. It has become the purpose to my life."[15]

Individuals don't have to be in crisis, however, to discover how to live with a clearer sense of purpose. One of the most encouraging aspects of the V3 Movement is not only that they are empowering a new generation of church planters. They are enabling members in these new plants to reach high, as followers of Jesus, for their best lives. They do this by empowering members to create both a new rule and rhythm of life.

They often start by encouraging people to discern a new purpose for their lives that enables them to live with more intentionality. They follow up by encouraging them to create a new rhythm of life to steward their lives to follow their rule of life in circles of voluntary accountability.[16] I would love to find established churches offering similar opportunities to enable members to live with a clearer sense of purpose.

Some readers will remember the book *The Seven Habits of Highly Effective People,* by Stephen Covey, which was published several years ago. Covey was one of the first to encourage people to develop a personal mission statement and argued that "personal character, purpose and self-discipline" are what matter.[17]

I'm sure that most readers remember Rick Warren's book *The Purpose Driven Life,*[18] which was extremely popular among Christians everywhere. Believe it or not, Christine and I wrote a book that came out three months earlier titled *Living on Purpose.*[19] As we like to tell people, we have not been "afflicted" with thirty million in sales. Apparently the Kindle version is still available on Amazon.

We were motivated to write *Living on Purpose* because even though there are a number of processes designed to help clergy discern their calling, we found little available for those of us in the pews. As a consequence, instead of intentionally giving our lives to a sense of biblical purpose, too many of us settle for less.

Often we settle for life as a very frustrating balancing act—one that often lacks any clear sense of purpose. Not surprisingly, for these struggling individuals, a sense of biblical faith too often plays a very small role

15. Brooks, "Hearts Broken Open," par. 7.

16. Catchim, "Developing a Rule of Life and a Rhythm of Life."

17. "Stephen Covey, RIP," 58.

18. Warren, *The Purpose Driven Life: What on Earth Am I Here For?*

19. Sine and Sine, *Living on Purpose: Finding God's Best for Your Life.*

in enabling them to direct their lives as they struggle to make it through the week.

In *Living on Purpose*, we started with the assumption that every follower of Jesus is called, not just the "full-time workers" in the church. Christine and I believe that we can all discern how to connect our lives a little more directly to God's purposes for a people and a planet. That sense of purpose can become our North Star, which allows us to discern with much more clarity how God might use our mustard seeds, in common cause with others, to make a little difference in our neighborhoods and our world.

We found as people used the book to draft a mission statement that they often also found a way to reinvent their lives. Mission statements seem to enable people to create much more helpful ways by which to orchestrate their entire lives—including how they steward their time and money—instead of chronically struggling with the old balancing-act way of life. Their mission statements often also become an orchestrating center for the stewardship of their entire lives.

For a number of parents, mission statements have enabled them to raise their children with a growing sense of compassion for others. For example, Andrew and Joan Collins in Britain drafted a family mission statement with their three kids. They sensed God calling them to be the hospitality home in their suburban community. Different members of the family took turns deciding which neighbors to invite over for dinner. Joan and Andrew reported that they witnessed their three kids not only beginning to take a greater interest in other people's lives but also becoming more sensitive and generous with both the adults and kids the family connected with.

Ivan was a Christian businessman Christine and I met in Melbourne, Australia. He told us that his life was paralyzed by busyness, fear, and the struggle to get his life balanced at work and at home. He told us that only after he had drafted his mission statement and started living into it did his life begin to change—as did his stewardship of his time. The opportunity for compassionate response for Ivan was working with disabled kids for whom people didn't seem to have much time. Once he focused his life on creating ways to empower these kids, everything else in his life came into focus. The last time we were in touch, we heard that his wife and he had started a small business so that he would have more time to invest in working with the kids he cared about so much, and he reported that he was finding his life much more fulfilling.[20]

Here it is important for me to define my notion of vocation. I know there are some in the church who would define whatever they do as a job as their Christian vocation. It is true, of course, that all that we do, we should do "as unto the Lord." However, I find no biblical basis for assuming, as some do, that whatever one does as a job is automatically one's Christian vocation. In fact, a case could be made that many products and services offered by the firms where many Christians work reflect a very different notion of what is important and of value than is reflected in the mustard seed empire of Jesus. Clearly, it is not only those who are involved in the work of the church who are advancing God's purposes but also those who are directly involved in both human empowerment and environmental restoration.

In many businesses, however, it is possible to create innovative ways to give concrete expression to the biblical concern for economic justice. For example, several years ago I learned about a Canadian Christian who owned a furniture business. He expressed his sense of calling to make a difference in a very concrete way—he put a cap on his own salary and the salary of his administrative team for three years in order to increase the benefit package for his lowest-wage workers.

Christine's living-on-purpose statement is: "To be a voice for those who have no voice and bring glimpses of God's shalom kingdom into people's lives." My statement reads, "God calls me from my mother's womb, my grandparent's farm and through the church to be a voice of compassion, hope and joy, giving expression, and inviting others to give expression, to the new world that is already here in the risen Christ."

You are invited to begin the process of creating your best life by drafting a purpose statement. You might discover how God can use your life to play a more active part in this new changemaking celebration. I hope your mission statement will enable you and your compatriots to find a clearer sense of how to connect your life to something of God's loving purposes.

20. Sine and Sine, *Living on Purpose*, 76.

Reaching for Your Highest by Drafting a Purpose Statement for All of Life

I encourage you to start by finding a small group in your church or in your network of friends. Make a commitment to help one another over seven weeks not only to draft a mission statement for your entire life but also to identify one specific way to make a difference in the lives of others. Then you can start the very satisfying journey of reaching for your best life. You will also discover how all of life can become a design opportunity to create a less stressful, more festive way of life. Christine and I call this an "active listening process." Let me briefly suggest some active listening steps that might enable you and those in your group to find a clearer sense of purpose for your lives during this seven-week process:

- First, take time to get to know each other better by sharing your stories and your struggles. Also, share as openly as possible how you would like to see your lives changed.

- Second, spend some time in prayer to identify those needs in the lives of neighbors near and far that particularly stir your heart. Those stirrings could be an important part of God's call on your life. Be sure to write them down and share them with others in your group. Help one another identify why these needs and opportunities stir you and your initial ideas on how you might be able to join others in engaging these opportunities.

- Third, spend time reading scriptures that focus particularly on a sense of God's loving purposes for people and the world, which we explored in chapter 4. Write down those specific purposes that seem to both stir your head and connect to some of the needs you listed in the last response. In fact, I would encourage you to write down a portion or two of Scripture that directly connects your area of concern and your desire to create a way to respond. Share this with your small group and help one another craft a beginning mission statement. Explore specific ways God might use both your strengths and your weaknesses.

- Fourth, since all of life is a "design opportunity," invite the Spirit of the Creator God to ignite your imagination and to create innovative ways for you to use your life and gifts, in concert with others, to engage the new opportunity that also reflects something of God's purposes that you discerned in your biblical reflection last week. During this fourth week, add a specific action step that enables you to become more involved in the changemaking celebration.

- Fifth, research whether there are those in your community, your church, or perhaps online who are already involved in a similar form of changemaking to what you imagined that you might join. Take time to discover "best practices" of those who are involved in any similar forms of innovation so that you can draw on and learn from both their successes and their struggles. Seek the discernment of your group to identify a place to make a small beginning on putting wheels on your mission statement.

- Sixth, identify the concrete ways in which you will need to reinvent your timestyle and lifestyle so that you have the time to become involved in your changemaking opportunity. Create ways to free up daily time to be present to God in Scripture and prayer as well as a weekly time not only for worship but for continuing to meet with friends who will support you in your journey into a whole-life faith—a specific way to become involved in making a difference in the lives of others.

- During week seven, have every person share where they are in the active listening process. Not everyone will have the same level of clarity in terms of how to be more directly involved in changemaking and how to alter their timestyles and lifestyles. Next, have everyone develop a script that outlines their next steps, identifying who their ongoing partners will be; share those scripts with the group, and pray for each other. End with a meal and celebrate your new beginnings, your new mission statement, and your way forward. Finally, create a way to keep everyone in your group informed as you seek to reinvent your lives, to put your sense of God's call on your life at the center.

Reaching High for Your Best Life by Improvising New Ways to Put First Things First

Since life can be a new design opportunity, imagine yourself taking a position as an actor in a large theater company to put on a drama. Sound a bit terrifying? Now imagine that this is an *improvisational* theater company. In other words, you will need to use your imagination to create your own lines and interact with the other players as the story spontaneously unfolds. Now that's really terrifying!

Many believers assume that the story of God begins in Genesis and concludes with the resurrection of Jesus and the creation of that first community of believers. However, I'm in the ranks of those who believe that the story that began with Abraham and Sarah is an ongoing drama. All of us who follow Jesus, in every era, are invited onstage to improvise, in community with others, what faithful discipleship looks like in the place and the time in which we live.

In *The Practice of Prophetic Imagination*, Walter Brueggemann challenges us to develop "an emancipated imagination" so that we might be set free from the seductions of all imperial narrative. He urges us also to rediscover a narrative of compassion and hope that calls us beyond ourselves, and to re-imagine the world as God intends it to be. He reminds us that our narrative looks forward to a great homecoming celebration in which healing comes to the broken, justice to the poor, peace to the nations, and we all celebrate coming home to a restored creation! Brueggemann also reminds us of the evidence Jesus offers John's disciples that he is indeed the one who will lead us all into this future of restoration and hope: "Go tell John what you have seen and heard; the blind receive their sight, the lame walk, the lepers are cleansed, the deaf hear, the dead are raised, the poor have the good news preached to them" (Luke 7:22).[21]

In other words, as followers of Jesus we are all invited to be a part of a large, sprawling drama that involves our entire lives and actually brings change to the lives of others. The Creator God wants to ignite our imaginations to create both a whole new way of being and a whole new way of doing that reflects something of God's purpose to bring restoration and hope to our world.

"Jesus was offering as a counter-agenda an utterly risky way of being Israel, the way of turning the other cheek and going the second mile, the way of losing your life to gain it," writes N. T. Wright in *The Challenge of Jesus*. "This was the kingdom-invitation he was issuing. This was the play for which he was holding auditions."[22] He adds that "along with this radical invitation went a radical welcome. Wherever Jesus went, there seemed to be a celebration; the tradition of festive meals at which Jesus

---

21. Brueggemann. *Practice of Prophetic Imagination*, xv, 123–27.
22. Wright, *Challenge of Jesus*, 44–45.

welcomed all and sundry . . . The meals spoke powerfully about Jesus' vision,"[23] which included the invitation to take up our crosses and follow him, thus "embracing Jesus' utterly risky vocation."

Risky or not, this is your invitation. Following this Jesus is not just about showing up at church once in awhile, giving a little bit of our left-overs and shooting up a prayer when you're stuck in traffic. The call to follow this servant Jesus is a call to a radical whole-life faith. It is clearly an invitation to leave the passive spectators' gallery and join the actors on stage. It is the opportunity to discover the great satisfaction of joining others in creating new forms of changemaking.

Reaching for Your Best Life by Taking More Time to Party

One of the major changes Christine and I have made in recent years is that we spend more time partying and doing hospitality than most of our friends. Ever since those early days on my grandparents' farm, I have been strongly motivated to find ways to bless and honor all those whom God places in our lives.

For example, Jackie, a delightful young volunteer who shared her gifts with us at Mustard Seed Associates over a number of months, an-nounced that she was going to marry another friend of ours named Wolt. They traveled back to Michigan, where their families hosted an engage-ment celebration. I urged them to let us host an engagement bash here in Seattle where they live.

They welcomed the opportunity to share their good news with friends. We planned a Saturday morning brunch, to be held in our home from 9:30 to 11:30. It was the first time we had ever hosted an event where the invitations went out over Facebook. Even though we asked for an RSVP, only a few of Jackie and Wolt's friends responded, so we estimated that maybe thirty people would show up.

I prepared a brunch of Mexican black bean frittatas with salsa, sour cream, cilantro, and green onions, along with a large tropical fruit salad of pineapple and mango, a luscious, almond-filled Scandinavian pastry, and large pots of coffee.

Thank God we scheduled brunch over a two-hour period. There is no way that Christine and I could have managed to feed more than seventy twenty-and-thirty-somethings if we had limited the event to one

23. Ibid., 47.

hour. Most importantly, Wolt and Jackie had a great time sharing the good news of their wedding plans with their friends. We all enjoyed a taste of the wedding feast that Jesus assures us will be a part of the great homecoming celebration.

I'd like to conclude this chapter by inviting you to imagine and create new ways to use your time and money for what matters most. First, let me offer you the short version of getting your life organized; the secret, according to the author of *The Life-Changing Magic of Tidying Up*, is this: "Start by discarding. Then organize your space, thoroughly, completely, in one go."[24] Now, a little longer and more focused approach.

Reaching for Your Best Life: Creating New Ways to Use Your Time and Money for What Matters Most

Mark and Lisa Scandrette, in their book *Free: Using Your Time and Money on What Matters Most*, urge us to take time to name the things that matter most to us. They mention everything from working for justice and healing in our society to working for greater wholeness in our own personal lives.[25] Mark and Lisa know that most of us want to learn how to live "gratefully, creatively and sustainably." Their seven steps represent a good way to begin the journey toward becoming not only whole-life disciples but also whole-life stewards:

1. Name what matters most to you.

2. Value and align your time.

3. Practice gratitude and trust.

4. Believe you have enough.

5. Create a spending plan.

6. Maximize your resources.

7. Live generously and spend wisely.[26]

They also urge us to identify the time and money "bandits" that take our time and money and terrorize our lives. In fact, it might be helpful to start by naming the bandits: the cost of those four lattes a day, or all

24. Kondo, *The Life-Changing Magic of Tidying Up*, Introduction.

25. Scandrette and Scandrette, *Free*, 54.

26. Ibid., 19–20.

those expensive lunches, or the bundles of time the bandits steal when you spend hours on Instagram, Twitter, Facebook, or gaming. Naming the bandits is the first step in putting them out of business.

I have a friend who is studying law at the University of Washington and simply can't afford to allow the bandits to steal his time. In fact, Ryan has his Facebook page programmed so that it is available for one and a half minutes once a day. Because of what matters most to Ryan, he simply will not allow the bandits to rip off time that he needs for his books.

Make a list of the bandits that are stealing your time and money. Find imaginative ways to defeat your bandits. Then share them with your small group and ask them to hold you accountable to dispatch each bandit one at a time. Be sure to party after every victory!

Speaking of stewarding time and money, let me urge all of my friends who are involved in church plants or in churches that aspire to be missional to offer courses for their members on how to become whole-life disciples and whole-life stewards. Wouldn't that enable them to become much more fully invested in the success of missional ventures, including having time to be present to neighbors?

I also want to offer a very direct word to my evangelical friends. Following Jesus was never a 10-percent proposition. Sure, it would be great if everyone in the church gave 10 percent of their income. But a growing number of New Testament scholars have convinced me that tithe stewardship has never been a part of what it means to follow Jesus. Zacchaeus gave half of his wealth to the poor, and to anyone he cheated he gave four times the amount. Jesus invited the rich young ruler to give away all his wealth. Hasn't becoming a follower of Jesus always been a call to whole-life faith and whole-life stewardship too?

Let me offer a very direct word to my mainline Protestant friends, too. I strongly support your call for economic, racial, and environmental justice. But I have to ask: if you care so deeply about these urgent issues, then why is your per capita giving often significantly lower than that of the evangelical, Pentecostal, and Adventist churches? As I've had the opportunity to work with different denominations, I've found that mainline giving in the US often hovers between 1 to 3 percent, while in some other groups giving often hovers between 4 and 7 percent.

I strongly urge Christians of all stripes to consider embracing the kind of whole-life stewardship created by Mennonites called the "graduated tithe." Meet a young Mennonite couple we will call Peter and Edith Miller. Let's travel back to when Peter graduated from medical school and started his medical practice in Elkhart, Indiana, in 1965. They started with a baseline budget that supplied all their needs, plus a little set aside for emergencies. As three children came along they increased their budget accordingly, but they never moved out of the three-bedroom house where they started their lives together.

As a consequence, as Peter's income as a doctor and Edith's income as a librarian increased over three decades, they were able to dramatically increase their giving. They invested most of their giving in a micro-investment fund in Mozambique. People in that region were able to borrow from that fund to start small businesses, not only to move their families out of poverty but also to enable their children to go to school. As Edith and Peter moved into their senior years, they had the satisfaction of realizing their graduated tithe had been a key to thousands of people being able to move out of poverty and become self-supportive.

Isn't this an impressive example of how many of us could find creative ways to increase the amount we give and also the amount we invest in funds that will have an impact on the changemaking celebration?

In recent decades, the Mennonites have published some very important books that call us to a more radical whole-life faith that focuses on working for the well-being of the neighbor and of God's good creation. My favorite is *The Upside-Down Kingdom*, by Donald Kraybill.[27] However, I have seen very few Christian books recently, including those by Mennonite authors, that show us practical ways to develop a more purpose-focused, whole-life faith. I have also found few courses on discipleship or formation that outline practical steps to enable us to change our entire lives in order to more fully live into God's purposes for our neighbors and our world. The best stewardship resource I have found in North America is the Faith and Money Network started by Church of the Savior.[28]

Reaching High for Your Best: Creating a Rule and Rhythm for All of Life

Christine and I decided when we were married to create a new rhythm for our lives that several young couples we know have embraced as well. We go on quarterly prayer retreats to a doggie-friendly motel in Anacortes,

27. Kraybill, *The Upside-Down Kingdom*.
28. See www.faithandmoneynetwork.org.

north of Seattle, for two days. The first day is always a tough one for me because our focus is reading over and sharing the last three months of journaling. I always find it a bit disheartening to see how slowly I am able to establish new disciplines in my life.

Day two is always a day of refocusing. Our respective mission statements have really become the integrating center of both our lives and our marriage. But on our quarterly retreats, on the second day we always set goals for the next three months to enable us to continue to take new ground, to try to live more fully and authentically into a sense of God's call on our life and our marriage. This includes setting goals for how we plan to use our time and resources in the next three months, as well as how we plan to set aside time to be more present to family, friends, and neighbors. One of our favorite things is hosting friends and neighbors and celebrating the good times and tough times in all of our lives.

As a result of this practice, Christine has created one of the most practical and creative blog sites on spiritual practices I have seen, and you too may find it valuable. She has given voice to numbers of people all over the world who have never had voice before. For example, for Advent one year she asked people to write on the question, "How do we wait as children wait?" She had rich posts from friends from Malaysia to Britain. Again, you might find it helpful. Go to godspace-msa.com.

As followers of Jesus, we are called not to simply limp though life but to join those who are reaching as high as they can to create their best lives. We have the opportunity to invite the Spirit of the living God to ignite our imaginations and so discover surprising new ways to be a difference and make a difference in these turbulent times.

Shane Claiborne reminds us that we can all be a part of a movement that simply "looks like Jesus again." He observes that

> *The most remarkable thing about the Pope is that what he is do-ing should not be remarkable.* He is simply doing what Popes and Christians should do—care for the poor, critique inequity, interrupt injustice, surprise the world with grace, include the excluded and challenge the entitled.
>
> Pope Francis is leaving off the fragrance of Jesus. He is fasci-nating the world with Christ. Maybe his witness will invite more folks to give Jesus a chance despite the embarrassing things we Christians have done in his name. I hope so. I want the world to see a Christianity that looks like Jesus again, a Christianity that is not just known for who we have excluded but for who we have embraced. Wouldn't it be wonderful if Christians were known

for our love again . . . not for our picket signs, or our bumper
stickers, or T-shirts, or dogma . . . but for our love?[29]

Dreaming and Scheming

It's time to get out your iPad or notebook and start with a little dreaming.

1. Can you name a few friends—at church, in your neighborhood, or
   online—whom you plan to contact to see if they would like to join
   you in discerning a clearer sense of God's call on your life?

2. When you gather with them, begin by reading aloud some of the
   Scripture in chapter 4 or from your Bible that reflects something of
   God's loving purposes, and start the journey through all seven steps
   of the discernment process, if possible.

3. What is one specific form of changemaking you are going to explore
   as you begin to live into your mission statement?

4. What are your creative design ideas for giving expression to the aspirations and values of the mustard seed empire of Jesus in all of life
   (beginning with throwing better parties)?

---

29. Claiborne, "First Year of the Pope's Revolution," pars. 7–8; emphasis in
original.

8

Imagine Gen Next Joining Us to Create Our Best Churches for Tomorrow

Climbing Higher, Higher, Higher

"WE ARE CLIMBING JACOB's ladder, every rung goes higher, higher ... every rung goes higher, higher ..." Reverend Jackson's voice boomed, drowning out both the congregation and the choir at All Nations Nazarene Church on a chilly October Sunday evening in Portland, Oregon, in 1954. "If you love him, why not serve him? If you love him, why not serve him? If you love him, why not serve him, soldiers of the cross?"

As the singing stopped, I slipped into the back of the church—I was fifteen minutes late to the Sunday night service. Three weeks earlier I had traveled by train from San Francisco to Portland to attend Cascade College. I was thanking God they had admitted me on probation. I realized my chances of actually completing a four-year degree were very slim, given my poor academic performance in high school. As a young Christian, I sensed (to my surprise) that God might be able to do something of value with my struggling life. So I was highly motivated to start climbing. I decided I should get involved in some kind of ministry as I started college. So I had signed up two weeks earlier to teach the high school Sunday school class at All Nations Nazarene Church, a predominantly black church near Cascade College.

As I was trying to slip in unobtrusively and find a seat the singing stopped. Reverend Jackson pointed directly at me and declared, "The Lord has told me that brother Tom Sine has the message for us tonight!"

I stood frozen in the aisle, clutching my Bible. "Brother Sine, come on up here right now and share the word the Lord has given you for us tonight!" A deeply committed introvert, I was terrified, but headed to the front, along the way fumbling to find Ephesians 4, which we had discussed in our dorm prayer meeting two days earlier.

Standing in the pulpit, I read slowly: "As a prisoner of the Lord, I urge you to live a life worthy of the calling you have received. Be completely humble and gentle: be patient, bearing with one another in love. Make every effort to keep the unity of the Spirit through the bond of peace" (Eph 4:1–3). I think I shared something about the struggle we all have in learning to be patient with friends at church, just as I struggled with my dorm mates at college. I offered a brief prayer and sat down. I am certain that was the shortest sermon ever offered from that pulpit. Reverend Jackson said, "Everyone please stand. Brother Sine is right—we do need to live a life worthy of our calling. We all have peaks in our lives we need to climb. Let's sing 'We Are Climbing Jacob's Ladder' one more time."

Can you remember when you launched your life? What were your aspirations? What peaks did you need to scale to start a new job, go to school, or get married to achieve your aspirations? What were the economic, family, and cultural challenges you faced when you launched your life? Could you have used a little encouragement and practical help to reach your summit?

In this chapter I want to invite you to consider the very high peaks facing both Gen Next and the church in the West to achieve their respective aspirations.

CONVERSATION 1—DOES THE CHURCH HAVE A GEN-NEXT FUTURE?

Taking Seriously the Compassion, Concerns and Creativity of Gen Next

We began this book by asking the important question, does the future have a church? We will end this book with a related question, one that is even more urgent: Does the church have a Gen Next future?

There are no easy answers to either question. However, both questions offer us a new opportunity. They offer us the opportunity to collaborate with a new generation to create both new forms of change-making and new forms of churchmaking that more authentically reflect the way of the servant Jesus.

Generations Y and Z are no longer content with a church that too often seems to exist primarily for those under the tent. They are no longer content with many of our churches that seem to be satisfied with being chaplains to the dominant culture instead of challenging it. However, as you will see, many are eager to be a part of vital communities of faith that become significantly invested in making a difference in the lives of their neighbors. Many are also eager to participate in communities that both challenge and enable them to become serious followers of the way of Jesus—with their entire lives.

I am confident that if we invite Gen Next to join us in discovering new ways the Creator God can use our mustard seeds to create our best communities, our best world, and our best lives many will join us. However, it will also require a willingness for those of us under the tent to "up our game" and to seek to become more authentic followers of Jesus in our lives. It will also require many of us to do the hard work of re-inventing our existing congregations as well as joining those who are creating new forms of churchmaking—in other words, the hard work of climbing higher to scale the high peaks that await us all in these turbulent times.

We need to prepare for our ascent by listening again to the concerning reports of the growing disengagement of Gen Next from our churches, recognizing that we have a very brief time in which to respond. Our response to this daunting challenge must begin by not only inviting the voices and views of Gens Y and Z but also by joining them in creating forms of changemaking and churchmaking. We need to start our climbing together. (This book is written to those of us who are over thirty-five to encourage us to invite the concerns and creativity of the under-thirty-five. However, this book is also written for the under-thirty-five who are already a part of the changemaking celebration and for those who want to be.)

Waking Up to Empty Pews and the "Nones"

CNN Religion Editor Daniel Burke recently reported that millennials are "leaving the church in droves." "Almost every branch of Christianity in the United States has lost a significant number of members," he writes, "mainly because millennials are leaving the fold." Mainline Protestant churches have been particularly affected by this exodus; they have "by far the worst retention rate among millennials, with just 37 percent staying in the fold."[1] Thirty-six percent of Gen Y now identifies as "nones" (not affiliated with any religious group). That is a much higher percentage than in earlier generations. Mission-Net in the UK likewise expresses concern: "With less than 2% of Generation Y (GY) the church and related organizations are facing a massive deficit."[2]

Reportedly, ethnic and immigrant churches in North America, Britain, and Australia are retaining a larger percentage of Gen Y than most predominately white, middle-class congregations. However, these churches do appear to be facing a "massive deficit" in not only the presence but more importantly the participation of creative young leaders. This deficit could, of course, accelerate the decline of many of our churches. Alan Roxburgh and his collaborators in The Missional Network are working with established churches in the West to help them both reimagine how to be the church in times like these and how to engage a new generation.[3]

To successfully engage these new generations we must start with the right question. Some are asking, "How can we make what we're offering more hip and attractive to Gen Next?" Wrong question! Instead, we should ask, How can we secure the creative ideas and leadership of the young, who can show us how to become more innovative changemakers and how to transform our churches into churches for others?

Inviting the Voices of Gen Next

I suggest we begin by asking another question of Gen Y and Gen Z: How would you like to see the church and followers of Jesus change in ways that would be valued by your generation? Let's start by listening to the voice of Rachel Held Evans and several other younger leaders. Evans is the author of *Searching for Sunday*[4] who arrested everyone's attention when, in an article for CNN's Belief Blog, she shared why many of her generation are leaving evangelical churches: "Young adults perceive evangelical

1. Burke, "Millennials Leaving the Church in Droves."
2. Smith, "Who Are We Engaging?," 1.
3. See www.themissionalnetwork.com.
4. Evans, *Searching for Sunday: Loving, Leaving and Finding the Church.*

Christianity as too political, too exclusive, old-fashioned, unconcerned with social justice and hostile to lesbian, gay, bisexual and transgender people."[5]

Stephanie Vos, who is a millennial and a Lutheran minister in Minnesota, declares, "The church needs the millennial hunger for authenticity, innovation and social change. There is an amazing opportunity to learn and grow from the inspiring individuals that are coming into adulthood . . . and [to] help them live their lives with more meaning and purpose."[6]

Dori Baker, an ordained elder in the United Methodist Church, states, "I spend a lot of time talking to diverse twenty-something Christians who are looking for a way to make a difference in the world. That work takes on stark urgency . . . in light of Ferguson, Baltimore, and other recent events that tore the mask off the myth that we live in a post-racial society. Fourteen people—six of them under thirty—just completed a deep dive through the Southern sites where nonviolent protesters challenged racism and won the Voting Rights Act 50 years ago." These journeys—a "holy pilgrimage," Baker says—were hosted by the School of Conversion, which grew out of Rutba House in Raleigh-Durham.[7]

Two years earlier Dori had led sixty young Christians on a pilgrimage from churches and colleges all over the US to Atlanta. Their dreaming started at the gravesite of Dr. Martin Luther King Jr., where they celebrated the fiftieth anniversary of his hope-giving "I Have a Dream" speech. Baker shared that while getting to know these young leaders better, she was encouraged by their own dreaming. She recalled that they dreamed of starting "entrepreneurial ministries that gather communities and re-unite neighborhoods around shared meals, celebrations and lament."[8]

Kenny Conley, a young pastor at Gateway Church in Austin, Texas, urges us to take seriously not only Gen Y but also Gen Z. He encourages us to invite the participation of Gen Z (those who are eighteen or younger). He explains that 25 percent of them are already volunteering and 60 percent want jobs that have a social impact, and that they are savers not spenders. "We can't patronize their intelligence," he says, "but [we

5. Evans, "Why Millennials Are Leaving the Church."

6. Vos, "Why the Church Needs Millennials," pars. 1–2, 4.

7. Baker, "Will Millennial Christians Save Our Cities?," pars. 1, 9.

8. Baker, "Worried about the church?," .

must] allow them to explore their faith, ask difficult questions and wrestle with the complexity to develop a true and authentic faith."[9]

Do you see why I am convinced that many of our young people are ready to lead our churches into some welcome new dreaming and scheming in our lives, congregations, and communities? Join me as I take you on a tour of a few churches that are finding a range of ways to engage Gen Next. Let's start by learning from business and social entrepreneurs how to take young leaders and their ideas seriously.

Are You Ready to Invite the Creative Ideas of Gen Next?

Christie Garton, a millennial social entrepreneur and author, offers some sound advice to corporate executives: "Millennials have an unparalleled thirst to participate and co-create with the brands they love."[10] She encourages executives to invite their creative ideas on both product design and marketing strategies. I would urge pastors and church leaders to be as smart as many corporate leaders have been by inviting creative input from the young.

Start with the teens, twenty somethings, and thirty somethings who are still a part of your church. Set up a time to walk around your neighborhood or community and ask them what issues they are most concerned about. Then invite their ideas of innovative ways that they might engage several of the challenges they identified—with the support of the church. Have a follow-up meeting with older people in your congregation who could serve as coaches or mentors. Select one or two of the most feasible ideas and empower the young to actually launch those ideas.

Here is the "secret sauce": If you invite the ideas of young people and take these ideas seriously, it will not only make a difference in their lives and those of your neighbors, it will also make a difference in your church. It will communicate that you value them, their ideas, and their participation. I think you will see an immediate difference in how they relate to your church. When you take them and their ideas seriously then they will have a sense of ownership. Then they will not just show up out of loyalty to their parents—it will be their church, too!

9. Conley, "Take a Peek a the Next Generation."

10. Garton, "To Sell Products to Millennials," par. 2.

Are You Ready to Invite the Changemaking of Gen Next in Your Community?

Join Esther and Helen in Empowering Homeless Families in Torrance

Life Covenant Church[11] collaborates with a network of churches in Torrance, California, to assist homeless families. The church became an affiliate of Family Promise.[12] Most shelters focus on simply meeting the essential needs of homeless families and individuals. To provide safety for families, however, they divide them up, which isn't good for the integrity of the families. Family Promise actually enables them to become self-reliant again.

Family Promise does this by enlisting a network of churches in a community to work together to provide safe shelter for families without dividing them up. These churches also commit a certain amount of their resources toward hiring trained social workers, who can assist these families with finding jobs and safe housing. Tim Morey, the pastor at Life Covenant Church, told me that they currently have a sixty-day turnaround to get families back on their feet. Clearly, this is an example of a network of churches finding satisfaction in being a part of the changemaking celebration.

Tim was surprised that some of the key leadership for this venture in both family and community empowerment comes from two millennials who were not a part of the church—Esther and Helen. They jumped at the opportunity to join others in making a real difference in the lives of their homeless neighbors and became highly invested in this ministry. In fact, Esther, who has an MSW in social work, became one of the congregational leaders in this impactful initiative. Over time both Esther and Helen also became a vital part of the spiritual life of the congregation. I encourage other established churches first to invite young people in your community to become involved in changemaking and then to encourage their growth toward a more personal faith. I suspect that many of us may be surprised by how many become followers of the Jesus who calls us to more authentic lives of loving servanthood.

11. See www.life-covenant.com.
12. See www.familypromise.org.

From Seed to Harvest: Urban Farming in Atlanta

Scott Bessenecker, associate director of missions for InterVarsity Christian Fellowship,[13] shared a story with me about a student named Bethaney Harrington. Bethaney took time for an internship at an urban community in Chicago. InterVarsity's Urban Projects not only encourage students like her to learn to listen to the people and the places where they work but also to imagine and create new responses. Bethaney returned to Atlanta with a social-enterprise idea called Atlanta Harvest.[14]

Her ideas were taken seriously by Grace-Midtown Church,[15] where she was a community-development intern. She organized people in her church and community, as well as InterVarsity students from Emory University where she was studying, to start a major urban farm in an abandoned parking lot only two miles from downtown Atlanta. Her church not only supported her new social enterprise but also generously contributed to this innovative startup. So now, instead of Atlantans buying produce shipped in from hundreds of miles away, they can buy leafy greens grown practically in their own back yards. What might happen if your church took the ideas of young people like Bethaney seriously?

Join Innové and Invite the Creative Ideas of Gen Next in Your Community

Speaking of food, do you remember the mobile food bus designed to serve underserved neighborhoods that won funding through Colonial Church and their social enterprise incubator, Innové in 2013?[16] Colonial Church hosted a celebration recently announcing the outfitting of the second bus to become a mobile food market. As a part of the celebration, everyone was treated to sambusas—savory, meat-filled pastries that were prepared by Somali women in the community. Here is the backstory behind the sambusas.

Mike Glover was one of the winners of the Innové 2015 competition. He is a young millennial who has become increasingly concerned about eighty thousand Somali immigrants in the Twin Cities area who are

13. See www.intervarsity.org.

14. See www.harvestatlanta.com.

15. See www.gfc.tv/midtown.

16. See www.innoveprojects.org.

struggling to become self-reliant. He is particularly concerned for single moms who have very little schooling or job skills. He received $3,000 from Innové's 2015 competition to start HOYO, an enterprise employing Somali women to make sambusas to sell in a broad range of stores in the greater Twin Cities area. This changemaking celebration rarely has a more savory aroma.

Is your church ready to sit down with the young in your community and invite their ideas of how to make a real difference in the lives of their neighbors? Are you ready, like Colonial Church and its Innové incubator, to help them both create and launch their changemaking ideas?

Join Churches Who Are Reducing Overhead to Empower Neighbors

Remember Life Covenant Church in Torrance, where Esther and Helen helped launch the Family Promise program? Life Covenant is a part of a vibrant denomination, one of only a few in North America that are still growing. The Evangelical Covenant Church[17] plants ten to twelve churches every year in the US, half of which are multicultural. What makes these Covenant church plants different from most established churches is that they reduce their overhead costs so they have more time and money to invest in mission both locally and globally.

For example, they have no programs for those under the tent—no Christian aerobics or knitting circles. Life Covenant in Torrance meets in a rented facility for morning worship every Sunday. The only other time they meet is in a weekly missional home group. The focus of these groups is primarily on creating new ways to make a difference in the lives of their neighbors. Tim Morey reports that by keeping facility and staff costs at a minimum, they are able to free up more than 35 percent of their time and money to invest in local and global mission.

Mustard Seed Associates had Efrem Smith speak at a conference several years ago, when he was the pastor of a new church plant called Sanctuary Covenant in Minneapolis. At that point the church had four hundred members. Forty percent of them were African American, 40 percent Caucasian, and the remaining 20 percent were Latino or Asian. The church worshiped in an urban middle school and had its offices in a drug and alcohol treatment center; its members also formed small missional groups that met in homes. They started an economic development

17. See www.covchurch.org.

organization to empower those in inner-city Minneapolis where they were planted. Efrem told me that nearly 50 percent of their resources were invested in local and global mission projects.

I urge church leaders to identify how much of your resources and time are invested in serving those under the tent and how much is invested in changemaking. I also urge leaders to wake up to two new realities: (1) Given the mounting human challenges that could be a growing part of many communities in the 2020s, our churches will need to invest a greater share of their time and money in serious changemaking. (2) We also need to wake up to a new reality: most members of Gen Y and Gen Z have little or no interest in joining a church where 85 to 95 percent of the time and money never leaves the building.

Graham Cray, a bishop in the Anglican Church in the UK, calls this preoccupation with church maintenance "the Whirlpool Factor": "The more you are around church, the more you are drawn into its maintenance. Its need for our money, time and talents . . ."[18] Bishop Cray challenges us to reinvent our churches, to invest much more of our time and money in being a launch pad for mission to those outside our churches and in nurturing whole-life discipleship in our churches.[19]

Clearly, if we want the church to have a Gen Next future, then we will need to change. We will need to become as smart as those in the business world and not only invite but take seriously the ideas of the young. We will also need to start with their concerns for the needs of those in our community instead of our preoccupations with institutional maintenance. Congregations would be wise to follow Innové's model, inviting the ideas of the young outside the church, supporting their efforts to launch their changemaking innovations, and celebrating the change it makes in the lives of our neighbors.

Dreaming and Scheming with Gen Next

It is time to get out your iPads or notebooks again, to start creating an intergenerational group where you live.

- If you are under thirty-five, come ready to share your ideas for changemaking in your community. If you are over thirty-five, come

18. Cray, "The Church: Whirlpool or Launch Pad?"
19. Ibid.

ready to invite the changemaking ideas of those that are under thirty-five.

- List the names of some of those who are under thirty-five in your neighborhood and ask several of your friends to invite these young people over for coffee. Then invite their ideas for changemaking in your community too.

- Consider bringing both groups together to share the ideas from the first two sessions. Then invite them to respond and jointly create variations or whole new possibilities of ways to make a difference in the community, as well as ways to launch one or two of the best ideas.

CONVERSATION 2—JOIN THOSE WHO ARE PLANTING CHURCHES TO ENGAGE GEN NEXT

As we rush toward the second decade of the twenty-first century, we are witnessing the planting of a remarkable array of innovative forms of church in the West. It would take a very large book to capture all the innovative forms of churchmaking that are seeking to engage new generations as well as the nonaffiliated from all generations, but I want to give you a glimpse.

Tim Catchim, one of the leaders along with J. R. Woodward of the V3 Church Planting Movement, reminds us how challenging it is to become an entrepreneur of any kind—including a church planter. "Ask anyone who has ever started something from scratch and built it from the ground up and they will likely tell you it is one of the most challenging things they have ever done. Church planting is no exception. It is rewarding, but quite challenging." Catchim says that "being a pioneer" brings a unique set of challenges: "you are often misunderstood, lack sufficient resources, [and] have to play multiple competing roles, all the while navigating lots of uncertainty and setbacks."[20]

Lifeway Research,[21] which provides church-planting resources primarily for evangelical church planters, reports that more than 4,000

20. Catchim, "Here Is V3's Method That Is Helping Church Planters to Grow a Movement." Be sure to check out the new IVP book: *The Church as Movement:Starting and Sustaining Missional-Incarnational Communities* by J. R. Woodward and Dan White Jr.

21. See churchplanter.lifeway.com.

new Protestant churches have been planted in the United States recently, while 3,700 have closed.[22] However, since there is a growing likelihood of accelerated closure of mainline churches as we race into the 2020s, that balance could change rapidly.

The Anglican Church in Britain and Down Under has been at the forefront of this movement, creating what they call New Expressions. I recently discovered they are even enabling some United Methodists in the US to plant new expressions here as well. We are also seeing a more recent import from the UK that is going global, called "Messy Church." Messy Church creates a very informal gathering of children and adults around hospitality, food, storytelling, scripture, and creativity that also provides opportunities to make a difference in the local community.[23]

Virtually every major denomination in the United States is now energetically planting an array of new forms of church. The Southern Baptists have always been heavily involved in church planting. The American Baptists are also becoming more active. I believe the two branches of Reformed Church are among those who have been at it the longest. The Presbyterian Church (U.S.A.) has set a goal of planting 1001 new churches.[24] The Methodists have innovators like Elaine Heath, who teaches at Perkins Seminary and is enabling grads to create "New Day communities" that are inwardly focused on spiritual practices and out-wardly focused in local mission. These plants are typically connected to larger Methodist congregations.[25]

The Disciples of Christ are seeking to plant a thousand new churches in a thousand different ways. I already mentioned one of their new plants in chapter 1: Hatchery LA. They aspire to offer an MDiv degree to enable young church planters to create common-cause communities in the way of Jesus that are also incubators for social-entrepreneurial ventures.[26] I am a big supporter of the Mennonite Church in North America. How-ever, they are one of the few denominations that seem to have no national church-planting program to engage a new generation. I suspect if they did, they would find the under-thirty-five would be particularly attracted

22. Green, "Church Planting 201."

23. See www.messychurch.org.uk.

24. White, "Supporting Planters as They Grow."

25. See www.missionalwisdom.com/new-day/worshipping-communities.

26. See www.hatcheryla.com.

to their advocacy for economic, racial, and environmental justice and peacemaking as well as for simpler, more sustainable lifestyles.

Sampling Startups to Engage Gen Next and the Rest

Let me offer you a very small sampling of some of these innovative start-ups, including two that I find particularly promising, Catacombs and Axiom, which not only engage the young but also offer new possibilities for established congregations.

Unplug from the Noise of Life

The Episcopal Church is investing $1.7 million in giving birth to some innovative new expressions. For example, Unplug from the Noise of Life in Boynton Beach, Florida,[27] seeks to engage twenty- and thirty-some-things who are interested in creating new forms of music for worship that connects to their generation. Rachel Held Evans, who has joined an Episcopal church, is right: many millennials do prefer more traditional liturgy than "contemporary" evangelical worship. She is also right when she reminds us that millennials would like to bring their own creative touch to traditional worship.

The Abbey: Sinners and Coffee

The Abbey is an Episcopal church plant in Birmingham, Alabama. Influenced by the tradition of monks and nuns teaching, nursing, crafting, and even brewing beer both to support themselves and to serve others, they are starting a coffee shop church. The Abbey doesn't intend to be an Episcopal Starbucks but rather a place to rediscover and reimagine the traditions of the Christian Church.[28]

St. Lydia's Dinner Church

St. Lydia's Church in Brooklyn is a dinner church. People come together to prepare and enjoy a meal on Sunday and Monday nights while pastor

27. See www.stjoesunplugged.org.
28. See www.theabbeybham.com.

LIVE LIKE YOU GIVE A DAMN!

Emily Scott shares a reflection on the Scriptures and invites a conversation about people's live and struggles. St. Lydia's is funded by the ELCA. The church rents out the property during the week as a co-working space for people in the community.[29] This could be a new model for a generation for whom the cost of constructing and maintaining a church building will be out of the question.

Valley & Mountain Community

Valley & Mountain, a Methodist church plant in an intercultural neighborhood in Seattle, just celebrated their fifth birthday. John Helmiere is the pastor. The church is deeply committed to being a radically hospitable community that works for justice and reconciliation in the way of Jesus. They have been active in addressing recent issues of racial justice in Seattle. They offer yet another model of providing a gathering place. They partnered with Community Arts Create to start the Hillman City Collaboratory, a cooperative multipurpose space shared by grassroots organizations and individuals who care about social change. Its mission would appeal to many millennials: "To become an instrument of transformation that provides space and programs to create community and equip change makers."[30]

Catacomb Communities: Political Action and Personal Accountability

Catacomb Churches, also here in the Seattle area, are being developed by Terry Kyllo and Sister Liz Colver from the Northwest Washington Synod of the ELCA.[31] Liz explained that these new house churches come together twice a month for a time of fellowship, food, story sharing, and liturgy. House churches, of course, have very little maintenance costs. These gatherings comprise six to nine people, many of whom are millennials. In addition to becoming a mutually supportive community where people share their lives and stories, they participate in a liturgy and a time of prayer. All of the house churches also come together once a month for a meal, story, and a worship experience.

29. See www.stlydias.org.
30. See www.valleyandmountain.org.
31. See www.lutheran-n.w.org/content.cfm?d-523.

One of the things that makes the Catacomb Churches unique is that they commit to work together in an important kind of changemaking called community organizing. For example, one Catacombs House Church with eight members in Mount Vernon took a lot of time to visit people to build authentic relationships and, in the midst of listening, identified some of the most urgent issues facing their neighbors. They discovered that wage theft was a huge issue among their neighbors who included many Skagit Valley farm workers. They decided to do community organizing around wage theft. They researched which organizations in the region help farm workers with the problem. Then they designed a website and produced flyers informing farm workers where they could secure assistance with this urgent issue, which they posted all over the community.

The other important dimension of Catacombs house churches is that members participate in intentional groups to live fully and authentically in their call to follow Christ. They hold one another accountable for how they relate to others and how they steward their lives. I would love to see a few of these groups started in all our established churches as the first step toward joining the changemaking celebration.

Axiom Church: Empowering Members to Put First Things First

Axiom, in Syracuse New York, is another model I am convinced established churches could learn from.[32] Join Dan White Jr. and his family as they share a meal of roasted eggplant, ground lamb, and rice with the Hiram family from Syria.[33] This is a reminder for all of us that we are called to be the hospitality of Christ to those who have suffered so much.

For the sixty people who are a part of Axiom, offering hospitality to the growing number of refugees settling in their neighborhood every week is as normal as going to church. In addition to weekly worship that involves scripture and stories, they also meet every other week in discipleship pods to grow their own lives as whole-life followers of Jesus.

In these pods, they help one another as followers of Jesus develop both a new rule of life and a new rhythm of life. Together they learn to reorder their lives around a much greater sense of purpose that connects to

---

32. See www.axiomchurch-ny.com.

33. See www.danwhitejr.blogspot.com/p/axiom.church.html.

a sense of God's purposes. In this process they help each other conduct a timestyle and lifestyle audit to enable one another to put first things first.

For example, Beth, a thirty-two-year-old basketball coach at the local high school, was surprised by what she learned from her audit. She discovered that she had created a lifestyle that was so jammed with social activities and a little extra work that she really didn't have much time to be present to God or to those around her. As a result of her audit, and with the support of her pod, she took her life back. She cut back on a major portion of her social activities to ensure that she had time to be present to God and to those people God had placed in her life.

God's Spirit awakened her to three young women on the basketball team who really needed her support and guidance. She is not only mentoring and tutoring them but also helping them make good life choices, since their parents don't seem to be very invested in their lives. Dan reports that Beth is enjoying life a lot more because she is living with a clearer sense of purpose and also learning how God can use her mustard seed to make a real difference in the lives of three young women she now cares deeply about.

Does the Church Have a Gen Next Future?

While Axiom, Catacombs house church plants, and thousands of other startups offer promising possibilities, no one knows if we are going to successfully engage significant numbers in the next ten to fifteen years to turn the ship around. We also don't know if enough established churches in the West will be motivated, like Innové, to invite both the ideas and leadership of Gen Next to create new forms of changemaking to move from token handouts to serious community empowerment.

However, I am convinced that people from all generations can learn a lot from younger followers of Jesus in churches like Axiom and the Catacomb house churches who are determined to be whole-life followers of Jesus and to put first things first! Can't we start a few small groups in all our churches to enable us as disciples of Christ to up our game and seek to become more authentic whole-life followers of Jesus? Can't we start discipleship pods or mustard seed groups, as we discussed in the last chapter, to enable us to discover a clearer sense of God's purpose for our lives and practical ways to reorder our personal lives to free up more time for God and neighbor, as well as to create a more festive way of life?

Climbing Higher: Launching Life in a New Millennium

As we mentioned at the beginning of this book, a surprising number of those in both Gens Y and Z are highly motivated to create innovative forms of changemaking. As we have just seen, some are committed to creating innovative forms of church as well. However, what many don't realize is that these two generations have more daunting peaks to scale to successfully launch their lives than any prior generations.

Ed Stetzer reminds us that money to fund these new church plants is limited, and it is already beginning to run out. I'm sure he's right. "The bi-vocational option needs to be seen as an opportunity, not as a penalty," he concludes. "It needs to be seen as a preferred option for planters." Stetzer recalls that he installed home insulation to support himself while he planted his first church.[34] I know his comments are well intended, but I find that many older Christians like him often don't realize how much more expensive it is for young people to launch their lives today than when we began our lives.

Here is one candid description of how large the mountains that millennials face loom: "The most educated generation in history is on track to becoming less prosperous, at least financially, than its predecessors." So writes Steven Rattner in the *New York Times*. "Millennials who didn't attend college have found their wages particularly squeezed, perhaps because of the decline of middle-skilled jobs in sectors like manufacturing." Rattner adds that "another drag on the finances of younger Americans is the mountain of student debt that has been piled up in recent years. Members of this year's graduating class left their campuses owing an average of $35,051, about twice the levels borne by their counterparts two decades earlier." Millennials, Rattner concludes, are "saddled with debt and thin paychecks." In the face of these economic challenges, they put off buying cars and new homes, even with mortgage rates being quite low. "By June this year," Rattner notes, "homeownership among Americans under 35 fell to 34.8 percent, down from a high of 43.6 percent in 2004."[35]

Of course, millennials launched their lives at the tail end of the recession, which made it difficult for many of them to make a strong beginning. They have had to find ways to cut their expenses by participating in the new sharing economy. While Gen Z will probably not have to deal with launching their lives in the wake of a recession, they still face some

---

34. Stetzer, "Rethinking Church Planting Funding."
35. Rattner, "We're Making Life Too Hard for Millennials."

daunting economic challenges as well. Their school costs and housing and transportation costs are likely to be even higher than those of their older sisters and brothers. These are very steep mountains for both Gens Y and Z to scale.

Can you think back to when you launched your life in the seventies, eighties, nineties, or early 2000s? What mountains loomed before you when you were eighteen? What were the economic challenges you faced? Maybe you had to choose between going to school or going to work. What were the family challenges you faced? How did you scale those mountains, and who gave you a hand?

Let me return to my story one more time not only to share some of the peaks I had to scale but also to illustrate how much more daunting it is for these generations that it was for mine. I am also very grateful for those who gave me a hand up. When I finish my story, I will invite you to imagine creative new ways you can help Gen Next launch their lives as well as innovative new forms of church and changemaking.

Climbing Higher: Launching My Life in the 1950s

In 1954 I was standing in line with my classmates waiting to enter the auditorium at San Mateo High School and receive my diploma. I turned to Kris, a classmate standing next to me, and asked, "What are you going to do after you graduate?" He said, "I want to go on to college and become an author." When I attended San Mateo High School in the fifties, I gave little thought to what I wanted to do with my life. In fact, I hung out with an aspiring group of young delinquents. As it turned out, we were not even that good at delinquency. As a consequence, I made my parents' lives hell, and my grades were in the toilet. I was headed into a future like many millennials today who, without additional education, face a very uncertain employment future.

However, late in my high school experience, I had a dramatic conversion experience, and suddenly I realized that I wanted to do something with my life that would make a difference in the lives of others. However, because of my terrible grades, I found myself at the bottom of the largest peak I had ever confronted. I was admitted to Cascade College on probation. I realized that I had a very limited chance of making it through the first year. That was peak number 1. That first year I virtually lived in the library![36]

As you will remember from my chapter-opening story, Reverend Jackson invited me to come forward on that October Sunday in Portland to offer the sermon. He did it again later that year—not just once but *twice*. Those traumatic experiences made me aware that the second peak I had to climb was to overcome my fear of speaking in public. So I changed my major from psychology to communication, wound up on the debate squad, and found myself scaling my second peak in sheer terror.

Around the same time, my folks, Tom and Katherine, found they were facing a major crisis. My mom left my dad shortly after I started at Cascade, and she took my ten-year-old brother, Jack, and headed back to her mom's in Blackfoot, Idaho. She made the decision in an effort to wake my Dad up to his need to deal with his growing alcohol addiction. This became, of course, the third peak I needed to climb with my family.

Looking back on my first week of college, during freshman orientation, the instructor, Dr. Grace Nash, stayed after class a number of times to show me how to create and maintain a time schedule. She taught me basic study skills. She was responsible for my making a strong beginning in my first semester at Cascade College. Dr. Lee Nash, her husband, was a historian and my advisor. He encouraged every forward step I took and was a mentor to me the rest of his life.

Without doubt I owe my greatest debt of gratitude to one of the most "oppressive" communications professors who ever worked on a college campus, Dr. Vic Walters, who helped me overcome my terror of speaking in public. I will forever be in his debt because he also taught me how to do research and write solid term papers. For every ten-week class, we were assigned one speech a week, a midterm, and a final exam covering textbook and lectures as well as assigned readings—plus a thirty-page term paper that had to meet his strict technical requirements. Often I had three courses at a time with Dr. Walters, which translated into the completion of ninety pages in one quarter.

With the kind help and prayers of these good people and so many others, including my classmates and Reverend Jackson, I climbed higher than I expected. In 1958, I graduated from Cascade College with a BA in communications. It was such a gift for my family to come to Portland for

36. By the way, my classmate Kris not only went on to college but also became a Rhodes Scholar. And he did write, but it wasn't the serious fiction he planned on. Kris Kristoffereson is, as many readers know, a leading singer/songwriter and a gifted actor.

my graduation. My mom and brother came by train from Idaho, and my dad flew in from San Francisco.

In spite of the many prayers of my friends at school and church, I was totally surprised when I received a call from my mom six months later. "After sixteen months your dad put down half a glass of whiskey in the bar and announced, 'This is the last drink I'm ever going to have.' He said that people laughed him out of the bar. He locked himself in his apartment and went through withdrawal with no medical help—which, of course, could have killed him!" My mom took a deep breath and added, "He has been sober for three months. Thank God, Jack and I are headed home at the end of the week."

For the next four years my dad and mom sought to scale their own Mount Everest. My dad offered to do free take-offs for contractors to get his business started again. My mom is one of the strongest and most loving women I have ever known. She took over the finances and kept my dad's books. They both started going to First Baptist Church in Burlingame. Incredibly, by the end of those four years, my dad had not only reestablished his business; he had become the president of Rotary and was awarded Citizen of the Year in Burlingame, California.

He acknowledged his great debt to my mother, and they were so grateful to God. Remarkably, he never had a single relapse. Years later I discovered that he often visited people in the hospital who had very few friends or family to look in on them, but he did it quietly, without need of acknowledgment.

One of the consequences of his recovery was that he went from being a very conservative dresser to being the "Christmas tree" of Burlingame. He often wore beautifully color-coordinated outfits, with expensive sport coats and slacks. At other times he would wear strange combinations. He simply loved the attention. Of course, he got a lot of attention, from both friends and the local paper, which he relished.

One Sunday, Tom and one of his Rotary friends, Fred Adams, who also attended First Baptist, wore loud, violently clashing outfits and sat together near the front of the church. Pastor Bob Johnson, a fellow Rotarian, interrupted the service just as the congregation finished singing the opening hymn.

Pastor Johnson pointed directly at my dad and said, "Tom Sine and Fred Adams, you both come to the front of the sanctuary right now!" My dad and Fred complied. When everyone in the pews saw their clashing apparel, as my mom put it, "They were stunned too." Then Pastor Johnson announced, "Tom and Fred, I am fining you $150 each for wearing those outrageous outfits in this church" (just as if they were in a Rotary meeting). My dad was beaming, and he and Fred were ready. Each of them put $150 in the offering plate Pastor Johnson held out to them. As they returned to their seats, Pastor Johnson called after them, "If you ever do it again it'll be $300 apiece next time!"

My folks, my brother, and I made it to the peak of our Mount Everest and never looked back, and we were all so grateful to God. Now, I realize that there may be a number of readers who have loved ones struggling with alcohol and drug addiction whose stories may not have ended so well. I, too, have lost loved ones who were not as successful as my dad and mom at scaling their peaks. However, all of us who have life and breath can, by God's grace, not only overcome our hang-ups but also, like the one we follow, become people for others, just as he was a man for others—"climbing higher, higher, higher!"

Climbing Higher: Enabling Gen Next to Launch in 2020s

Gen Y and Gen Z face some of the same challenges we all face as we make a beginning. However, what often is not recognized is that they face much steeper economic peaks than any prior generation. When I graduated from Cascade College in 1958, the cost of room and board, tuition, fees and books was $700 a year. I worked as a janitor during the summer and paid that bill off. None of my classmates had to take out loans to pay for an education at a private college. In the intervening decades, the rate of pay for my summer job has probably gone up five times. However, the cost of a private college education has gone up closer to forty times.

After completing my degree at Cascade College, I earned a master's degree in counseling from San Jose State University, and in 1961 I returned to work on staff at Cascade College for $4,000 a year (the same amount as I would have earned on public welfare). I was able to purchase a completely restored 1920s bungalow with four bedrooms, two and a half baths, and an unfinished basement for $14,000; my monthly mortgage payments were $100. A young couple graduating from a private college in Portland today would probably have significant school debt. Since the price tag for a restored house in that neighborhood would likely be around $800,000, they would probably not qualify for a loan even with two incomes for a house in the same condition today.

The cost of a middle-class lifestyle continues to rise much more rapidly than the income of each successive generation. There is also a growing concern that there may not be as many jobs available when Gen Z starts graduating. Those members of Gens Y and Z who haven't had the opportunity to attend college may very well wind up joining the growing underclass of the working poor that we discussed in chapter 3.

I would urge all who are as excited as I am about seeing members of Gen Next plant new churches and start new social innovations to generously support and enable them to launch both their lives and their changemaking ventures. For example, I would encourage those who have extra space in their homes to offer free or reduced rent to students and recent grads. Christine and I so enjoy the benefits of intergenerational living and would encourage older couples to give it a try. Older generations should also consider deeding their homes to Christian organizations that are serving as incubators to provide inexpensive living and co-working space for the next generation of social innovators. I would also encourage churches to invite the young to join them in reimagining how they might repurpose church properties to provide Gen Next innovators affordable housing (where codes permit) as well as to host incubators for both social innovators as well as makers, crafters, and artists.

Climbing Higher: Reimagining Properties for Gen Next in the 2020s

St. Luke's Episcopal—Seattle

On a bright sunny Saturday May morning in 2015, Reverend Britt Olson, the Priest in Charge at St. Luke's Episcopal Church, Seattle, warmly welcomed a group of us to her church. Our team included Forrest Inslee, Dwight Friesen from the Seattle School of Theology and Psychology, and myself from Mustard Seed Associates, to run a prototyping session on creative ways to repurpose church properties.

Essentially, we tested a process for repurposing escalating numbers of church properties that will become available in the coming decades. We wanted to demonstrate creative ways to reimagine use of properties that both reflected something of the mission of the church and engaged some of the emerging opportunities of the local communities.

We offered this as a part of our new consulting services for our change to a center for imagination and innovation. We invited twenty participants, including young church planters, to participate in an idea-storming process to imagine some possible new uses for properties like those at St. Luke's in the rapidly growing Ballard neighborhood here in Seattle. Britt took us on a tour of two sanctuaries and a range of other houses and a community garden. We also visited the church kitchen, where the eighteen members of St. Luke's were busy preparing breakfast for the homeless.

After reminding participants that St. Luke's Episcopal Church was at the center of the Charismatic Movement in the seventies that had an impact on the lives of thousands of people, we took them on a quick tour of the Ballard neighborhood, which attracts a number of younger people and young families. Then we broke people into four creativity groups.

One of their inclusive ideas envisioned this space becoming the "living room" of Ballard with a Christian community on the site to offer hospitality since it is right in the heart of the neighborhood. Participants also imagined using part of the property to create both low-income housing and housing for young millennials interested in being a part of a monastic community of contemplation and action to offer the hospitality of Jesus to all the new arrivals. Another particularly compelling idea was to create an eatery on the property that specialized in offering festive local, sustainable meals using produce from their community garden; as well as operating a program to train some of the homeless to work in restaurants. This group also suggested inviting young performers to create new forms of liturgical worship as well as well as Spirit-led open mic nights that that would engage younger participants. This imagery of hospitality included providing the capacity of the historic sanctuary to not only serve the small congregation but also to host weddings and funerals for the community.

Please understand that what I have just described was not actually planning the future use of the property at St Luke's Episcopal Church. Rather, we were testing a process for enabling churches to repurpose properties in ways that could extend their ethos and mission into the coming decades in ways that engage a new generation.

Church of the Eighth Day—Melbourne

Pastor Gary Heard at the Church of the Eighth Day in Melbourne is in the midst of redesigning the property for his church, in a poorer urban area in Melbourne, Australia, to better serve the needs of their neighbors. This small Baptist church with about twenty members, which is asset rich and cash poor, has been working to convert its property into a ministry center appropriate to the needs of its context and community in the twenty-first century. It is developing an apartment complex on the site with a mixture of housing options for different family and individual needs, such as those on low-incomes, or people with disabilities. A variety of community spaces have been built into the design, including a community hub where the church can gather and worship and serve the needs of its community. A commercial kitchen, rooftop garden, open courtyard, and a variety of spaces for the community to gather have been incorporated into the design. The outcome will release some of the funding tied up in property for income-generation to fund ministry in the community. This is one of the creative alternatives that congregations that need to re-purpose facilities should check out.[37]

Regardless of whether you join a new generation in the changemaking celebration, the churchmaking celebration, or the church-repurposing celebration, we need to invest more of our life together in throwing better parties that help us more fully enter into the way of Jesus.

Join Us: Celebrating the Great Homecoming Feast of God!

Christine and I relish throwing parties. Several years ago on the first Sunday of Advent we hosted a party around the theme "Celebrating the Great Homecoming Feast of God." Since we can seat only ten people at our table, we imposed on Mark and Anna Mayhle, who own the Shafer Baillie Mansion, and can seat eighteen at their table. We invited fourteen others including several young church planters. We began the evening by watching the classic European film *Babette's Feast* and asking a single question: Where do you see the loving purposes of God in this film about feasting?

For those who haven't seen the film, it is set in a small village in Denmark in the late 1800s. The father started a small house church in his home with the help of his two daughters, Martine and Filippa. When their father passes away, Martine and Filippa try to keep this small Christian community together—with much difficulty.

One day a refugee from France, named Babette, appears at their door. She asks if she can come in and cook for the sisters. They explain

37. See www.theeighthday.org.au.

that they have no money. Babette replies that she is a refugee and at risk and doesn't need compensation but simply a safe place to live. The sisters accept her offer and she prepares the simple Danish fare they are used to. Babette has a little money and every year she buys one ticket in the French Lottery. One year, to her amazement, she actually wins ten thousand Francs, and the sisters are very happy for her.

As Martine and Filippa are planning to have a celebration of the one hundredth birthday of their father with their small community, Babette insists on preparing the meal. The sisters relent. What they don't realize is that Babette spends her entire fortune on this one meal. As the sisters and their small community come in to dine, they are overwhelmed by the sensuous fare, which includes roast fowl, turtle soup, huge plates of fresh fruit, and vintage wine. They all resolve to eat this rich food in spite of the fact that they find it a bit intimidating. To their surprise they discover that they enjoy it. As they eat, grudges and divisions that have broken their relationships begin to disappear and their mutual care for one another slowly returns.

Lorens, a famous general, is their guest for the celebration. He can't find words to express how impressed he is by this remarkable feast. He remarks, "Only one other time have I been so privileged. Only once before have I eaten such elegant food . . . in Café Anglais in Paris." Of course, Babette is the former chef of that cafe.

When we asked our guests where they saw the loving purposes of God in the film, they responded immediately. "We see God's loving purposes in the extravagant generosity of Babette as well as in the incredible abundance and beauty of God's good creation," one person stated. "We see it in 'the restoration of the bond of peace' described in Ephesians 4" as they dined on this rich fare. Another person added that it was in "Babette's extraordinary generosity as she gives everything she has to express her gratitude to those who took her in as a refugee in her time of desperate need." Our guests also saw in this magnificent feast imagery of the great homecoming celebration of God featured in the prophets and the gospel.

We followed this viewing and discussion with a lovely liturgy that Christine prepared, drawing on the homecoming feast portrayed in Isaiah 25: "On this mountain the Lord Almighty will prepare a feast of rich food for all peoples, a banquet of aged wine—the best of meats and the finest of wines. On this mountain he will destroy the shroud that enfolds all peoples, the sheet that covers all nations; he will swallow up death forever. The Sovereign Lord will wipe away the tears from all faces." Imagery of hope, restoration, and feasting.

My very favorite thing is cooking for people. I have never cooked French food before, however. I spent all day cooking for our feast. So, after the film and the liturgy, we invited all our guests to sit down and experience, over the next hour and a half, something of the great homecoming feast we had just viewed. We had wild mushroom soup, a goat cheese and walnut salad, stuffed pheasant (fortunately we had someone who knew when to take the pheasant out of the oven), French wine, and abundant fruit. Everyone seemed to fully enter into the joy of God's homecoming feast in which justice finally comes to the poor, healing to the broken, and peace to all peoples and the restoration of God's good creation through the risen Christ.

Are You Ready to Join the Changemaking Celebration?

Our journey began with celebrating the very good news that in the last ten years we have witnessed the arrival of a new changemaking celebration that is making a remarkable difference in many of our lives as well as the lives of our neighbors near and far, and bringing much-needed social and environmental justice.

We also began with some bad news about not only the graying and declining of the church in the West but also the concerning levels of declining participation and the rapid exodus of Gen Next. If these trends are not reversed it will mean a declining witness to the way of Jesus in many Western countries, as well as a significant reduction in the church's capacity to be something of Christ's compassion to respond to some of the daunting challenges we will face in the 2020s

However, as we have seen, every challenge is actually a new opportunity. I sincerely believe the Spirit of God is seeking to use these social innovators to wake up followers of Jesus to the reality that we could be missing out on the good life of God—we could be missing the feast. We could be missing out on discovering how God might use our mustard seeds, in concert with others, to give people a taste of that great homecoming feast where all things will be made new in the risen Christ.

Dreaming and Scheming as We Scramble Up
All Our Mountains

This is the last time I am going to invite you to take out your iPad or note-book, get together with your friends, and prayerfully do some dreaming and scheming. I encourage you to do it over a special meal this time.

- What are your ideas for creating new forms of church that are more invested in the changemaking celebration, or for starting a mustard seed group in your congregation to enable you to create your best communities and your best lives?

- If you are a Gen Next reader, what difference would you like to make, and what kind of support would you like to receive from older generations? (Be sure to tell them!)

- If you are not a Gen Next reader, in what ways can you help them launch and create new forms of changemaking and new forms of church?

- Before you do anything else, plan a party and be sure to ask a range of other generations and strangers to come and get a taste of God's great homecoming feast.

- Finally, be sure to contact us and let us know the creative ways God is using your mustard seed to make a little difference in the lives of others! www.msaimagine.org

Invitation to Join Those Climbing Higher

As you know, this journey for me began at the SOCAP conference in San Francisco in 2013. When I came home to Seattle, I felt God challenging me to get out of the bleachers and back in the field of play. Frankly, I felt challenged by a new generation of innovators to start living like I give a damn. Since I have worked with college and grad students most of my adult life, I am going to start volunteering with schools like the Seattle School of Theology and Psychology one morning a week. I will use the second morning to join my Mennonite friends and my friends in Lake City Future First to create flourishing, resilient neighborhoods in north Seattle.

I urge all my readers to join me in living like you give a damn, too. I realize some of you are already involved to the hilt in changemaking in your workplace, your community, or your church. However, I urge you, wherever you are involved, to consider becoming more a part of the changemaking celebration by taking seriously

- connecting our lives more directly to God's loving purposes for people and world;

- anticipating new opportunities in our rapidly changing local and global contexts; and

- asking the Creator God to ignite our creativity to join those creating our best communities, our best world, and in the process often our best lives as well as our most vital communities of faith for times like these.

As you will remember, this book began with very good news. God seems to be at work not only through people of faith but also through people of compassion who are bringing welcome change to our world in what we call a "changemaking celebration." As we have seen, this new changemaking celebration is led largely by a new generation of social innovators who derive real satisfaction from impacting the lives of others. They are inviting those of us in the church to move beyond token handouts and to join them in creating new forms of local community empowerment and social entrepreneurship to make a lasting impact in the lives of our neighbors locally and globally.

Remember, many of these young people, leading this celebration, tell us they would take our faith more seriously if they saw more of us "walking the talk," seeking more fully to live into the radical way of Jesus. As I reflect over my life on the many authentic followers of Jesus I have known, one name particularly comes to mind—Steve Hayner. From his early days as pastor at University Presbyterian Church here in Seattle and Vice President of Student Affairs at Seattle Pacific University, Steve was a close friend and mentor.

When I worked at World Concern in the mid 80s, Steve was so moved by the Indochinese refugee crisis that for months he volunteered a morning a week to help however he could. When he took over the leadership of InterVarsity Christian fellowship, he enable this ministry to rapidly become one of the most intercultural Christian organizations in the US, giving voice to many young people in IVCF from all races and cultures.

When Steve left IVCF, he did something I have seen few church leaders do. He took a much less prestigious position and became an assistant pastor in a black church. Throughout his entire life he modeled a welcome form of servant leadership. I have never met a Christian leader who more authentically modeled the way of Jesus.

Steve went on to accept a teaching position at Columbia Seminary. In 2009, he was invited to become the President of Columbia Seminary. As many readers know, Steve recently lost his yearlong battle with pancreatic cancer. At his memorial service on February 23, 2015, a number of us celebrated the gift that Steve Hayner had been to our lives.

However, in those months before he discovered he had cancer, Steve sent me a stream of emails about young Christian innovators that he was meeting in his travels. He shared rich examples of those who were creating a host of new ways to be the church and to make a difference in the lives of their neighbors. In our final exchanges, we both expressed a desire not only to support these young innovators but also to find ways to join them.

This book is my small attempt to live into our dreaming. It is also my attempt to do my own scheming about how to join the remarkable array of young innovators who live like they give a damn. I think it is becoming clear, as we gallop into the increasingly turbulent 2020s, that business as usual in our lives, communities, and congregations will no longer serve.

I am convinced that the Creator God longs to ignite our imaginations not only to create new ways to make a difference but to also be a difference. I believe God is inviting us to join those who are creating both more flourishing communities and more festive lives as a part of the changemaking celebration.

Why would anyone want to miss God's best and settle for less? Why would anyone want to miss preparing for God's great homecoming feast where healing finally comes to the broken, justice to the poor, peace to the nations, and where God's good creation is restored through the risen Christ?

Do send us your stories of how you, your friends, and your congregations are creating new ways to make a difference and be a difference in times like these! We want to share your participation in the flourishing of the changemaking celebration. mail@msaimagine.org

Bibliography

Alsop, Ronald. "Why Bosses Won't 'Like' Generation Z." *BBC.com*, March 5, 2015. http://www.bbc.com/capital/story/20150304-the-attention-deficit-generation.

Anderson, Lane. "The Instagram Effect: How the Psychology of Envy Drives Consumerism." *Deseret News*, April 15, 2014. http://national.deseretnews.com/article/1294/The-Instagram-effect-How-the-psychology-of-envy-drives-consumerism.html#45f6s17aA68MPHVz.99.

Assange, Julian. "Who Should Own the Internet?" *New York Times*, December 4, 2014. http://www.nytimes.com/2014/12/04/opinion/julian-assange-on-living-in-a-surveillance-society.html?_r=0.

Associated Press. "U.N.: World Population to Reach 8.1B in 2025." *USA Today*, June 13, 2013. http://www.usatoday.com/story/news/world/2013/06/13/un-world-population-81-billion-2025/2420989/.

"Back to the Drawing-Board." *Schumpeter* (blog), *The Economist*, July 6, 2013, 62.

Baker, David. "The States Experiment with 'Anticipatory Democracy.'" *The Futurist* 10 (1976) 262–71.

Baker, Dori. "Will Millennial Christians Save Our Cities?" *OnFaith* (blog), June 23, 2015. http://www.faithstreet.com/onfaith/2015/06/23/can-millennial-christians-save-their-cities/37095.

———. "Worried about the Church? Meet These Young Christian Leaders." *Faith and Leadership*, August 26, 2013. https://www.faithandleadership.com/dori-baker-worried-about-church-meet-these-young-christian-leaders.

Barber, Benjamin R. *If Mayors Ruled the World: Dysfunctional Nations, Rising Cities.* New Haven: Yale University Press, 2014.

Bass, Diana Butler. *Christianity After Religion: The End of Church and the Birth of a New Spiritual Awakening.* New York: HarperOne, 2013.

Bayrasli, Elmira. *From the Other Side of the World: Extraordinary Entrepreneurs, Unlikely Places.* New York: Public Affairs, 2015.

Beaty, Katelyn. "The Top 10 *This Is Our City* Stories: Editor's Pick." *Christianity Today*, January 15, 2014. http://www.christianitytoday.com/thisisourcity/7thcity/10-top-this-is-our-city-stories-editors-pick.html.

Berry, Wendell. "Thoughts in the Presence of Fear." Orion Magazine, May 5, 2007. https://orionmagazine.org/article/thoughts-in-the-presence-of-fear/.

Bollier, David. "Fab Labs, Time Banks and Other Hidden Treasures You Didn't Know You Owned." *Yes! Magazine*, Summer 2014, 61.

Bornstein, David, and Susan Davis. *Social Entrepreneurship: What Everyone Needs to Know.* Oxford: Oxford University Press, 2010.

Brooks, David. "Communities of Character." *New York Times*, November 27, 2015. http://www.nytimes.com/2015/11/27/opinion/communities-of-character.html?_r=0.

———. "Hearts Broken Open." *New York Times*, June 19, 2015. http://www.nytimes.com/2015/06/19/opinion/hearts-broken-open.html?_r=0.

Brown, Kerry. "In Many Ways, the 'China Dream' Is Not Different from the American One." *The Guardian*, January 30, 2014.

Brown, Tim. *Change by Design: How Design Thinking Transforms Organizations and Inspires Innovation*. San Francisco: HarperCollins, 2009.

Brueggemann, Walter. *Journey to the Common Good*. Louisville: Westminster John Knox, 2010.

———. *The Practice of Prophetic Imagination: Preaching an Emancipating Word*. Minneapolis: Fortress, 2012.

———. *The Prophetic Imagination*. Philadelphia: Fortress, 1978.

———. *Sabbath as Resistance: Saying No to the Culture of Now*. Louisville: Westminster John Knox, 2014.

Burke, Daniel. "Millennials Leaving the Church in Droves." *CNN*, May 14, 2015. www.CNN.com/2015/05-12/pew-religon.study.

Burn-Callander, Rebecca. "Jamie Oliver and David Cameron Join Forces to Celebrate Social Enterprise." *The Telegraph*, September 11, 2014. http://www.telegraph.co.uk/finance/businessclub/people/11087165/Jamie-Oliver-and-David-Cameron-join-forces-to-celebrate-social-enterprise.html.

Calamur, Krishnadev. "Google's Stake in SpaceX Puts It Closer to Goal of Internet Access for All." *NPR.org*, January 21, 2015. http://www.npr.org/sections/thetwo-way/2015/01/21/378816375/googles-stake-in-spacex-puts-it-closer-to-goal-of-internet-access-for-all.

Campaign for a Commercial-Free Childhood. "Stop Matell's 'Hello Barbie' Eavesdropping Doll." March 11, 2015. http://www.commercialfreechildhood.org/action/shut-down-hello-barbie.

Catchim, Tim. "Developing a Rule of Life and a Rhythm of Life." http://thev3movement.org/2013/12/developing-a-rule-and-rhythm-of-life/

———. "Here Is V3's Method That Is Helping Church Planters to Grow a Movement." http://thev3movement.org/2014/03/here-is-v3s-method-that-is-helping-church-planters-to-grow-a-movement/.

Chan, Melisa. "American Muslims are Raising $1,000 an Hour for San Bernadino Vicitms." *Time*, December 9, 2015. http://time.com/4143416/san-bernardino-shooting-muslims-donald-trump-fundraising/.

Claiborne, Shane. "The First Year of the Pope's Revolution." *Huffington Post*, March 13, 2014. http://www.huffingtonpost.com/shane-claiborne/pope-francis-revolution-_b_4959736.html.

———. "Imagine a New World." *Relevant Magazine*, Spring 2011. www.relevantmagazine.com/tags/shane-claiborne.

Collum, Danny Duncan. "Cultivating a Better America." *Sojourners*, July 2013, 42.

Comstock, Craig K. "The 'Transition Town' Movement's Initial Genius." *Huffington Post*, November 27, 2010. http://www.huffingtonpost.com/craig-k-comstock/the-transition-town-movem_b_788693.html.

Conley, Kenny. "Take a Peek at the Next Generation." *ChildrensMinistryOnline.com*, August 5, 2014. http://childrensministryonline.com/fresh-ideas/take-a-peak-at-the-next-generation/.

Cook, T. J. "4 Benefits That 4 B Corps Didn't See Coming." *Huffington Post*, August 17, 2015. http://www.huffingtonpost.com/t-j-cook/4-benefits-that-four-b-corps-didnt-see-coming_b_7980258.html.

Cray, Graham. "The Church: Whirlpool or Launch Pad." *freshexpressions.org*, April 1, 2012. https://www.freshexpressions.org.uk/news/whirlpoolorlaunchpad.

Crouch, Andy. "A New Kind of Urban Ministry." *Christianity Today*, October 28, 2011, 22–25.

Dearborn, Kerry. *Drinking from the Wells of New Creation: The Holy Spirit and the Imagination in Reconciliation*. Eugene, OR: Cascade, 2014.

Dees, J. Gregory. "Toward an Open-Solution Society." *Stanford Social Innovation Review* 11.2 (2013). http://ssir.org/articles/entry/toward_an_open_solution_society?id=422600001.

Dunkelman, Marc J. *The Vanishing Neighbor: The Transformation of American Community*. New York: Norton, 2014.

Eavis, Peter, and David Jolly. "Stocks Dive as Worries about Asia Reverberate." *New York Times*, September 1, 2015. http://www.nytimes.com/2015/09/02/business/dealbook/daily-stock-market-activity.html.

The Economist. "Back to the Drawing-Board." Schumpeter blog. July 6, 2013, 62. Online: http://www.economist.com/news/business/21580444-design-companies-are-applying-their-skills-voluntary-and-public-sectors-back.

———. "Past and Future Tense: The World Economy in 2015 Will Carry Troubling Echoes of the Late 1990s." December 20, 2014, 13.

Eggers, William D., and Paul Macmillan. *The Solution Revolution: How Business, Government, and Social Enterprise Are Teaming Up to Solve Society's Toughest Problems*. Boston: Harvard Business Review Press, 2013.

Evans, Rachel Held. *Searching for Sunday: Loving, Leaving, and Finding the Church*. Nashville: Thomas Nelson, 2015.

———. "Why Millennials Are Leaving the Church." *CNN Belief Blog*, July 27, 2013. http://religion.blogs.cnn.com/2013/07/27/why-millennials-are-leaving-the-church/.

Field, Anne. "Social Entrepreneurs Create 3D Printed Wrench from Recycled Ocean Plastic." *Forbes*, June 8, 2014. http://www.forbes.com/sites/annefield/2014/06/08/social-entrepreneurs-create-3d-printed-wrench-from-recycled-ocean-plastic/.

Fischer, Karen. "Chinese Students Lead Foreign Surge at U.S. Colleges." *The Chronicle of Higher Education*, November 30, 2014. http://www.nytimes.com/2014/12/01/education/chinese-students-lead-foreign-surge-at-us-colleges.html.

"Forbes Announces $1 Million Global Change the World Social Entrepreneurs Competition." *Forbes*, July 22, 2015. http://www.forbes.com/sites/forbespr/2015/07/22/forbes-announces-1-million-global-change-the-world-social-entrepreneurs-competition/.

Fox, Bob. "Reconciliation of Christians and Muslims." Accessed February 18, 2016. http://www1.cbn.com/spirituallife/reconciliation-of-christians-and-muslims.

Francis, Pope. *Evangelii Gaudium*. November 26, 2013. http://w2.vatican.va/content/francesco/en/apost_exhortations/documents/papa-francesco_esortazione-ap_20131124_evangelii-gaudium.html.

―――. "Pope Francis Urges Young Cubans to Keep Hope Alive," September 20, 2015. http://en.radiovaticana.va/news/2015/09/20/pope_francis_urges_young_cubans_to_keep_hope_alive/1173395.

Frankl, Viktor. *Man's Search for Meaning*. Translated by Ilse Lasch. Boston: Beacon, 1946.

Freire, Paulo. *Pedagogy of the Oppressed*. New York: Bloomsbury, 1970.

French, Rose. "Religion Beat: Colonial Church in Edina to Share Business Talents." *Star Tribune*, November 30, 2012. http://www.startribune.com/religion-beat-colonial-church-in-edina-to-share-business-talents/181618731/.

Frost, Michael. *Incarnate: The Body of Christ in an Age of Disengagement*. Downers Grove: InterVarsity, 2014.

Gallagher, John. "Vertical Farming Sprouts in Detroit's Brightmoor District." May 2, 2015. http://www.freep.com/story/money/business/michigan/2015/05/02/detroit-farm-urban-agriculture-brightmoor-vilsack/26300041/

Garton, Christie. "To Sell Products to Millennials, First Invite Them to Help Develop It." *Entrepreneur*, October 1, 2014. http://www.entrepreneur.com/article/237925.

Gelles, David, and Michael J. de la Merced. "Google Invests Heavily in Magic Leap's Effort to Blend Illusion and Reality." *New York Times*, October 22, 2014, B7.

Godfrey, Neale. "Business Not as Usual: The Millennial Social Entrepreneur." *Forbes*, August 23, 2015. http://www.forbes.com/sites/nealegodfrey/2015/08/23/business-not-as-usual-the-millennial-social-entrepreneur/.

Goldenberg, Suzanne, John Vidal, Lenore Taylor, Adam Vaughan and Fiona Harvey. "Paris Climate Deal: Nearly 200 Nations Sign in End of Fossil Fuel Era." *The Guardian*, December 12, 2015. http://www.theguardian.com/environment/2015/dec/12/paris-climate-deal-200-nations-sign-finish-fossil-fuel-era

Goodman, Michelle. "Don't Quit Your Day Job." *Entrepreneur*, September 2015, 89–90.

Gorbis, Marina. *The Nature of the Future: Dispatches from the Socialstructed World*. New York: Free Press, 2013.

Gratz, Roberta Brandes. *We're Still Here, Ya Bastards: How the People of New Orleans Rebuilt Their City*. New York: Nations Books, 2015.

Green, Josephine. "Democratizing the Future: Towards a New Era of Creativity and Growth." Philips Corporation, 2007. http://www.design.philips.com/philips/shared/assets/Downloadablefile/democratizing-the-future-14324.pdf.

Green, Lisa Canon. "Church Planting 2015: Who Attends and What Attracts Them." *Christianity Today*, December 8, 2015. http://www.christianitytoday.com/gleanings/2015/december/church-planting-2015-who-attends-what-attracted-lifeway.html.

Green America. "7 DIY Cooperatives at Home." *Green American*, September/October 2012. http://www.greenamerica.org/pubs/greenamerican/articles/SeptOct2012/DIY-cooperatives-at-home.cfm.

Hamm, Trent. "22 Ways to Reduce Your Spending without Making Your Life Miserable." *The Simple Dollar.com*, August 26, 2015. http://www.thesimpledollar.com/21-ways-to-reduce-your-spending-without-making-your-life-miserable/.

Hansen, Drew. "Imagination: What You Need to Thrive in the Future Economy." Interview with Rita King. *Forbes*, August 6, 2012. http://www.forbes.com/sites/drewhansen/2012/08/06/imagination-future-economy/.

Harper, Lisa Sharon. "One Year Later: The Evolution of a Movement." *Sojourners*, August 12, 2015. https://sojo.net/articles/how-blacklivesmatter-changed-my-theology/one-year-later-evolution-movement.

Hempel, Jessi. "The Woman Finding Tech Jobs for the World's Poorest People." *Wired*, July 28, 2015. http://www.wired.com/2015/07/leila-janah-samagroup/.

Huddleston, Trevor. "Beyond the Walls of the Church." Review of *The World Is Learning Compassion*, by Frank C. Laubauch. *The Saturday Review*, May 24, 1958, 13.

Islam, Anna, et al. "Negative Environmental Impacts of American Suburban Sprawl and the Environmental Argument for New Urbanism." http://sitemaker.umich.edu/section007group5/consumption_and_the_american_dream__a_new_identity.

Jackson, David, and Neta Jackson. *Living Together in a World Falling Apart*. Carol Stream, IL: Creation House, 1974.

Jarvis, Brooke. "Empowered by the Past: Red State Co-ops Go Green." *Yes! Magazine*, April 3, 2013. http://www.yesmagazine.org/issues/how-cooperatives-are-driving-the-new-economy/empowered-by-the-past-how-red-states-grow-green-co-ops.

———. "Growing Local: Interview with BALLE's Michelle Long." *Yes! Magazine*, November 29, 2009. http://www.yesmagazine.org/new-economy/a-globe-of-villages-interview-with-balles-michelle-long.

Jiang, Steven. "Living the American Dream in Jackson Hole, China." *CNN.com*, July 5, 2013. http://www.cnn.com/2013/07/04/world/asia/china-jackson-hole-jiang/.

Jones, Kevin. "The Local Funding Kit Feeds Giving." *NeighborhoodEconomics.org*, July 21, 2014. http://neighborhoodeconomics.org/the-local-funding-kit-feels-giving/.

Kelly, Marjorie. "The Economy under New Ownership: How Cooperatives Are Leading the Way to Empowered Workers and Healthy Communities." *Yes! Magazine*, Spring 2013, 18–22.

Kennedy, Dan. "The Return of Hometown News." *Yes! Magazine*, Summer 2014. http://www.yesmagazine.org/issues/the-power-of-story/the-return-of-hometown-news.

Kerr, Graham. *Flash of Silver: The Leap That Changed My World*. Mt. Vernon, WA: Kerr, 2015.

Kjaer, Anne Lise. "Urbanisation and the Smart Society." http://global-influences.com/scientific/emergent-technologies/urbanisation-and-the-smart-society/.

Klare, Michael T. "The Future of Climate Change Is Widespread Civil War." *The Nation*, November 3, 2015. http://www.thenation.com/article/the-future-of-climate-change-is-widespread-civil-war/.

Kondo, Marie. *The Life-Changing Magic of Tidying Up: The Japanese Art of Decluttering and Reorganizing*. Translated by Cathy Hirano. Berkeley: Ten Speed, 2014.

Koppel, Ted. "Where Is America's Cyberdefense Plan?" *Washington Post*, October 30, 2015. https://www.washingtonpost.com/opinions/lets-talk-about-a-cyberdefense-plan/2015/10/30/efb19060-7cd7-11e5-b575-d8dcfedb4ea1_story.html.

Korn, Peter. "The Spirit Moves . . . and So Do People—into Houses." *Portland Tribune*, October 1, 2015. http://portlandtribune.com/pt/9-news/275047-148694-the-spirit-moves-and-so-do-people-into-homes.

Kraybill, Donald B. *The Upside-Down Kingdom*. Scottdale, PA: Herald, 2003.

Laskey, Alex. "Climate Change Is Divisive. Climate Solutions Are Not." *The Christian Science Monitor Weekly*, May 19, 2014, 35.

Lawrence, Howard. "Gluing a Place Together, One Neighbor at a Time." October 15, 2013, Abundant Community.com.

Leong, David P. *Street Signs: Toward a Mission Theology of Urban Cultural Engagement.* Eugene, OR: Pickwick, 2012.

Lipka, Michael. "Millennials Increasingly Are Driving the Growth of the 'Nones.'" Pew Research Center, May 12, 2015. www.pewresearch.org/fact-tank/2015/05/12/millennials-increasingly-are-driving-growth-of-nones/.

Liu, Eric, and Scott Noppe-Brandon. *Imagination First: Unlocking the Power of Possibility.* San Francisco: Jossey-Bass, 2009.

Lubetzky, Daniel. *Do the Kind Thing: Think Boundlessly, Work Purposefully, Live Passionately.* New York: Ballantine, 2015.

Lufkin, Brian. "The New Tech Times: How Makers at the *New York Times* Are Inventing the Future of Media." *Make*, July 20, 2015, 24.

Mair, Aaron. "Labor Day 2015: Uniting Labor, Climate, and Racial Justice Movements Our Best Hope for a Better Future." Compass, The sierra Club, September 2, 2015.

McAnnally-Linz, Ryan. "A Watershed Moment." *Sojourners*, May 2014, 21–24.

McKibben, Bill. "IPCC Report Says Climate Change Is 'Severe, Widespread and Irreversible.'" *EcoWatch.com*, November 2, 2014. http://ecowatch.com/2014/11/02/bill-mckibben-ipcc-report/.

McKnight, John, and Peter Block. *The Abundant Community: Awakening the Power of Families and Neighborhoods.* San Francisco: Berrett-Koehler, 2010.

McNeal, Marguerite. "Rise of the Machines: The Future has Lots of Robots, Few Jobs for Humans." Interview with Martin Ford. *Wired*, no date. http://www.wired.com/brandlab/2015/04/rise-machines-future-lots-robots-jobs-humans/.

Mead, Nick. "Fikay Eco Fashion: Banking on Buses and Boats." *The Guardian*, November 20, 2013. http://www.theguardian.com/small-business-network/2013/nov/21/banking-on-buses-and-boats.

Meadows, Donella H., et al. *The Limits to Growth: A Report for the Club of Rome's Project on the Predicament of Mankind.* New York: Universe Books, 1972.

Mehr, Hila. "Why Every Social Entrepreneur Needs to Read This Book." *Huffington Post*, May 6, 2014. http://www.huffingtonpost.com/hila-mehr/why-every-social-entrepre_b_5268764.html.

Middleton, J. Richard. *A New Heaven and a New Earth: Reclaiming Biblical Eschatology.* Grand Rapids: Baker Academic, 2014.

Millard, Cheryl. "Young People and Placemaking: Engaging Youth to Create Community Places." January 2, 2015, www.pps.org.

Miller, Caroline Adams, and Michael B. Frisch. *Creating Your Best Life: The Ultimate Life List Guide.* New York: Sterling, 2009.

Moe-Lobeda, Cynthia D. *Resisting Structural Evil: Love as Ecological-Economic Vocation.* Minneapolis: Fortress, 2013.

Monbiot, George. "*Interstellar*: Magnificent Film, Insane Fantasy." *The Guardian*, November 11, 2014. http://www.theguardian.com/commentisfree/2014/nov/11/interstellar-insane-fantasy-abandoning-earth-political-defeatism.

Moore, Jina. "'Extreme Poverty' Cut by Half." *Christian Science Monitor Weekly*, January 7, 2013, 30.

"Muslims Form 'Ring of Peace' to Protect Oslo Synagogue." *The Telegraph*, February 22, 2015. http://www.telegraph.co.uk/news/worldnews/europe/denmark/11427713/Muslims-form-ring-of-peace-to-protect-Oslo-synagogue.html.

O'Connell, Gerard. "Pope Francis: 'The Gospel of the Marginalized Is Where Our Credibility Is Found and Revealed.'" *America: The National Catholic Review*,

February 15, 2015. http://americamagazine.org/content/dispatches/pope-francis-gospel-marginalized-where-our-credibility-found-and-revealed.

Packard, Josh, and Ashleigh Hope. *Church Refugees: Sociologists Reveal Why People Are Done with Church but Not Their Faith.* Loveland, CO: Group Publishing, 2015.

Palmer, Parker. *A Hidden Wholeness: The Journey Towards an Undivided Life.* San Francisco: John Wiley, 2004.

Parker-Pope, Tara. "In with the New Mission Statement." *New York Times,* January 6, 2015, D4.

Peterson, Hayley. "Millennials Are Old News—Here's Everything You Should Know about Generation Z." *Business Insider,* June 25, 2014. http://www.businessinsider.com/generation-z-spending-habits-2014-6.

Platt, David. *Radical: Taking Back Your Faith from the American Dream.* Portland: Multnomah, 2010.

Prickett, Sarah Nicole. "Look Out, It's Instagram Envy." *New York Times Magazine,* November 6, 2013. http://www.nytimes.com/2013/11/06/t-magazine/sign-of-the-times-look-out-its-instagram-envy.html?_r=0.

Pullen, John Patrick. "Problem Solved: Hackathons Are No Longer the Realm of Just the Tech Set." *Entrepreneur,* November 2014, 58–60. [http://www.entrepreneur.com/article/238390]

Rachman, Gideon. "Nationalism Is Back." *The Economist,* December 20, 2014, 92.

Rangan, V. Kasturi, et al. "The Truth about CSR." *Harvard Business Review,* January-February 2015. https://hbr.org/2015/01/the-truth-about-csr.

Rattner, Steven. "We're Making Life Too Hard for Millennials." New York Times, August 2, 2015. http://www.nytimes.com/2015/08/02/opinion/sunday/were-making-life-too-hard-for-millennials.html?_r=0.

Restakis, John. *Humanizing the Economy: Co-operatives in the Age of Capital.* Gabriola, BC: New Society, 2010.

Rivera, Erica. "Twin Cities Mobile Market Rolls into 'Urban Food Desert.'" *Minnesota Business Magazine,* November 22, 2014. http://www.minnesotabusiness.com/twin-cities-mobile-market-rolls-urban-%E2%80%98food-deserts%E2%80%99.

Rodin, Judith, and Margot Brandenburg. *The Power of Impact Investing: Putting Markets to Work for Profit and Global Good.* Philadelphia: Wharton Digital Press, 2014.

Ronsvalle, John L., and Sylvia Ronsvalle. *The State of Church Giving through 2013: Crisis or Potential.* Champaign, IL: Empty Tomb, 2015.

Roxburgh, Alan J. *Structured for Mission: Renewing the Culture of the Church.* Downers Grove, IL: InterVarsity, 2015.

Rowe, Jonathan. *Our Common Wealth: The Hidden Economy That Makes Everything Else Work.* Edited by Peter Barnes. San Francisco: Berrett-Koehler, 2013.

Satyanarayana, Megha. "Urban Farming Invigorates Detroit Neighborhood." *Detroit Free Press,* May 20, 2013. http://archive.freep.com/article/20130520/NEWS01/305200021/urban-gardening-detroit.

Scandrette, Mark, with Lisa Scandrette. *Free: Spending Your Time and Money on What Matters Most.* Downers Grove, IL: InterVarstiy, 2013.

Schewitz, Manny. "70,000 Muslim Clerics Issue Fatwa Condemning Terrorism." *Forward Progressive,* December 12, 2015. http://www.forwardprogressives.com/70000-muslim-clerics-issue-fatwa-condemning-terrorism/.

Schmidt, Eric, and Jared Cohen. *The New Digital Age: Reshaping the Future of People, Nations and Business.* New York: Knopf, 2013.

Schuman, Michael. "The BRICs Have Hit a Wall." *Time*, January 10, 2014. http://business.time.com/2014/01/10/brics-in-trouble/.

Schwartz, Beverly. "From Gargabe to Gold." *beinkanddescent.com*, June 2013. http://www.beinkandescent.com/articles/1757/Albina+Ruiz.

Seager, Charlotte. "Generation Y: Why Young Job Seekers Want More than Money." *The Guardian*, February 19, 2014. http://www.theguardian.com/social-enterprise-network/2014/feb/19/generation-y-millennials-job-seekers-money-financial-security-fulfilment.

Sengupta, Somini. "Global Populations of Youths Is Highest Ever, U.N. Reports." *New York Times*, November 18, 2014, A6.

Shapin, Steve. Review of *The Innovators*, by Walter Isaacson. *Wall Street Journal*, October 3, 2014. http://www.wsj.com/articles/book-review-the-innovators-by-walter-isaacson-1412372231.

Sherter, Alain. "Goldman Sachs: 2016 Looks Like a Dud for the Economy." *CBS Moneywatch*, September 29, 2015. http://www.cbsnews.com/news/goldman-sachs-2016-looks-like-a-dud-for-the-economy/.

Sider, Ronald J. *Rich Christians in an Age of Hunger: Moving from Affluence to Generosity*. Nashville: Thomas Nelson, 2005.

Sine, Christine, and Tom Sine. *Living on Purpose: Finding God's Best for Your Life*. Grand Rapids: Baker, 2002.

Sine, Tom. "Are You Recession Ready?" *Leadership Journal*, January 25, 2009. http://www.christianitytoday.com/le/2009/winter/areyourecessionready.html.

———. *Cease Fire: Searching for Sanity in America's Culture Wars*. Grand Rapids: Eerdmans, 1995.

———. "Creating Communities of Celebration, Sustainability and Subversion." In *New Monasticism as Fresh Expression of Church*, edited by Graham Cray et al. Norwich, UK: Canterbury, 2010.

———. *The Mustard Seed Conspiracy*. Waco, TX: Word, 1981.

———. *Mustard Seed vs. McWorld: Reinventing Life and Faith for the Future*. Grand Rapids: Baker, 1999.

———. *The New Conspirators: Creating the Future One Mustard Seed at a Time*. Downers Grove, IL: InterVarsity, 2008.

———. *Wild Hope*. Dallas: Word, 1991.

Slade, Hollie. "The Crowdsourced Incubator on Track to Create a New Generation of Social Entrepreneurs." *Forbes*, April 3, 2014. http://www.forbes.com/sites/hollieslade/2014/04/03/meet-the-crowdsourced-incubator-on-track-to-create-a-new-generation-of-social-entrepreneurs/.

Smith, C. Christopher, and John Pattison. *Slow Church: Cultivating Community in the Patient Way of Jesus*. Downers Grove: InterVarsity, 2014.

Smith, Emily Esfahani. "There's More to Life than Being Happy." *The Atlantic*, January 9, 2013. http://www.theatlantic.com/health/archive/2013/01/theres-more-to-life-than-being-happy/266805/.

Smith, Gerry. "Christian Tech Entrepreneurs Find Funds, Support among the Faithful." *Huffington Post*, December 4, 2012. http://www.huffingtonpost.com/2012/12/04/christian-tech-entrepreneurs_n_2198154.html.

Smith, Rachael. "Who Are We Engaging? A Closer Look at the Millennial Generation." March 7, 2011. http://www.globalconnections.org.uk/sites/newgc.localhost/files/papers/Mobilisers%20Forum%20Consultation%20Notes%207-3-11.pdf.

Solnit, Rebecca. *A Paradise Built in Hell: The Extraordinary Communities That Arise in Disaster*. New York: Penguin, 2009.

Sparks, Paul, Tim Soerens, and Dwight J. Friesen. *The New Parish: How Neighborhood Churches Are Transforming Mission, Discipleship and Community*. Downers Grove, IL: InterVarsity, 2014.

"Stephen Covey, RIP." *Schumpeter* (blog), *The Economist*, July 21, 2012, 58.

Stetzer, Ed. "New Research: Less than 20% of Churchgoers Read the Bible Daily." *The Exchange* (blog), September 13th, 2012. http://www.christianitytoday.com/edstetzer/2012/september/new-research-less-than-20-of-churchgoers-read-bible-daily.html.

———. "Rethinking Church Planting Funding: What to Do When the Well Runs Dry? You Dig Another Well." *The Exchange* (blog), January 26, 2015. http://www.christianitytoday.com/edstetzer/2015/january/rethinking-church-plant-funding.html.

Stoll, Shannan. "Too Much Stuff in Your Life? Seven Ways to Turn It Around." *Yes! Magazine*, September 5, 2013. http://www.yesmagazine.org/issues/the-human-cost-of-stuff/7-ways-to-unstuff.

Stone, Brad. "Inside Google's Secret Lab." *Bloomberg Business Week*, May 22, 2012. http://www.bloomberg.com/bw/articles/2013-05-22/inside-googles-secret-lab.

Sunde, Joseph. "When a Church Matches Missions with Entrepreneurship." *Acton Institute PowerBlog*, October 15, 2013. http://blog.acton.org/archives/61292-matching-missions-entrepreneurship.html.

Taylor, Peggy, and Charlie Murphy. "10 Things Creative People Know." *Yes! Magazine*, April 11, 2014. http://www.yesmagazine.org/issues/education-uprising/ten-things-creative-people-know.

Tetlock, Philip E., and Dan Gardner. *Superforecasting: The Art and Science of Prediction*. New York: Crown, 2015.

Thorpe, Devin. "SOCAP Adds Gratitude Awards to Celebrate Social Entrepreneurs." *Forbes*, August 23, 2014. http://www.forbes.com/sites/devinthorpe/2014/08/23/socap-adds-gratitude-awards-to-celebrate-social-entrepreneurs/.

Tomlinson, Heather. "Ruth Padilla DeBorst." *Premier Christianity*, March 2015. http://www.premierchristianity.com/Past-Issues/2015/March-2015/Ruth-Padilla-DeBorst.

United Nations. "Charter of the United Nations." http://www.un.org/en/documents/charter/index.shtml.

Vanston, Jon. "In the Age of Imagination, Small Trends Have Big Impacts." September 16, 2012. https://gigaom.com/2012/09/16/in-the-age-of-imagination-small-trends-have-big-impacts/.

Vatican Radio. "Pope Francis Urges Young Cubans to Keep Hope Alive." September 20, 2015. http://en.radiovaticana.va/news/2015/09/20/pope_francis_urges_young_cubans_to_keep_hope_alive/1173395.

Vos, Stepanie. "Why the Church Needs Millennials, but Millennials Don't Need the Church." *thesaltcollective.org*, October 9, 2014. www.thesaltcollectiv.org/why-the-church-needs-millennial-but-millennials-don't-need-the-church.

Wallis, Jim. "America's Flirtation with Fascism." *Sojourners*, December 8, 2015. https://sojo.net/articles/americas-flirtation-fascism.

(Un)Common Good: How the Gospel Brings Hope to a World Divided. Grand Rapids: Brazos, 2014.

Warren, Rick. *The Purpose Driven Life: What on Earth Am I Here For?* Grand Rapids: Zondervan, 2002.

Weems, Lovett H., Jr. "It Is Not Enough to Be Right," *Faith & Leadership*, October 10, 2011. www.faithandleadership.com/qa/lovett-h-weems-it-not-enough-be-right.

Weigel, David. "American Dreams in China Storms the Box Office." June 17, 2013. http://www.slate.com/articles/news_and_politics/foreigners/2013/06/american_dreams_in_china_storms_the_box_office_the_chinese_version_of_the.html.

"What Is a Watershed?" *WatershedDiscipleship.org.* http://watersheddiscipleship.org/what-is-a-watershed/.

White, Vera. "Supporting Churches as They Grow." Presbyterian Church (U.S.A.), Association for 1001 New Worshipping Communities, November 21, 2012.

Wilk, Karen. "Exiled to Discover God at Work in the World and in Us." *MissioAlliance.org*, July 8, 2015. http://www.missioalliance.org/exiled-to-discover-god-at-work-in-the-world-and-in-us/.

Woodley, Randy. *Shalom and the Community of Creation: An Indigenous Vision.* Grand Rapids: Eerdmans, 2012.

Wright, N. T. *The Challenge of Jesus: Rediscovering Who Jesus Was and Is.* Downers Grove, IL: InterVarsity, 1999.

———. *Surprised by Hope: Rethinking Heaven, the Resurrection, and the Mission of the Church.* New York: HarperOne, 2008.

Yardley, Jim. "Under Francis, a Bolder Vision of Vatican Diplomacy Re-emerges." *New York Times*, December 19, 2014, A18.

Zimmer, Carl. "Ocean Life Faces Mass Extinction, Broad Study Says." *New York Times*, January 16, 2015, A1 and A3.

Zweig, Jason. "The Trick to Making Better Forecasts." *The Wall Street Journal*, September 25, 2015. http://www.wsj.com/articles/the-trick-to-making-better-forecasts-1443235983.